Alex Duff is a journalist and communications expert. He has worked as a reporter in the UK, Brazil and Spain, covering the business of sport for fifteen years for Bloomberg News. He lives in the Netherlands. *Le Fric* is his second book.

Praise for *Le Fric*

'Rollicking' *Times Literary Supplement*

'Sports book of the year' *De Tijd*

'The compelling story moves effortlessly from the empty boulevards of German-occupied Paris to the heart of the City of London, from a quiet house in Tring, Herts, to the 21 lung-busting hairpin turns on the ascent to Alpe d'Huez. One of the best books you will read this year' *Daily Mail, Sports Books of the Year*

'*Le Fric* lifts the veil on the obscure family who run the world's most famous bicycle race, the Tour de France . . . Duff welds together the sporting and business worlds in a way that is always entertaining – like the race itself' *Sunday Times, Sports Books of the Year*

'A rip-roaring read about war, money, politics and sport . . . The 300 pages flew by . . . Deftly covers the big stories and personalities without getting sensational, it's a page-turner but informative and well-sourced. Sports fans should enjoy it and anyone with an interest in media history in France would do well to read it too' *Inner Ring*

'Brilliant . . . a business history with the rhythm and suspense of a mystery thriller and plenty of curious revelations you will surely be repeating in conversation' *Stelvio*

'Le Fric brings new insight to the Tour de France . . . A welcome attempt to unravel the secretive business model and ownership of cycling's best-known event' *Road.cc*

Le Fric

Family, Power and Money:
the Business of the Tour de France

Alex Duff

CONSTABLE

CONSTABLE

First published in Great Britain in 2022 by Constable
This paperback edition published in 2023 by Constable

3 5 7 9 10 8 6 4 2

A CIP catalogue record for this book
is available from the British Library.

ISBN: 978-1-40871-672-4

Typeset in Bembo by Hewer Text UK Ltd, Edinburgh
Printed and bound in Great Britain by Clays Ltd, Elcograf S.p.A.

Papers used by Constable are from well-managed
forests and other responsible sources.

MIX
Supporting
responsible forestry
FSC® C104740

Constable
An imprint of
Little, Brown Book Group
Carmelite House
50 Victoria Embankment
London EC4Y 0DZ

An Hachette UK Company

www.hachette.co.uk

www.littlebrown.co.uk

For Silvia, Madalena and Carlota – and *el Monte Abantos*
which got me into cycling.

Contents

Introduction

Once a year, an eighty-year-old widow and her two forty-something children gather in a Paris office to sign off on the financial accounts of the Tour de France and some other smaller sports events. The meeting occurs every June, and is a formality. After all, they speak to each other almost every day. After agreeing to award themselves a dividend, often worth tens of millions of euros, they go their separate ways. The rendezvous has taken little more than an hour, and is over for another year. As the trio leave, they disappear on to the streets, unrecognised.

Yet the cycling race that finishes on the Champs Élysées in a mark of its stature is owned by this closely knit triumvirate. Between them, these three have the right to set the route, invite some of the teams, sell television rights, decide the prize money and pocket the profits.

For decades, the family has stayed out of the public eye. It is shielded from scrutiny by a small group of management executives, a ring of steel protecting its privacy. Typically, the matriarch appears before her staff once a year for a New Year's toast with champagne. The son gives a five-minute speech each autumn at the unveiling of the following year's race route. His words are ceremonial, designed to avoid headlines.

For most of the last century, sport was not big business and the Tour de France was a money-losing marketing vehicle to promote a portfolio of newspapers the family owned. Today, its media empire is shrinking and the cycling race has become its biggest cash machine. To protect its heirloom, the family works hard to strengthen the race's bond with the state. In the sport of professional cycling, perhaps the only person who wields more power than the race's matriarch and her children is the President of the French Republic.

Broadcast on French public television, it provides lingering helicopter shots of châteaux, patchwork farmland and snow-covered peaks worth tens of millions of euros in advertising for the French tourism industry. In an act of calculated diplomacy, the family each year charters a jet that is on hand to fly in to mountain stages public officials such as the mayor of Paris and Government ministers along with executives of the race's sponsors. Maintaining good relations with the state as well as business is important because it's the Interior Ministry that issues a decree each year that temporarily shuts off 2,300 miles of roads on the race route, loans the President's motorbike cavalcade as a security detail and generally makes life as easy as possible to organise the logistics of the travelling circus.

Since the 1970s, sports from tennis to football and motor racing have developed from amateur pursuits to commercially driven behemoths. The sale of television rights has turned them into lucrative businesses, in which athletes and teams share in most of the spoils. Cycling, in contrast, has stayed true to a feudal business model formulated a century ago and, for more than half a century, controlled by the same Parisian family.

The teams that compete in the Tour de France have long searched for a way to modernise. Like a group of cyclists in a Grand Tour – comprising the three most prestigious multi-week stage races in professional road cycle racing – the teams have tried to launch a breakaway attack to wrest control of the race. To defend its prize asset, the family leans on the state and a Gallic distrust of foreign intervention. To this day, in no small measure because of the family's conservatism, professional cycling's business model is nothing like that of the ATP men's tennis tour, the UEFA Champions League or the FIA Formula One championship.

In recent years, as private equity began buying up strategic stakes in sports for the first time, the family has rejected buy-out attempts by everyone from China's richest man to Lance Armstrong's buddies on Wall Street and in Silicon Valley before his spectacular fall from grace.

Dozens of books have covered the rich history of the Tour de France. This book takes a different approach. It looks at its changing relationship with money or cash – *le fric* – during the eras of newspapers, television and the Internet. But, more than anything, it is the first book to unravel how, over the last seventy-five years, one Parisian family gained and maintained control over the world's most famous bicycle race.

Prologue

Marie-Odile Amaury occasionally came across them at private functions. With her unassuming manner and simple but stylish clothes, she chatted amiably about the weather, house prices and holiday destinations. Peering out from under her blonde fringe, and fixing the middle-aged men from Belgium, Italy, Spain, the UK and the United States with her piercing blue eyes, she was always polite and spoke respectable English to those with no French. The owner of the Tour de France kept her public profile so low that many of them did not recognise her.

While drinking tea out of china cups on the balcony of the Belgian king's residence outside Brussels on the eve of a recent Tour de France start, she was chatting with one of them about their grand surroundings for several minutes. They joked about their holiday homes, how theirs also had similar décor, marble columns and chandeliers, and a garden with its own golf course. The man thought the unassuming lady he was talking to was an aide to the Belgian royal family, or perhaps a member of its catering staff. It was only when she introduced herself that he realised he was chatting to a woman who was richer than their host, King Philippe.

Those of the Tour de France team managers who recognised Marie-Odile Amaury would often try to steer the conversation to the business of cycling. Face to face with the matriarch who controlled the purse strings, they reminded her they received a mere €51,234 in compensation to attend the Tour de France, with a few free hotel rooms thrown in. The money barely covered their expenses for petrol for the team buses and cars during the three-week race. Under Madame Amaury's feudal system, the teams could use the profile of her race to reap their own income from private sponsorship deals, but they did not have the right to share in any of the television and race sponsorship money which was said to approach €100 million a year. This was a highly unusual situation in modern-day sport, and made the team managers bristle when they met her in person.

Their complaints would turn the air cold within seconds. At first, Madame Amaury would, with a thin smile, refer them to her senior executives for further discussion. But if they persisted with their gripes, she could turn prickly. Striding up to her purposefully, one of them exchanged a kiss on each cheek in line with French custom before he asked her abruptly if he could iron out some differences, face to face, right away. Hardly skipping a beat, she said, 'Happy New Year . . .' – it was mid-July – and walked past him.

At the dawn of the twenty-first century, two-thirds of French listed companies remained partly family-owned, according to the economist Thomas Philippon. That compared to fewer than one-quarter of those in the US and UK.[1] The fortunes of the very wealthiest of these French dynasties from the Bettencourt

1 Thomas Philippon: *Le Capitalisme d'héritiers. La crise francaise du travail*, 2007

family, custodian of L'Oréal, to the Arnaults, owners of Louis Vuitton, are picked over by the media. Perhaps none of these clans is more secretive than the Mulliez family, the controller of Decathlon, the sports retailer. The structure of its holding company means that the only shareholders allowed to join are the members of the family tree who can be traced back to a wool-factory owner born in 1877.

Leaders of most family-owned companies tend to be more risk averse. They are more conscious of threats that may weaken their 'heirloom' as they endeavour to pass it on carefully to the next generation. Among them, Marie-Odile Amaury. She and her family owed their wealth from the Tour de France to a media empire started in 1944. In this historical context, the cycling team managers who confronted her were not just coming up against the iron will of a proud pensioner, but against what they felt was the immoveable force of the French way of doing things. Sometimes, they felt all the energy they used up to achieve change in the sport was like trying to run through a brick wall.

But one day at the start of 2011, a plot was hatched. A dozen of them filed into the hall of a grand building in the City of London to discuss how to bring down cycling's antiquated business model. Rothschild & Co, around the corner from the Bank of England, was so embedded in the financial district of London that it owned St Swithin's Lane, the narrow street where it was located. It was on this same site in 1814 that the Duke of Wellington had hired the founder of this family dynasty to finance Britain's flagging war effort against France. By secretly obtaining large amounts of gold through its network of couriers, dealers, brokers and bankers, the bank said it provided the financial firepower to rescue British troops from 'almost certain defeat' against Napoleon.

The Rothschild & Co office today looks more like a museum than a banking institution; it has oil paintings on the walls, a library and an unusual ornament – a 1960s safe with four billion different combinations. In one room, until recently, five pasty-faced bankers from gold trading houses in the financial district fixed the price of gold at 10.30 a.m. each day. In a century-old ritual, each would raise a mini Union Jack flag on their desk when they agreed with the day's opening price. All this history and tradition was a bit of a surprise for the cycling team managers who were used to meeting in French no-frills chain hotels with little more luxury than free wi-fi and a buffet breakfast. They were more familiar with the workings of bicycle components than high finance. As they took in their surroundings, they were curious as to what would come next. A couple of days earlier, they had received by email a twelve-page prospectus outlining the business plan for a new championship – World Series Cycling.

In a wood-panelled room, Jonathan Price, the Englishman chairing the meeting, sported curly dark hair tinged with grey and swept back off his forehead, and an expanding middle-aged girth straining against his pressed shirt. In his forties, he was pale with brown eyes, and wore the top two shirt-buttons undone; he could have passed for a middle-aged pop impresario. He spoke slowly because there was a lot to take in; he explained who he was and went through the details of the prospectus. In truth, like most British people, he knew almost nothing about professional cycling. He was a football man. A decade earlier, he was one of the young executives who had turned Manchester United into a commercial superpower after its listing on the

London Stock Exchange. Price's job had been to replace provincial advertisers like the local travel agencies and car dealerships with global brands at Old Trafford stadium. Now, he told the group of men staring at him, there was a tremendous opportunity to modernise cycling.

Incorporating the Tour de France and other major races, Price said World Series Cycling would also include events on the east and west coasts of the United States, and in Asia. And the best news of all, the teams would get 64 per cent of the equity. Currently, their equity stood at zero. To pull off this exciting new championship, all the teams would need to be united. Until everyone was on board, this project had to stay under wraps. There was no question of going to Madame Amaury to ask her to surrender her family's position. 'Pepsi would not go to Coca-Cola to tell them their plans,' Price would say, conspiratorially, to one confidant.

Sitting alongside Price was an Asian man with a well-kept beard. Majid Ishaq, head of Rothschild & Co's Consumer, Retail and Leisure department. A Manchester United season-ticket holder, five years earlier he had brokered the Glazer family takeover of the club he supported. At the time, Rothschild became a target for fan activists outraged at the Americans loading the club with debt. At one point, they shut down its computer network, and broke into its offices. Ishaq coolly underwrote the deal for forty-five minutes when, because of a clerical error, the family's funds did not come through on time. The Glazers were so impressed they offered him the job as United chief executive.[2]

---

2 Author interview with source: the Manchester United job was accepted by Ed Woodward, then a JP Morgan banker who also worked on the takeover deal.

Ishaq had drawn up the World Series Cycling financial model. If he helped get the project over the line, Rothschild & Co would get a cut of the income. Using the bank's maths models, he predicted the series would have annual pre-tax profit of €39 million by its fourth year. That would give the teams €25 million to share between them, and that was just the start; the revenue would continue to rise exponentially if the series was able to market itself effectively as a brand like, say, the UEFA Champions League. Cycling was, of course, nowhere near as popular as the $1 billion football tournament, but there was still a lot of untapped potential.

As the gaggle of team managers prepared to leave the City of London for the airport, they took one last look at their noble surroundings. The bottom line, they knew – World Series Cycling would need to include the Tour de France to be successful. Price could organise as many startup races as he wanted, but the French race brought in up to 80 per cent of the teams' media exposure during the nine-month cycling season. That exposure was worth tens of millions of euros in publicity for their sponsors such as American tech company Garmin, Spanish phone company Movistar and Belgian floor maker Quick Step. Most team bosses desperately needed to be at the Tour de France start line to get these big sponsorship deals. And they knew that Madame Amaury, who would not even entertain them for a chat unless it was about the weather, would not agree to dilute her family's patrimony.

That would be like Napoleon surrendering to the Duke of Wellington.

Price had an answer to this conundrum. In 1973, he explained, leading tennis players had transformed the sport, wresting control from organisers of the Wimbledon championship. The grass-court tournament was the tennis equivalent of the Tour de

France, the standout event in what, at the time, was a fragmented circuit of year-round events. Based at an ivy-walled club house with eighteen lawn tennis courts in a London suburb, the championship was managed by the All-England Lawn Tennis and Croquet Club, an invitation-only members club that considered itself the guardian of the game. Etiquette maintained men had to bow and women curtsy when there was a member of the UK royal family in attendance. Occasionally, Queen Elizabeth II would make an appearance. Among the house rules were players who had to wear white, with no sponsor logos.

The man in charge of compliance at Wimbledon was a former army captain called Captain Gibson, the tournament umpire. In the summer of 1972, he had marched on to the Centre Court in his dark woollen suit and ordered a twenty-four-year-old Californian player to go to the locker room and change her dress because it contained the purple logo of a sponsor, a cigarette maker. The following year, the Wimbledon committee banned a gangly six-footer from Yugoslavia after he skipped a Davis Cup match for his country to earn a bigger cheque in a new event in Montréal.

Fed up with being pushed around like this, the Association of Tennis Professionals, a newly formed player group led by Americans with little respect for tradition, announced a stunning move − a Wimbledon boycott. Defending champion Stan Smith was among eighty players to pull out. Instead of stars like John Newcombe and Rod Laver, journeymen that few people had ever heard of filled the men's draw. A little-known Czech, who admitted he didn't much like playing on grass, won the title. Within weeks, the boycott had paid off. Tennis authorities granted players the right to play wherever they wanted. It was a pivotal moment, moving power into the hands of the athletes, and paved the way for broadcast and sponsorship revenue, much of which flowed down to them in prize money.

In the City of London, the group of cycling team managers were told that, if push came to shove, they could pull off the same kind of coup against Madame Amaury. It would undercut the business empire that her father-in-law had launched more than six decades earlier during the Second World War with a helping hand from the gentlemen around the corner at the Bank of England.

Part I

Rise & Fall of a 'Bastard': the Tour de France in the Newspaper Era

1

War

Rue du Bac, Paris, 1944

On a summer's morning, a lone cyclist rode down the rue du Bac towing a parcel in a wooden trailer. Inside was 27 million francs (then the equivalent of about $500,000) in tightly packed banknotes. He went past shuttered stores. Only a few shopkeepers in this part of Paris were still open for business but even they did not have much to offer after four long years of German occupation; within an hour of opening, the local baker had sold all the bread he could eke out from the small supply of wood he had to fire his oven. A few doors down, a restaurant in the street had tried to get around rationing rules but was now closed after a Government search found waiters serving black-market beef.

With petrol hogged by the Germans for their war effort, bicycles outnumbered cars on the city's boulevards in occupied Paris. The air was cleaner than before the war and you could even hear birds singing. People used bikes to carry firewood, sacks of coal or even their young children and elderly parents. The cyclist sometimes carried newspapers in his trailer, but this time he was transporting cash through the half-functioning city. A few minutes earlier, in the south of the city, he had collected the parcel from a British spy.[1]

The British had been sending cash through enemy lines to finance Resistance groups for years; some of it came from reserves, some of it was stolen from the German-controlled banks. Now Britain and the US were making their own French francs — hundreds of millions of them — in readiness for the defeat of the Nazis. With Paris on the verge of liberation, they planned to use literally ton after ton of newly minted banknotes to restart the French economy.

Six months earlier, the US Federal Reserve had arranged the printing of a dizzying amount of money — 40 billion French francs — at a private press in Boston, packing bundles into more than 7,000 boxes. Each casket bore no more than a stencilled code on each side. They were shipped across the Atlantic to Bank of England vaults for safekeeping ahead of D-Day. There was so much of the stuff that the bank hardly knew what to do with it all.[2]

After exchanging a code word with the English spy, the cyclist received his tranche of the money, put it on the trailer of his bicycle and began riding north. He pedalled past Chapelle Notre-Dame de la Médaille Miraculeuse where, on one wall, worshippers had engraved messages into stone tablets thanking the Virgin Mary for protecting their family during the war.

---

1 Guy Vadepied: *Émilien Amaury: La véritable histoire d'un patron de presse du 20ᵉ siècle* (2009) cites the 27 million francs figure and the handover by an English spy. In 1944, the dollar was worth about 50 francs, according to the *New York Times*, 'A Farewell to the Franc' (27/12/2001).
2 Bank of England archives: correspondence between UK Treasury and Washington, February 1944.

He was heading for a back street near the Seine. There, behind two sturdy wooden doors, was the advertising agency that he and his colleagues used as cover for their role in the Resistance. By day, they had worked on advertising campaigns for France's wartime Government that sought to boost the morale of the hungry, deflated nation that had surrendered to Hitler. At night, they prepared clandestine new bulletins supporting the call to resistance of the exiled Charles de Gaulle, the general court-martialled and sentenced to death by the same Government.

As part of this secret operation, the single-page updates were printed on the subterranean floors of a building on Boulevard Raspail. Between walls of clean white tiles over three floors, there was a machine to make lines of type from hot molten lead and a printing press that made the floor shake when the black iron contraption sprang into action. When the electricity went down, the Resistance men took off their overalls and took it in turns to produce the power themselves, pedalling on a stationary bike by the light of kerosene lamps. In the morning, concealed in the sacks of postmen and railway workers, the newspapers were sent across the country.

Once, when the cyclist was carrying a batch in the wooden trailer behind his bike, it overturned and the papers were blown across the road by the wind, just as a group of German soldiers were passing. Instead of fleeing, he coolly asked the uniformed men for help to gather them up. They obliged. Fortunately, none of them read French.[3]

---

3 Vadepied, *ibid*

Then, one afternoon in midwinter, the Gestapo called at the door of the building above the printing press. They forced their way in and, as they clambered down the winding iron staircase in black leather boots, they barked orders in German. The Resistance men in overalls looked up from the metal plates they were filling with typeset of anti-Nazi rhetoric. They were taken away for questioning. The cyclist arrived that evening to find typeset and lead plates scattered about the floor. He gathered them up, placed them in his wooden trailer, and, under the veil of night, took them to another press in Montmartre.

Each evening, he tuned in to the BBC. With the volume turned down low – you never knew who was listening – he heard how Allied forces were driving back German troops across northern France. Senior Nazis had started leaving Paris, stealing fine art from the walls of townhouses they had called home and driving away in black limousines. Cafés and restaurants that were their regular haunts on the Champs Élysées now stood empty. Only rank-and-file soldiers remained to defend the city.

From rue du Bac, the cyclist emerged on to a wide boulevard. As he looked up, he saw a group of soldiers in uniform with the insignia of a silver eagle perched on the Nazi symbol, embroidered above the breast pocket. They were manning a field gun which was surrounded by sandbags and barbed wire – and blocking his path to the office. If they stopped him, he could be detained, questioned and searched.

Barely pausing, he changed direction, turning right. He kept riding, his heart pounding. In a few seconds, he was at his family home. He parked the bicycle, picked up the parcel, and shut the large front door behind him. He checked that nobody had followed him. The street was empty. The soldiers had probably not taken a second glance at him or his trailer. From home, he telephoned the office. He asked to speak to the leader of the secret network, codenamed Jupiter.

★ ★ ★

Jupiter was a newspaper advertising executive in his thirties with broad shoulders, dark features and sparkling eyes. His real name was Émilien Amaury.

After the Gestapo raid, Amaury's group had scaled back publishing and turned its attention to reviving a free press once France was liberated. A set of proposals was typed out in a blue notebook and sent through enemy lines to Charles de Gaulle for approval. For the first time in some 350 years since the first newspaper appeared in France, the press was about to start afresh. And Amaury was the man trusted with overseeing the startup capital.

A few days after the cash drop, the city was liberated. Church bells rang around the city. It was the beginning of the end of four years of miserable drudgery and shame. Parisians had their freedom again. They caroused in bars, tossing back wine, cognac and any other alcohol they could get their hands on. They thanked the American troops and cheered the return of De Gaulle as he paraded down the Champs Élysées for a photo opportunity in military garb topped by his trademark kepi cap shaped like a cake box.

That same week, Amaury moved out of a back-street office and installed himself on the top floor of a building on the famous boulevard. The space had been hastily abandoned by an official of the Vichy Government who had fled not long after the Nazis.

The building, number 114, was in a cream corner block with a portico decorated with elaborate stone details. There was an impressive view from his new workplace. From the window looking to your right, above the rows of trees, you could see the Arc de Triomphe, from which the flag bearing the swastika had flown for the last four years. Now an enormous French flag was draped over the edge of the monument.

Across the road was the trademark awning of the upmarket restaurant Fouquet's, the establishment that had served high-ranking German officers. The bill delivered on the starched white tablecloth after a dinner of *foie gras*, *steak tartare* or *sole meunière* could easily top 1,000 francs, a month's rent for a one-bed apartment. Since the Nazis had left, the spacious dining area was mostly empty, out of the price range of most people. Even on the most prestigious avenue in France, electricity was distributed for only twenty minutes during the evening. When winter arrived, Amaury and his staff would wear coats and gloves at their desks, and warm themselves with piping hot bowls of beef stock. The atmosphere was said to be friendly, the boss benevolent, as together they enjoyed the return of freedom.

In his office, Amaury smoked throat-burning cigarettes – Gauloise smokes did not yet have a filter – and worked his network of contacts as he figured out how to play his part in the return of a free press.

★ ★ ★

Twenty years earlier, Amaury had arrived in Paris as a poor fourteen-year-old boy, part of an influx of workers in the capital in the 1920s that included Russians, Italians and North Africans who crammed into tiny rooms in 50-franc-per-week hotels or set up in homes in the suburbs, where Renault and other big factories were based. Amaury, who could barely read and write, managed to find a job as a *plongeur* in a restaurant on the boulevard Raspail.

He was already used to manual work. From the age of twelve in his hometown of Étampes, he had delivered milk pails door to door to boost his family's income. His father, a road mender on a paltry 80 francs a month, had left home to work as a chauffeur in Paris. He sent back some money but barely stayed in touch. Amaury's mother stitched together empty potato sacks for him and his five siblings to keep them warm at night.[4] Even when Émilien arrived alone in Paris, he barely saw his father.

Long hours and modest pay meant most *plongeurs* had enough to live off but, hidden away from sunlight all day, they had little chance of escaping their mundane existence. At midday – the hour known as *coup de feu* (gunshot) – in the space of an hour dozens of white-collar workers – lawyers, journalists and businessmen – streamed in for their lunch, leaving Amaury an enormous stack of dirty plates and cutlery to clean.

He was not entirely confined to the kitchen. Part of his job was carrying coffee and bread baskets to white-collar workers who came for the three-course *prix-fixe*. In doing so, he got to know a kindly fifty-year-old newspaper proprietor called Marc Sangnier, who came from a wealthy family. His father had owned a large portfolio of real estate in Paris and he now lived in a grand building a few doors down from the restaurant. From the building next door to his home, he edited a series of worthy but boring Catholic periodicals.

---

4 Vadepied, *ibid*

Taking pity on the young lad slaving away every weekday at the restaurant, Sangnier invited him to dine at the family home and meet his twelve-year-old son Jean. Over the following months and years, Amaury would become a regular visitor at the *hôtel particulier* with its large windows and high ceilings. He and Jean saw each other almost every day and became close friends. Before long, Amaury was practically part of the family and Monsieur Sangnier continued to treat him as such. He offered him work at his newspaper business, allowing him to escape the grind of restaurant work.

Amaury started out doing odd jobs at the Catholic newspaper group, which had a crucifix in one of the editorial meeting rooms. One summer, he used the brawn developed from carrying milk pails to build an outdoor auditorium in Normandy for a conference hosted by his patron. Eventually, he settled in the advertising department, which carried small ads for the makers of priest's robes and funeral services.

At age twenty-one, and after a brief adventure in the French Army in north Africa, he married his pregnant girlfriend Geneviève and they moved into an apartment on the rue de Rennes. They had met on a military parade ground north of Paris. The daughter of school teachers, she persuaded him to go to night school to complete his education. Amaury was a little self-conscious about his lack of schooling but that was mostly overshadowed by his natural self-confidence.

In his twenties, he gradually became part of the bourgeoisie, a well-dressed man in tailor-made suits with rugged looks, a slightly crushed boxer's nose and a dimple in his chin. With his high-school diploma completed, his wealthy benefactor helped him set up his own advertising agency, installing him in his own office.

Amaury carved out a niche in the market with his staff producing ready-made ads, with catchy slogans and, in the years before the war, adding to the dry news pages of the Catholic periodicals brands like Suchard chocolate and Moët champagne.[5]

At the time, *Le Petit Parisien* was the biggest newspaper in town, selling about two million copies a day. Its masthead boasted that it was the most-read daily in the world. Over ten inky broadsheet pages, it packed in politics, crime, cartoons and football results. Small ads were scattered untidily across its pages, which cascaded off vast rolls of paper near the Gare de l'Est to become bundles of newsprint dropped at the kiosks painted the same bottle-green colour as Metro entrances, street lamps and *pissoirs*.

Even at 25 centimes a copy – half the price of a black coffee – it had been highly profitable. Its spacious offices included leather armchairs and sofas, oil paintings and a Steinway grand piano. The payroll had correspondents in Berlin, Brussels, Geneva, London, Rome and Shanghai, and a globe-trotting star foreign reporter who filed stories from Lebanon to the Soviet Union. When the Nazis arrived in Paris in 1940, they found 29 million francs in the newspaper's bank account, plus 1.5 million francs of cash squirrelled away in a vault.[6]

By then, the owner of *Le Petit Parisien*, a New York-born widow called Madame Dupuy – *née* Helen Brown – had retreated to Manhattan. Her staff were instructed to take care of her apartment and the family's sprawling nine-bedroom château near Versailles. Madame Dupuy, her grey hair still elegantly coiffured

---

5 Bibliothèque Nationale de France: Back copies of *Sillon* newspaper from 1930s
6 Micheline Dupuy: *Le Petit Parisien*, 1989

in the US according to French style, listened to the worrying events from Europe through American radio broadcasts.

The German occupiers appointed their own managing director of her newspaper, and the front page she had gently vetted began to carry news releases issued by the Nazi propaganda office. To the disgust of Amaury and his peers, the newspaper described Resistance men and women as 'terrorists'. Within months, sales had tumbled to fewer than 500,000, and the newspaper quietly dropped its claim to be the world's most-read. By now, because of a paper shortage, there were just two pages of news each day.

For four years the newspaper survived as a shell of its former self, hardly making any money.

★ ★ ★

When the interim German boss of *Le Petit Parisien* abandoned his post as American troops neared Paris in 1944, Madame Dupuy's nephew attempted to reclaim the newspaper, and holed himself up in its offices for two days. However, De Gaulle's aides had already approved the nomination of five Resistance men to take over. Journalists and production staff were ushered from their posts and told there was new management in charge. It was the end of *Le Petit Parisien*.

By the next morning, a new title was in the works – *Le Parisien Libéré*.

Émilien Amaury and four of his Resistance peers were the men placed in charge of the new title. The first edition on 22 August 1944 ran to only two pages and was more of a public service than a commercial operation. With no time to distribute the paper to kiosks, piles of the first edition – despite the printed cover price of two francs – were dropped in piles around the city and given away for free. Some of them were left on the street barricades assembled by the Resistance. In the top left-hand corner was a quote by De Gaulle: 'We are all united in one cause: the greatness of France.'

The same day, a newly authorised radio station played 'La Marseillaise'. Parisians turned up the volume and opened their windows.

The blue-collar staff who manned the printing presses during the occupation and had been led from their workplace out on to the street were summoned to a meeting to learn their fate. Some carried bundles of clothes and personal posses-sions with them, expecting to be taken to prison with other Nazi collaborators. The envoy of De Gaulle who addressed them had a grey pointy beard and stared at them through round spectacles.

'We are going to liberate the press,' he told them.

The workers looked back at him anxiously. He paused. Rather than tell them they were going to be imprisoned, he surprised them – they would keep their jobs. The linotype machines that placed words on to hot metal and clanking presses often malfunctioned, and there was nobody else with their know-how to keep them running.[7] And so, they were likely paid for their post-liberation services services with the US-issued banknotes delivered to Amaury by bicycle. (There was no way back on to the payroll for most journalists and editors, who were replaced with Resistance publishers.)

---

7 Emmanuel Schwartzenberg: *Spéciale dernière, Qui veut la mort de la presse quotidienne française*, 2007

Le Parisien Libéré was initially incorporated as a workers' co-operative and, because of his experience, Amaury was placed in control of ads. But, empowered by his Government contacts, he had loftier plans than to return to his pre-war life as a small-business advertising executive. He found himself in the swankiest address in France thanks to his work serving De Gaulle, the spiritual leader of the Resistance. In the last twelve months of the occupation, he was part of a small group of Resistance men who had worked on the ground rules for the phase that was now taking place – the return of a free press.

The first rule of the new media landscape was iron-clad – anyone who had owned newspapers during the occupation, obeying the Nazi censors, must give up their publications. This action would strip out the barons who remained in an industry already ravaged by war, and leave plenty of opportunity to exploit for entrepreneurially minded Resistance men. As he settled into his new office, Amaury felt confident he was very much part of the new post-liberation establishment. His big hands, like slabs of meat poking out from his suit jacket, rested on his large desk. Three black finger-dial telephones sat before him.

* * *

On a Saturday morning a few days after the liberation, Amaury was taking a pause for breath in his apartment on the rue de Rennes. Before the war, it had been a bustling road full of shops and cafés and he had lived happily with his wife Geneviève and their daughter Francine. On the other side of the street was Les Deux Magots, where crowds had spilled on to the street to swap gossip and drink coffee and liquor. Amaury and Geneviève had often dined with friends in local restaurants, or taken in a movie nearby in one of the cinemas in the cobbled streets of the Latin Quarter.

But on this weekend morning, he would have been on his own. Life had not yet returned to normal. His wife and their two children – their son Philippe was born at the start of the occupation – were out of town, staying with his mother-in-law in the countryside north of Paris. Outside, the war had dimmed the street's pre-war verve; the walls of the grand Haussmann buildings were smoke-blackened. Not far from his front door was a messy barricade made up of sandbags, furniture and barbed wire.

There was a rap on the door. On the doorstep, Amaury found a stout man from Brittany. The son of a cattle farmer, he had made the long journey from his homeland, navigating bombed-out roads in a stuttering car powered by charcoal. Brittany was a world away from Paris, a windswept rural area known for hardy farmers with their own language and traditions. The most western zone abutting the waves of the Atlantic, called Finisterre – Land's End – was an eight-and-a-half-hour train ride from Paris.

Amaury welcomed his visitor, who introduced himself as Paul Hutin, and they sat down to talk.[8] Before the war, Hutin explained, he was general secretary of *L'Ouest-Éclair*, a newspaper serving western France. He left the office, a cream-coloured rococo building in Rennes, at the outbreak of war. After helping to shelter stranded British soldiers during the occupation, he hid out in a priest's house in the countryside. When German soldiers fled the oncoming US Army, he followed them into the

---

8 Vadepied, *ibid*

university town and returned to his old newspaper with an envoy of De Gaulle.

As the Stars and Stripes and Tricolore flags were raised side by side in front of the town hall, Hutin told staff that, under a directive of the general, the newspaper must cease publication and be replaced by a new title – *L'Ouest France*. A group of more than fifty assembled staff, not sure whether they were celebrating the return of a free press or about to be fired, drank a glass of champagne to mark the occasion.

As the bubbly went flat, Hutin needed money to cover the newspaper's production costs. That was why he had come to see Amaury, now the main fixer in the newspaper business who had secured a share of the 342 million banknotes that were heading to France via England. Under De Gaulle's mandate, Amaury was to distribute his quota of cash among nine newspapers. He agreed to provide Hutin with the capital he needed and, in return, negotiated a stake in the Breton newspaper; it was an early manoeuvre by Amaury on the way to becoming a publishing magnate.

When the statutes of *L'Ouest France* were approved in a temporary office by civil servants a few days later, Amaury widened his influence from the Champs Élysées to Finisterre.

2

Freedom

Le Champs Élysées, 1944

As the provisional Government rushed to impose some kind of order on the city and establish a free press, Émilien Amaury was in a commanding position and hungry for more deal-making. At his new office at 114 Champs Élysées, he received another unannounced visit from the editor of sports newspaper *L'Auto*.

Jacques Goddet left his bike on the pavement and walked into the building's hallway, with its concave ceiling and *beaux-arts* features befitting a Renaissance church. The wooden balustrade on the grand marble staircase was as ornate as the splendid stonework in the entrance. Goddet walked up to the fifth floor.[1] He had a habit of climbing the staircase in the city's smarter buildings even when the lift was working. It helped him stay in shape, and gather his thoughts.

During the occupation, he had edited a four-page skeleton version of the newspaper under the title *L'Auto-Soldat*. There was not much sport to write about – no World Cup, no Olympics, no Tour de France. He was obliged to publish coverage of military sport and Nazi propaganda, but he was

---

1 Vadepied, *ibid*

determined to keep the newspaper alive with a small group of correspondents because, well, it was his family legacy. He had inherited it from the co-founder Victor, his father.

For most of his thirty-nine years, Jacques had enjoyed a prosperous lifestyle. He grew up around the Paris theatreland and sport. On some nights he went to plays with his family, and on others he watched the human drama of sport. He saw riders whizz around the wooden boards of his father's indoor Velodrome d'Hiver, roared on by crowds. Ernest Hemingway, a visitor one afternoon at that time, described tobacco smoke wafting up to the glass roof, shafts of light, the sound of a sputtering motorbike pace-setter and a Belgian rider sucking cherry brandy through a tube to numb the pain.

Goddet's father had remodelled the velodrome from a glass-roofed exhibition centre, and it was a box-office hit. But, with the outbreak of war, the glass was covered with layers of blue paint in an effort to stop it being a target for bombings. After the armistice, the darkened venue only staged the occasional boxing match.

In July 1942, the velodrome was used by French police to hold 12,884 Jews – including 4,051 children – wearing the yellow Star of David stitched into their clothing. They were driven to the venue by a publicly run bus company and kept in the stands and on the wooden indoor racing track without water or food for days. Aware of their fate, thirty of them committed suicide. The rest were sent by train to their deaths at German concentration camps.

After the war, Goddet barely mentioned what had happened. In his 526-page autobiography,[2] he obliquely defended himself

---

2 Jacques Goddet: *L'Équipée Belle*, 1991

– 'I have never in my life judged people because of their race or religion.' During the occupation, he said, he regularly travelled on the Paris metro in the last carriage set aside for Jews.

As he arrived to meet Amaury, his usual ebullience was punctured. Publication of *L'Auto-Soldat* had been suspended a week earlier. The official reason, printed on the front page, was blamed on an electricity shortage. 'We are sure,' said the note, 'our readers will remember us fondly during this pause.' In reality, the assets were frozen by the provisional Government, as were Goddet's interests in the Velodrome d'Hiver and the Parc des Princes stadium.

The chances of him reviving the newspaper were slim. The man soon to become Information Minister had promised to bury the editors who had published newspapers during the occupation 'in a common grave of national dishonour'.

On the top floor, Amaury greeted Goddet at the door and fired a question at him – could he borrow his bike? He was sending a young assistant to the Information Ministry, to register the statutes of a weekly newspaper – *Carrefour* – that would launch the following day, a Saturday. In his plummy accent, Goddet responded, 'Of course.'

Specialising in long-form features, the periodical would be weightier than the quick-hit news of *Le Parisien Libéré*. Amaury's name would be printed at the top of the first edition, with De Gaulle, in his kepi, on the front page. Goddet had little interest in politics, but agreed to buy some shares to help fund the venture. Money was not the problem for Goddet right now; he needed someone with influence in the provisional Government.

He discussed with Amaury how else they could work together. Before the war, Goddet had also run the Tour de France to promote *L'Auto*. Perhaps the only saving grace from his embarrassing war effort was his refusal to organise the cycling race under German rule. The two men shook hands and agreed to help each other, where possible.

It was a sort of memorandum of understanding, a handshake deal. Amaury would make overtures to the provisional Government on Goddet's behalf to help him restart a sports newspaper. In return, they would agree, he would get a 50 per cent stake in *L'Auto*'s treasured asset – the Tour de France.

★ ★ ★

Over more than three decades, the Tour de France had become part of the national psyche, drawing fond memories of carefree summer days for millions of French men and women. The seed for the race was planted on a winter's day in 1902. A junior reporter of *L'Auto* suggested to the then editor that they organise a bicycle race around France to boost sales. Over lunch, the editor scowled as he heard the plan, asking whether he wanted to kill the riders from exhaustion. 'For me,' he said, 'it's a no.'[3]

However, Goddet's father Victor, the newspaper's financier, thought it was a good idea. At the time, novel sporting contests were all the rage. The sports pages of newspapers were filled with all kinds of bizarre sporting events, such as a 100-metre race between men on horseback and motorbike riders. At one point, a local motoring club came up with the idea of holding a non-stop, twenty-four-hour car race on the country roads around Le Mans. Some of the hair-brained schemes would be consigned to the dustbin, others would stand the test of time. In

---

3 Jacques Marchand : *Quel Tour pour demain?*, 2013

fact, the French have few peers when it comes to designing successful sports contests. A posh Parisian with a handlebar moustache called Pierre de Frédy – later known as Baron de Coubertin – convened a meeting at Sorbonne University that led to the first modern Olympic Games in 1896. A few years later, a grocer's son called Jules Rimet founded the Fédération Internationale de Football Association (FIFA) in rue Honoré and eventually worked on a plan to launch a national-team tournament called the World Cup.

On 1 July 1903, the junior reporter of *L'Auto* was sent to the Au Reveil Matin restaurant on a dusty road in a Paris suburb. He was to be the official timekeeper for the inaugural Tour de France.

At 3.00 p.m., sixty men from France, Germany, Belgium and Italy dressed in a rag-tag of jumpers, culottes and caps set off on a 1,509-mile journey. A couple of hundred people watched them leave. The experiment was under way. The newspaperman would follow them around France, using the rail network, as the competitors pedalled to the end of that day's stage. Each stage was a marathon endeavour.

Barely one-third of the riders finished the course. It was precisely the rigour of the race that caught the public's imagination. The riders rose at 2.00 a.m. and pedalled in the dark for the rest of the night and most of the next day. To try and dull the pain in their legs, they sipped whisky from a hip flask. A reporter for *Le Petit Parisien* called them 'convicts of the road'. When they had a flat tyre, they changed it themselves. When they were thirsty, they pumped their own water from wells. Organisers made sure they received no privileges, even refusing them an extra woollen jersey to ward off the early-morning cold.

For eager newspaper readers, the account of each stage was a fresh instalment in a summertime novella, complete with a cast of heroes and villains. Their exploits and traits were embellished by journalists, borrowing some of the artistic licence of novelists who captivated the public with popular serialisations. Within a few years, daily sales of *L'Auto* had soared to 300,000 during the race, and its initially sceptical editor Henri Desgrange became the ringleader of the travelling circus. Soon, the signing-on ceremony by cyclists at the start of the race was switched from the suburbs to the Place de la Concorde. Dozens of other newspapers began reporting on the race.

Better than a fictional serialisation, Le Tour was real and sometimes the protagonists jumped from the pages of newsprint. Across rural France, when the suntanned heroes came through town, mayors would bankroll concerts, outdoor film screenings and dances.[4] As they signed in for each day's stage in the early hours at a local café on the main square, the party would still be going and the patron doing a roaring trade would waive the charges for the riders as they topped up their flasks with alcohol or coffee – or whatever mix they were using. Extras such as amphetamines obtained from the pharmacy would be ground up with the back of a teaspoon, scooped up and tipped in before another day's slog through the pre-dawn chill and into the scorching midday sun.

But those were distant memories for now. The Tour de France had not taken place for six years. After his meeting with Amaury, Goddet found himself in purgatory. However much he used his affable charm, his war record counted against him. There was

---

4 Christopher S. Thompson: *The Tour de France – A Cultural History*, 2006

deep bitterness for those who had in any way helped the Nazis; retribution gangs handed out summary beatings and shaved the heads of women accused of sleeping with Germans. When, two months after the liberation, Goddet went to the trademark office to register the Tour de France as his own, it was more in hope than expectation.

He was no closer to getting back his paper, or the race. In 1945, there was again no Tour, nor would there be the following year.

The Communist party, the largest and best-funded political organisation in France, had designs on taking over the national festival. In the first elections after the war, the extreme-left party would secure the most seats, more than the Socialists and the Christian Democrat Party and their assets included twelve daily newspapers – including one called *Sport*. The Tour de France would be a showpiece event for the party whose supporters were massed in the suburbs of Paris, known as the red ring.

Envious at the power of the national fête, Communist newspapers had attacked the commercialism of the race organised by Goddet. There were logos on the jerseys of riders and a noisy caravan of advertisers who jostled for the attention of waiting crowds to promote everything from vacuum cleaners to salami and liquors. This caravan pushed the race, one left-wing daily said, towards sporting bankruptcy. The communists hoped to refashion the event in their own way.

But the struggle to run the Tour de France could wait. Sport was hardly a priority amid the stone-blackened façades, crumbling stucco and lingering food shortages. With a paucity of paper, Government minister Pierre-Henri Teitgen questioned why France needed sports news.

'What's the point?' he asked.

Waving away early requests by Amaury to allow Goddet to relaunch a sports daily, Teitgen was much more interested in political and foreign news. He approved the launch of sixty regional and national newspapers, including a reputable organ specialising in foreign affairs that aimed to be like a French version of *The Times* of London. *Le Monde* would devote only one article a week to sport. The reporter writing the column would be given a desk at the end of one corridor in an 8-square-metre room, not much bigger than a cupboard.[5]

* * *

Less than eighteen months after the liberation of Paris, Charles de Gaulle resigned from leading the Government, fed up with political fighting. He had led France out of the Second World War, but not back to economic health. There was still not enough fuel to heat or light Parisian apartments during the winter months and bread was rationed in smaller quantities than during the German occupation, with each person entitled to the equivalent of half a baguette a day, roughly one-third of what he or she would normally consume. 'For the Frenchman,' a US senator told his peers in Washington as they prepared a bailout, 'bread and wine and a little cheese are his life and he is hollering.'

Although De Gaulle had gone, the Information Ministry that regulated the press remained populated with Amaury's Resistance comrades. That meant that he was still well placed to further his business interests, which continued to prosper. A few weeks

---

5 Laurent Greilsamer: *L'homme du Monde – La Vie d'Hubert Beuve-Méry*, 2010

earlier, the ministry had finally caved in to his lobbying to give Goddet a second chance in newspapers. The ministry decided that a sports newspaper championing French sporting heroes would help raise national morale.

There were, however, a series of conditions on Goddet's return. His sport newspaper must not resemble *L'Auto* in any way. It could not have the same gothic masthead, the same yellow pages or use the same office where it was printed during the Nazi occupation. Nor could Goddet's name appear in its pages. The Government fixed the cover price at 2 francs. At least he could choose the title. It would be called *L'Équipe*. The newspaper appeared initially as a single sheet on Monday, Wednesday and Saturday. The print run was 150,000, two-thirds going to Paris kiosks.

Goddet nominally put in charge seventy-three-year-old motor-racing journalist Charles Faroux, who was one of the creators of the 24 Hours of Le Mans. Raising capital with a small group of friends, they hired thirty staff, including correspondents for boxing, football, cycling, gymnastics, rugby, fencing, tennis and swimming, and moved across the road into a four-room apartment above a cabaret club on the second floor of 13 rue du Faubourg-Montmartre. In the cramped newsroom, journalists heaped their raincoats on top of a bookshelf, smoked, swapped gossip and hammered out copy on typewriters.[6]

The lavish pre-war expenses of journalists in taking first-class travel were no longer possible. During the war, *L'Auto* had a single car powered by coal for journalists. After the war, they still got about on the metro or by bicycle. In more prosperous

6 *L'Équipe Raconte L'Équipe, 70 Ans de Passion*, Editions Robert Laffont, 2015

New York, the new *L'Équipe* correspondent dined in fancy restaurants and took cab rides to cover boxer Marcel Cerdan's fights, earning the nickname 'the Baron' from his jealous Parisian counterparts.

Cerdan, a French–Algerian middleweight, was the biggest sports story of the time. The first edition of *L'Équipe* carried a story about him being offered an eight-fight deal worth more than 10 million francs by an American promoter. The humble boxer charmed Parisians with his winning smile and dominance in the ring. His affair with the singer Edith Piaf meant that his fame climbed even further. When he fought at the Parc des Princes, 45,000 people bought tickets, and crowds who could not get in filled rooftops nearby to peer into the ring.

When he beat Tony Zale at Madison Square Garden to win the world title, sales of the new sports title rocketed to 800,000. The headline on top of the story, sent to Paris via a Western Union telex, was simple: 'MARCEL CERDAN, WORLD CHAMPION'. For a country that had succumbed to German rule in 1940 and needed financial aid from the Americans for flour to make baguettes, this was something to shout about.

Cerdan's promoter ran a cabaret next door to the *L'Équipe* office, and fed the newsroom with stories. Many years later, the boxer's son claimed that the extra-marital affair with Piaf was a marketing stunt, although that seems unlikely. Cerdan once told one of the newspaper's reporters he was besotted with the waif-like singer who was half his size – but would beat him up if he wrote about the affair.

For finding him a way back to newspapers, Amaury was paid in kind. Goddet ceded him a 50 per cent stake in the Parc des Princes. A few weeks later, a public official announced that the two men had obtained the rights to organise the 1947 Tour de France. The race remained under state control but Amaury and Goddet were now temporary licensees. A letter written by the official sent to the French Cycling Federation explained they alone could use the yellow jersey, and chart a course around the country's periphery traversing the mountain passes of the Alps and Pyrenees.

The typed two-page letter advised that if the federation gave another entity any of these rights, the Government would not hesitate to take legal action.[7] It was a warning to the Communist party which, the previous summer, had organised the five-day La Ronde de France to vie with Goddet's La Course du Tour de France, another mock version of the real thing.

The return of the Tour de France was much too important for morale for the Government to skimp on costs. With generous financial support, the organisers were able to acquire bicycles, vehicles and petrol, and put up almost 5 million francs of prize money, five times as much as in the last edition in 1939. National teams from France, Belgium, Italy, the Netherlands and Switzerland signed up, along with five French regional squads. A cheerful, pipe-smoking Government official was assigned to accompany the race to make sure public roads were cleared to let the bike race past.

On a Wednesday in late June, cyclists with goggles strapped to their caps gathered outside the *L'Équipe* office. Before the war, Goddet had helped organise four races as a deputy director, but now he had to answer to a new boss – the Government. He was under pressure to make the race a success. Cerdan made the

---

7 Copy of letter obtained by author from French national archives

official start and huge crowds lined the roads to send off the riders. 'I have never seen so many people,' one rider said.

In blazing sunshine, Goddet sat in the back seat of the cabrio-let car that drove across the Place de la Concorde, leading the peloton towards Lille. Showing a remarkable lack of foresight, he had ordered one tonne of meat, copious amounts of vege-tables and 800 kilos of bananas for the race to lug around in stop-start refrigerators powered by generators. With France sweltering under a heatwave, by the time they had got halfway around the clockwise traversal of the country, the vegetables were infested with maggots and the bananas were blackening. The rice cakes handed to cyclists at feed stations were stale and rock hard. The riders began to gripe about the quality of the food, much to Goddet's annoyance.

In another blunder, a light aircraft hired to take aerial photo-graphs of the race crashed into the side of the Tourmalet moun-tain pass, and was abandoned by the side of the route with the new logo of *L'Équipe* displayed on the wreckage for everyone to see. However, these episodes would turn out to be mere anec-dotes. The French welcomed back the Tour de France with spontaneous celebrations. It was like the good old days. In the midday heat, men danced with their wives in the street as they waited for the peloton to come past. The national festival had returned, bringing a welcome boost to morale.

On the last leg of the race, riders rode through Caen, where the last Tour de France had passed eight years earlier. Now, the Norman city was in ruins. The riders cycled past the bombed-out shells of buildings and Saint-Pierre church, whose spire had been ripped off by a mortar during fighting between British and German forces.

At the start of the final stage, Pierre Brambilla, a square-jawed, suntanned Italian, held the yellow jersey. There was still perhaps time for the French to claw back his three-minute lead over them on the last leg from Caen to Paris, which at 160 miles was one of the longest stages of the race. On a short, sharp climb into the town of Bonsecours, a Breton rider with the West of France team called Jean Robic launched an attack and dropped Brambilla. The race was on.

Goddet was keen to have a French winner. The problem was, to Goddet at least, Robic was hardly an icon. He was short, had protruding ears and was, well, ugly. He had 'a pockmarked face like a bitter apple, big ears and a little nervous body', according to one journalist. What's more, he did not even ride for the national team, but for a regional squad. More to Goddet's taste was the pin-up cycling star René Vietto with slicked-back hair and film-star looks.

The previous summer, when Robic threatened to win Goddet's mock race with a solo breakaway to Aix-les-Bains in the Alps, Goddet came to his hotel room on the rest day to have a chat. 'Mr Robic, you ride very well but you are . . .' he said, pausing, unsure how to put it politely.

Robic knew what he was getting at. 'My legs will decide what happens,' he shot back, according to one account.[8] 'They will do what they want.'

Robic was used to being looked down upon. When he delivered black-market coffee to bourgeois Parisians at the start of the war, they sent the 5ft 3in emissary on his way via the service

8 Christian Laborde: *Robic 47*, 2017: Laborde's book is a 'biographie romancée' meaning there is some artistic licence.

lift, without a tip. With the German Army bearing down on Paris, he had to cycle all the way back to Brittany, riding 60 miles per day with a suitcase balanced on his handlebars as the rich swept by in saloon cars.

On his return to Paris, he pedalled 50 miles out of town before dawn to a job digging ditches for nine hours to build an airfield, burning so many calories that the rationed food of the time was never enough.

Cycling was his ticket to fame and fortune.

The only trouble was, just as he was racing away from the Italian in the yellow jersey on the hill into the town of Bonsecours, another Frenchman sprinted past both of them. Robic strained to get back on Édouard Fachleitner's wheel and refused to budge. After an hour of riding steadily together, they had put the morning's leader out of the race. Robic had a three-minute advantage over Fachleitner in the general classification and so, if he could track him all the way to Paris, he would win the Tour de France.

Fachleitner turned to the little Breton and proposed not to attack in return for one-fifth of his first prize of 500,000 old francs. Robic accepted.[9] Even the amount he would have left over, about £35,000 in today's money, was a princely sum for someone who had made a living as a labourer.

By the time they were on the outskirts of Paris, the pair were ten minutes ahead as they entered the packed Parc des Princes. The huge crowd roared the Breton to the finishing line. In a daze, he sought out his wife Raymonde who was wearing a white dress in the front row of the crowd, pulling down the

---

9 Laborde, *ibid*

wire fencing to kiss her. Robic had married her four days before the start of the race, and promised he would bring back the prize money. It was a great story. In his village in Brittany, the local priest rang the church bells again to celebrate their man winning the Tour de France. The nation's favourite race was back – *Vive Le Tour, Vive La France*.

The following year, the Government gave its official verdict on Goddet's performance – he was named Chevalier de la Legion d'Honneur. He could finally start putting his name on his new sports newspaper again. His embarrassing war effort was forgotten. He could have his old life back again. He was back fully immersed in the worlds of sport and newspapers, and he loved them as much as ever.

On a typical weekday morning, Goddet awoke before dawn and travelled across town in a chauffeur-driven car, devouring the day's press by a lamplight in the back seat.[10] He was one of the first to arrive at *L'Équipe* each morning as concierges washed down the pavements and cleared the debris from outside the cabaret, bars, theatres and restaurants in rue du Faubourg-Montmartre. He strode through the cobbled-stone forecourt and up the stairs to be greeted on the first floor by the newspaper's Tunisian deliveryman dipping Turkish delight into his black coffee in the front office. Ali Neffati's dark skin and fez had made him something of a celebrity when he rode the Tour de France. Now in middle age, he was part of the newspaper's sporting heritage.

'Good morning, Monsieur Jacques,' Neffati said.

'Good morning, old boy,' Goddet responded.

---

10 *L'Équipe Raconte L'Équipe, ibid*

Almost everyone was known as 'old boy' in the upper-class parlance of Monsieur Jacques. This was in part, according to one former colleague, because he was not good at remembering the names of all of his staff.

By 10.00 a.m. Goddet was showing the heads of department where they had gone wrong in that day's paper, striking through stories with a red pencil. He packed his day with meetings, radio show appearances and editing duties. He kept his secretary busy until he left the office at 8.00 p.m. before heading back across town for a change of clothes and dinner.

Early one morning, as Goddet breakfasted in his brother's apartment, there was a radio bulletin – an Air France plane destined for New York and carrying Marcel Cerdan had gone missing near the Azores, the remote outcrop of islands about 1,000 miles west of Portugal. Cerdan was heading for a rendez-vous with Edith Piaf ahead of his rematch with Jake LaMotta. She was on a concert tour in the United States.

Goddet scrambled into action before he finished his coffee, dispatching a reporter to travel to the tiny island of San Miguel. *L'Équipe* was one of only three media outlets who made it to the island – the others were US agency United Press International and the French public radio station. Later that day, it emerged that the plane had crashed into a mountain and none of the forty-eight passengers had survived.

Cerdan was identified by his two watches; one, set on New York time, had been a present from Piaf.

3

Recovery

Paris, 1950s

After the brief post-liberation honeymoon period when American-issue cash was plentiful, things became much tougher for publishers. The Government managed newspapers tightly, controlling supplies of paper and continuing to set their cover price. Nevertheless, Amaury was already on the way to becoming established. He was soon able to extend his empire, taking ownership control of *Le Parisien Libéré* by converting the newspaper into a limited company and buying out two other board members. So as not to attract too much attention to this takeover, which ran contrary to the initial idealism of the paper's incorporation as a workers' co-operative, his equity was held in the name of one of his business associates.[1]

Rules that Amaury himself had helped draw up said that a newspaper owner could only control a single daily title, but there was scope to seed more enterprises. Amaury also founded news weekly *Carrefour*, acquired a stake in *L'Ouest France* and started women's magazines *Marie-France* and *Point de Vue*. He asked Jean Sangnier to run the magazines. He trusted his

---

1 Vadepied, *ibid*

boyhood friend completely; it was Sangnier he had asked to deliver the parcel of 27 million francs to him by bike. Now, working on separate floors of 114 Champs Élysées, the two pals saw each other nearly every day as they had done as teenagers.

In New York, Madame Dupuy – the pre-war owner of *Le Petit Parisien* – watched from afar Amaury's journey to becoming a media titan. On the death of her husband in 1927, she had taken charge of the newspaper with its fifteen daily editions, and a distribution network of more than 1,000 Paris kiosks and 18,000 out-of-town sales agents. For a Manhattan widow to have such power caused considerable interest back home before the war. When an American correspondent for *Time* magazine phoned her at home in 1928, she talked to him about her business strategy from her bed where she was recovering from an operation. Reclining on a pile of feather pillows, she explained that she would stick to her husband's principles of a news-packed daily edition and was coaching her two sons to one day take over the title whose premises Amaury was renting from the Government.[2]

From her exile in Manhattan, Dupuy invited diplomats with connections to France and the foreign office to society dinners and lobbied the US Government to give back her family's assets that also included her château near Versailles, whose last rent-paying tenants before the war were the recently abdicated English King Edward VIII and his American wife Wallis Simpson.[3] In the course of eighteen months, the US ambassador to Paris sent more than a dozen letters to the French Government

2 *Time* magazine : 2 April 1928
3 *New York Times*: 28 January 1938

supporting Madame Dupuy's claim that she had not collaborated with the Nazis.[4]

French officials were unsure how to respond. They were adamant that newspaper owners during the occupation should be punished. Madame Dupuy's claim was also weakened because the other major shareholder, her brother-in-law, was close to Hitler's ally Benito Mussolini. Nevertheless, civil servants did not want to upset the country's liberators. Eternally grateful for their freedom, town halls across Normandy had engraved the names of American military commanders into stone façades. Many flew two flags outside the local administration – the French Tricolore and the Stars and Stripes. The national Government was also conscious of the aid package that the United States Government was preparing for France. It was possible Washington would simply deduct the value of Madame Dupuy's assets, and those of other American expatriates. The bureaucrats dawdled, and American-owned wealth remained frozen.

French lawmakers were still knee-deep in the difficult job of trying to get to the bottom of what had really happened during the occupation. It was hard to verify facts because so much of what had happened was undocumented. Military and civilian courts were examining tens of thousands of cases, including that of the L'Oréal founder, whose dynasty faced the threat of nationalisation for selling paint to the Nazis to coat planes and tanks. There were even whispers in the corridors of power about one of De Gaulle's loyal allies – Émilien Amaury.

In 1941, Amaury had cosied up to the administration of

---

4 Annie Lacroix-Riz: *La Non-Epuration en France, De 1943 Aux Années 1950* (2019)

French leader Philippe Pétain who had shaken hands with Adolf Hitler to seal an armistice between France and Nazi Germany. Under the pact, Hitler ruled Paris and the northern part of France while Pétain controlled the south from the spa town of Vichy. The French administration set up temporary offices in the resort town, installing civil servants in hotel rooms. Pétain, a First World War veteran in his eighties, took rooms 124 and 125 of Hôtel du Parc in which to sleep and work. Amaury travelled to Vichy just as Pétain and his staff were getting their feet under their desks, using baths as filing cabinets and establishing the Interior Ministry in a casino.

Using his charm, Amaury courted the right people and won a rolling contract to create posters and information booklets on behalf of the Government. With the country starved of resources, these campaigns encouraged the French people to adhere to traditional family values and become self-sufficient by planting their own crops. (Even the grandest parks of Paris would be dug up and used to plant vegetables.) With the country no longer free, the national motto of '*Liberté, Egalité, Fraternité*' was replaced with a new one to fit the predicament of German rule and nationwide austerity: '*Travail, Famille, Patrie*'.

Under the public advertising contract that would be worth 50 million francs over three years, Amaury drew generous pay cheques to disseminate these messages and was able successfully to relaunch his advertising agency in Paris that had stopped operating during France's brief combat with Germany. To the left-wing lawmakers in parliament, one thing was clear – Amaury had made a money-spinning deal with the old man who had sided with Hitler. One day in parliament, a socialist politician questioned Amaury's right to accumulate all the assets he now enjoyed.[5]

How should history judge Amaury?

It was a question that was resolved swiftly by officialdom. Amaury's closest ally in Government immediately came to his rescue. Pierre-Henri Teitgen, one of De Gaulle's most senior ministers, took the floor in parliament to shoot down the upstart socialist. 'I'm astonished that you should question a man of such courage,' he said, sparking a round of applause by his colleagues. Teitgen had first-hand knowledge of the dangerous double game Amaury had played during the occupation. As Nazi officers hobnobbed in Paris at black-tie *soirées* in the German ambassador's townhouse, a few doors down in the same street, Amaury and his staff worked into the night to prepare Resistance newspapers. A few hundred metres away, the underground printing press they had used to churn out the text of De Gaulle's speeches functioned each night under the noses of the Gestapo. The press was a short walk from the Lutetia hotel, with Nazi intelligence officers in each of its 233 rooms.

In the man endorsing him, Amaury could not have had a better ally. Nobody questioned the legitimacy of Teitgen to be one of the most powerful men in the provisional Government. He had been arrested in Paris by the Gestapo in the last months of the occupation, tied up and questioned for thirty-five straight days in a windowless room.[6] After refusing to open up and reveal his identity to his inquisitors, he was eventually thrown on to a

5 Vadepied, *ibid*
6 Biography of Teitgen retrieved from *Ordredelaliberation.fr*

train heading for a prison in eastern France. He and his fellow captives managed to escape the Germans by carving a hole in the rusty roof with a blade fashioned from a fork. With the endorsement of this French wartime hero, the matter of Amaury's war record was officially closed, at least as far as the Government was concerned.

Just to make sure, Amaury worked behind the scenes to reinforce further his Resistance credentials, sending a scrapbook of the clandestine newspapers he had published to De Gaulle. They included the cuttings of the speeches the General gave to BBC radio while he was safely in exile in London. The General responded with a handwritten thank-you note. Reading the cuttings, he wrote, had made him emotional. It made Amaury's heart glow. One of his most treasured possessions was a black-and-white photograph of himself with De Gaulle on the gravel drive of his hero's ivy-covered home in a village near Lille. The gangly General, in civilian clothes, towered a full head above the media magnate. De Gaulle wrote a personal message with a fountain pen in the bottom-right corner: 'For E. Amaury, my friend'.[7]

When De Gaulle returned to politics with a new party, Amaury's *Le Parisien Libéré* was the first newspaper to rally round to support his administration, asking readers to send 50-franc stamps to his home to support the ailing public health service. Newsreels showed sacks of post being delivered; more than 100 million francs was raised. Meanwhile, Amaury's *Marie-France* magazine encouraged housewives to make the best of

---

7 A first edition of the photograph with De Gaulle's inscription was available in August 2021 for €2,500 at *Edition-Originale.com*

the hard times by getting creative in the kitchen with powdered eggs, and knitting their children winter clothes.

Perhaps partly thanks to this Government support, there appeared to be no hurry to call in the millions of francs sent through enemy lines to Amaury to help him and his Resistance peers establish a free press. It was not clear whether the money that had arrived via an English spy was a loan or grant. In fact, initially, it had not even been clear in France if the cash was legal tender at all. At first De Gaulle regarded the American notes issued in 1944 as no more valuable than Monopoly money.

De Gaulle did not get on with the American leaders, who had failed fully to endorse his mandate as French leader because he was unelected. He threw a tantrum when he found so many francs made in Boston were being circulated by the Allies across liberated Normandy. He had not been briefed about the bank-notes. Not only did he see them as a threat to French sovereignty by Washington, but he feared Allied troops – who got the monthly equivalent of $50 spending money – would buy essential food supplies, depriving hungry Frenchmen, women and children.

As the Allies pushed back the Germans, the fresh banknotes arrived by land, sea and air. On one occasion, a parachute drop of 9 million francs in a metal box plunked into a field in Brittany. Upset by this invasion of money, De Gaulle declared the new money 'phony'. In Normandy, shopkeepers were suspicious of the cheap-looking notes that soldiers used to pay for cigarettes, candy and other provisions. Seeking to dispose of the bills quickly, in case they were suddenly taken out of circulation, according to historian Vladimir Petrov, locals 'showed great zeal' in paying their taxes in advance, forming long queues at the tax office.[8]

A few weeks later, De Gaulle backed down and agreed to recognise the American-issue cash provided, according to a written agreement, it would be 'considered as having been issued by the French Treasury'.[9] The French would control the distribution of the billions of new francs. By the end of the Second World War, according to Petrov, up to 85 per cent of currency in France was printed abroad.

After the liberation, the Bank of France sought quickly to replace the foreign-made money not just for sovereignty reasons. It was becoming a target for forgers because the design was rudimentary. By 1946, it was already being swiftly phased out. According to his biographer, the editor of *Le Monde* was the only newspaperman to repay his three-million-francs share of the cash handout.[10] Hubert Beuve-Méry was scrupulous about editorial independence, and parsimonious to the point of neuroticism. The man from *Le Monde* was said to offset the financial risk of hiring each new reporter by buying a gold bar as security and depositing it in the office safe.

As part of his spartan lifestyle, Beuve-Méry holidayed in an isolated stone Alpine cottage with no telephone, no hot water and an outside toilet. Instead of burning through the money like Amaury and his peers, he repaid the Government and arranged a 1.25 million franc bank loan.

---

8 Vladimir Petrov: *Money and Conquest – Allied Occupation Currencies in World War II*, 1967
9 Bank of England archives: copy of memorandum seen by author
10 Greilsamer, *ibid*

As courts and bureaucrats slowly worked through the back-log of who should get what after the war, the Government eventually passed legislation that meant owners of newspapers during the occupation who had not actively collaborated with the Nazis could trade their assets at pre-war prices. By now, Madame Dupuy had returned to Paris. She died barely a year after the law was passed, at the age of seventy-six, but her children were able to sell the newspaper offices that now housed *Le Parisien Libéré* to an investor who, in turn, leased them to sitting-tenant Amaury.

With a capable editor running the newsroom, Amaury had turned his newspaper into a comparative success; it was selling up to one million copies a day. Certainly, it was half the amount of copies of its predecessor *Le Petit Parisien*, but it was still a profitable business at a time when many of the other post-war startups were struggling because of prohibitive initial costs. Amaury eventually bought the assets, including ageing printing presses, a full sixteen years after moving in.

★ ★ ★

While the Tour de France was not a money-spinner in its own right, it continued to be a hit in terms of popularity. The French enjoyed soaking up the carnival atmosphere of the summer soap opera. It was not just a bicycle race; it was a travelling fair. Each year, wrote author Christopher S. Thompson,[11] *Le Tour* brought a chance to party and cut loose from the drudgery of the long winter months of working on farms and in factories. In the month of July, the riders who took part were transformed from

---

11 Christopher S. Thompson, *ibid*

working-class grafters to Greek gods. In the breathless prose of newspapers, they were the 'giants of the road'.

In the early years of pre-dawn starts and all-day stages, these young men, representing their national or regional teams, skirted the entire circumference of France. A significant proportion of the riders were foreign – Belgians, Swiss, Germans, Italians and Spaniards – and their participation helped spread the popularity of the Tour de France. Lugging their heavy steel bikes around with them on overnight trains, the international bounty-hunters crisscrossed the continent to compete in what was probably the hardest slog in sport. With no appearance fees, they financed their own travel costs to chase prize money and fame.

The race was perhaps the equivalent of running a dozen marathons in a month, and it was not surprising some riders snapped at the unyielding determination of the race organisers to make *Le Tour* the ultimate battle of man against the elements. At 2 a.m. on a chilly night by the English Channel at Cherbourg, the defending champion Henri Pélissier was told he could not wear an extra jersey as he readied for that day's 250-mile stage. Cursing his tormentors, Pélissier and his younger brother pedalled for fewer than 50 miles before giving up at dawn and retiring to a café at Coutances train station to warm themselves with steaming bowls of hot chocolate.

Although participants could rest their exhausted bodies for a couple of days in between each stage, those who went the distance were surely among the fittest athletes on earth. Life on the road would get gradually easier as the years went by. What was initially an individual race – *mano a mano* – gradually became a team game as bicycle makers got involved. With bike sales booming in the age before mass production of cars, they were easily drawn to the potential of this popular drama. Based in the Paris suburb of Neuilly, Alcyon was among the bike companies that began organising its own team more efficiently. Junior riders shielded the star rider from the wind, fetched him water and even handed over their wheels if his own were damaged. The objective was to keep the star – with the company logo stitched into his jersey – in the media spotlight.

Alcyon and the other bike makers were ahead of the curve; this was the dawn of sports marketing as we know it today. Among a few other corporate visionaries at the time were Peugeot, which bankrolled some of the earliest motor racing teams, and Lipton tea, whose owner competed in the America's Cup to indulge his passion for sailing and advertise his global empire.

For the best part of twenty years, the cycle companies competed aggressively for success. In this marketing war, Alcyon was even reputed to stoop to race-fixing in 1929 as its star rider struggled to stay in the lead. According to one account,[12] the company paid his rivals to ease off and guarantee the brand a third straight victory. As a result of this chicanery, and in an effort to try and revive the Corinthian values of old, the race organisers decided to do away with commercial sponsors the next year, reverting back to national teams. This decision might have made racing purer but it meant organisers themselves had to cover team costs, everything from hotel rooms to bicycles and regular meals. Facing so many extra bills, the race introduced an advertising caravan to bring in a new funding stream.

---

12 Jean-Francois Mignot: *Histoire du Tour de France*, 2014

For a fee, companies could join the travelling procession around France and display their wares to the huge crowds lining the route.

Every year, the line of vehicles became louder, brasher and more carnivalesque as advertisers competed to grab the public's attention. The maker of a domestic insecticide spray constructed a giant bug on a truck which made a buzzing sound as it passed by. A clothes maker with a dove in its logo created an effigy of the bird that made a cooing noise. All the while, good-looking *animateurs* and *animatrices* on board the vehicles handed out chocolates, paper hats and soft drinks. At the end of each stage, after the caravan had come to a temporary halt, liquor companies Martini, Pernod and Ricard kept the party going by bankrolling evening shows by popular singers. The festival atmosphere was infectious, even outside France. When Amsterdam became the first foreign host city at the start of the 1954 race, canal-side bars and cafés were allowed to open all night and a fairground was erected on Dam Square in the centre of the city. Millions of Dutchmen and women lined the race route, some waving the French Tricolore.

For all its popularity in western Europe, the Tour de France's fame did not go much further than an overnight train ride from Paris, and failed to cross the choppy waters of the English Channel. In London, the *Daily Telegraph* did not send a reporter to cover the race, only bothering to list the previous day's results in small print on its sports pages that were amply covered with county cricket reports. Meanwhile, *The Times* managed only a few lines about each day's action. In 1955, the surprise appearance of a British team at the Tour de France was as strange to *L'Équipe* writer Antoine Blondin as a 'turban-wearing delegation from

Pakistan showing up for the world championship riding post-man's bikes'.

If they managed to make a name for themselves, the travelling cyclists zigzagging across Europe by train could become rich. And a select few did. In terms of celebrity, the profile of the best riders of the post-war years was similar to today's football stars. Thanks to the endorsement deals and appearance fees they could command at one-day races, there was more money on the table available to them than they could possibly gather. Fausto Coppi would become the sport's wealthiest post-war star. The Italian was probably earning more than the best-known footballers of the era, such as Real Madrid's Alfredo di Stefano, partly because cycling was more developed commercially than football. While Di Stefano played in a plain white t-shirt without any branding, Coppi banked a retainer to bear the logo of bike maker Bianchi.

Besides this regular income, Coppi collected pay cheques worth as much as 800,000 francs from promoters who paid him to take part in evening track races in the winter, according to one of his biographers.[13] That was a large sum by any standard, far more than a senior French business executive at the time would take home in a year.[14] Over the course of three winter months, at the peak of his fame, Coppi picked up fourteen cheques for appearing at velodromes in Antwerp, Brussels, Ghent, Nice and Paris. He would make the overnight journey by sleeper train from Milan to Paris to race at the indoor Velodrome d'Hiver.

If Coppi's name was on the card, it was almost certain to be a sell-out. As many as 20,000 fans piled in to watch him take on

---

13 William Fotheringham: *Fallen Angel – The Passion of Fausto Coppi*, 2009
14 Christian Baudelot, Anne Lebeaupin: *Les salaires de 1950 à 1975*, academic paper published in 1979

other riders in an individual or team pursuit. Some of the fans would queue all day to see him in action. The posh section of the velodrome crowd on the upper tier were served by waiters in starched white shirts. These shows under floodlights were easier and more glamorous for Coppi than the exhausting work of road racing. He would travel in the first-class carriage to Paris, arriving looking relaxed in a pressed white shirt and suit. For these short *séjours* away from his home in provincial Italy, he would be put up in the smartest hotels and enjoy some of the city's finest food.

Life on the road at the Tour de France was altogether tougher and more humble. Each day, riders would have to endure scorching sun, rain showers and the pain of hour upon hour in the saddle. A picture from the 1949 Tour shows Coppi in a hotel room on the west coast of France, wearing a vest and pyjama trousers, while soothing his tired feet in a bidet brimming with cold water. Next to him, paint is peeling from the skirting board. For all that sacrifice, the Tour de France was not even a very big payday – the first prize was not a whole lot more than he received from one of those big nights at the Velodrome d'Hiver in front of adoring fans.

Summer outdoor criteriums – exhibition races on street circuits – were another quick way to bump up earnings. In one summer month, Coppi was offered up to 53 million lire, another small fortune, to appear in a series of criteriums in July and August.[15] The races took place across continental Europe. To squeeze in as many as possible, riders would take amphetamines to keep going. Often, the money was paid tax-free in brown envelopes.

---

15 Fotheringham, *ibid*

Coppi had a chiselled jawline, a Roman nose and a troubled aura, his brow furrowing when he rode alone. As a celebrity even outside the sports pages, he was visited by Gina Lollobrigida and Maria Callas. On the Tour de France rest day, schoolboys followed him around as though he was a Hollywood star. His public persona took on another dimension when a beautiful woman in a white raincoat was photographed with him at a race. He was outed as having an affair with Giulia Locatelli, the wife of a doctor. Locatelli is credited with encouraging his stylish life-style – he owned two Lancia Aurelia sports cars and dressed in check suits. In Italy, his affair created a scandal at a time when adultery was a crime. He and his lover stood trial and Pope Pius XII expressed his dissatisfaction. The Catholic Church, instead, promoted his great Italian rival Gino Bartali, who attended mass before Tour de France stages and dedicated victories to Saint Thérèse of Lisieux. He was known as Gino the Pious.

Goddet was keen to bring this all-Italian storyline to the Tour de France narrative. For newspapers, scandal like this was gold dust. The gregarious, well-travelled Parisian editor had long encouraged links with the Italian sports journalists, inviting the correspondent of *Gazzetta dello Sport* to work out of the *L'Équipe* office. Both sports dailies had a common interest in promoting cycling to sell papers. In Italy, *Gazzetta* could sell 600,000 copies after a Coppi win; *L'Équipe* typically boosted sales by 50 per cent to some 300,000 during the Tour de France. Goddet had increased the prize money eight-fold in seven years but, to his frustration, it was still not enough to guarantee the presence of the sport's biggest star. Coppi had so many money-making options open to him that he could pick and choose. The Tour was not always his priority.

After his second Tour win in 1952, Coppi sat out the next year's race to focus on the one-day world championship race in Lugano despite an extra cash offer from *Gazzetta dello Sport* to race the Tour. Instead of competing in France, he hired a car and travelled to the Alps with his lover to watch by the side of the road as his peers battled up the mountains. He was a no-show the next two years as well. Three weeks of pain in the saddle and the risk of being eclipsed by arch rival Bartali was not a big enough draw. Those three straight absences incensed Goddet, who feared the Tour de France was losing its status as the premier race. After blaming his sponsor Bianchi for lacking class, Goddet (then on the second of three marriages) joined the Vatican in questioning Coppi's morals, writing in *L'Équipe* that he was 'cloistered in vanity'.

For every superstar at the Tour de France, there were dozens of grafters much further down cycling's pay grades. Among them was a journeyman rider from Algeria, Abdel-Kader Zaaf, who lived for a time in Belgium and cadged lifts from richer cyclists to races in Europe to avoid paying train fares. He was on a daily wage of as little as 7 francs while riding for a North African team. As the race contenders set their sights on the financial spin-offs that came with winning the Tour de France, Zaaf scrapped for mid-stage prize money bonuses that were inserted by organisers to try and keep the pace lively. In an early stage of the 1951 Tour, he raced ahead of the field and picked up at least one 20,000-franc bonus (then about £20). His job for the day mostly done, he sat down by the roadside to eat and watch the rest of the riders fly past.

Later in the race, Zaaf asked Coppi's Italian teammates if they could collaborate. If they let him win the stage, he would lead them in a breakaway move to pull away from the rest of the field. 'I'll work for you but let me win a stage,' he said. 'I have a lot of mouths to feed at home.'[16] The Italians tentatively agreed but when, in the heat of the moment, they could not find consensus on the right moment to break away, Zaaf decided to go solo with 40 kilometres left, just as a big group of cyclists had stopped for a toilet break. He was chased down by the angry peloton, and his chances of a money-spinning stage win disappeared like an illusory pot of gold at the end of a rainbow.

At this point, the Tour de France was not even very lucrative for the race's promoters. Sizing up the race's own commercial potential, Amaury had moved to shore up its intellectual property rights before the Amsterdam race start. In the name of *Le Parisien Libéré*, he extended the race's trademark to Belgium, Germany, the Netherlands, Italy and Switzerland. If companies in those countries wanted to be one of the official Tour de France brands, they would have to pay his newspaper for the privilege. The trademark covered everything from beer and cigarettes to wine and watches and sports equipment.[17]

For now there was no rush of new sponsorship money from Amsterdam-based Heineken to become the official Tour de France beer, nor did cigarette-maker Nazionali in Rome want to use the race's name in advertising because Bartali sometimes smoked one of its filter-less cigarettes to calm his nerves before races. In fact, no financial upside outside France would emerge for years to come. Nevertheless, Amaury and Goddet figured the marketing spin-offs for their newspapers at home outweighed

---

16 Max Leonard: *Lanterne Rouge – The Last Man in the Tour de France,* 2013
17 European Union Intellectual Property Office online documents

the costs of organising the race. For crowds lining the route, the brands of *Le Parisien Libéré* and *L'Équipe* were positioned each day from the start line banner to the chassis of the race director's car. In the sprawling caravan, every vehicle was obliged to carry a mini flag with the names of the two titles next to the headlights.

To be one of the two newspapers that arranged the Tour de France was prestigious and undeniably some of the gold dust rubbed off indirectly on their owners themselves. So in 1956, Amaury and Goddet worked out a deal with the Government to acquire the race outright, returning it to private ownership for the first time in eighteen years. Amaury, the son of a road mender, was buying part of France's cultural heritage and burnishing his credentials as a proud patriot. Goddet was buying back the confiscated family silver from the state. In a four-page contract, both men agreed to buy the race outright for 20 million French francs, then about £20,000.[18]

★ ★ ★

While 114 Champs Élysées was the axis of the Amaury kingdom, the centre of Goddet's smaller kingdom was at the foot of a long hill in Montmartre. The *L'Équipe* office was in cabaret land between the Moulin Rouge and Pigalle red-light district. The vibe reflected the style of the newspaper editor whose favourite word was 'fabulous' and who, as a boy, had a family season ticket to the best shows in town. Goddet's office contained a life-size white stone statue of Bacchus. He would shrug when visitors remarked on the presence of the god of wine in his

---

18 Copy of agreement obtained by author from French national archives

workplace. The room was designed in an art-deco style before the war by his older brother, he explained. Party-loving Maurice had long ago abandoned the family newspaper, and nights on the town, to live on the Côte d'Azur.

Jacques was not afraid of a little ostentation himself; he had the symbol of the Olympics – five interlocking rings – added as a detail to the building's faux marble stone façade. There was a bar on the ground floor, where waiters in white starched jackets served refreshments, just like in the theatre. The actors in this world were young athletes, and they often dropped by to the Paris sports mecca. On a tour with his club Santos, the young footballer Pelé arrived laden with packets of a Brazilian coffee that he was promoting. American boxer Sugar Ray Robinson, dressed immaculately in a suit and overcoat, came in a Cadillac with an entourage that included his own hairdresser and a dwarf-ish type of modern-day court jester he called 'Little Boy'.

At the end of July afternoons, Parisians gathered in the street outside the building to find out what had happened in that day's Tour de France stage. A junior *L'Équipe* journalist wrote in chalk on a slate board the time gaps between the leaders and held it out of the newsroom window.

At the race, Goddet dressed up in safari garb, wearing a pith helmet, khaki shorts and long socks when he was in the humid south of France. From an open-top car, he communicated with riders through a megaphone. Even though he owned half of the race, Amaury did not bother to follow the circus outside Paris. He was not a big sports fan, although he would have loved to be there on 16 July 1960 when it passed the village of Colombey-les-Deux-Églises in the Haute Marne region. With an artistic flourish, Goddet shouted through his megaphone for the riders to halt the race. He then addressed the crowds who were massed on the pavement of the village's main thoroughfare. They included a tall middle-aged man wearing a dark grey, double-breasted suit.

'The Tour affectionately salutes President de Gaulle,' Goddet boomed, to applause from the crowd.

De Gaulle, accompanied by a single gendarme, gave a royal-like wave to the riders who respectfully doffed their cotton caps. Race leader Gastone Nencini pulled up, leant forward on his bike and shook hands with the President. 'You are going to win,' De Gaulle told the Italian. The race would end the next day in Paris so it was not, by any means, a wild prediction.

Every day on the Tour de France, Goddet wrote a daily dispatch from the race that used more florid language than most of the journalists he employed. Because they had to queue up to transmit reports by a public telephone or telex machine, developing a concise style saved time and money. Laboriously, the telex operator would type in their story, open up a line to the *L'Équipe* teleprinter in Montmartre, and transmit the copy at the rate of sixty words per minute. The process could take hours. It was even more problematic when staff reported from abroad. At the 1956 Olympics in Melbourne, the reporting team of six were instructed to cut the use of adjectives and punctuation, and had the no-frills copy rewritten with more panache in Paris.

Eventually, Goddet acquired a telex machine – which took up most of the back seat of a car at the Tour de France – and hired two operators who transmitted the copy of journalists. No longer did they have to waste time queuing up at the local post office to send their articles. This allowed more time for creative writing, and Goddet employed well-known authors including Antoine Blondin on a freelance basis to cover the race, turning the tired clichés of working-class riders into golden prose. Every summer, Blondin followed the race in a red Peugeot cabriolet with the *L'Équipe* logo on the chassis. In that car, according to race historian Jacques Augendre, 'the art of telling the story of the Tour de France was born'.

One of the riders Blondin wrote about with panache was Charly Gaul, a timid slaughterman from Luxembourg who rode with a small crucifix around his neck. He became known as the 'Angel of the Mountains'. He ascended alone through the rain clouds to win the 1958 Tour de France even as motorbike riders struggled with the conditions. Gaul rode, Blondin wrote, with the pedal stroke of a ballerina. Referring to notes scribbled down in the back seat of the Peugeot carrying him and two colleagues, Blondin composed his daily report at the hotel bar after each stage, while drinking a glass of absinthe. He wrote in ink in clear looping handwriting on squared schoolboy workbooks.

The last-placed rider on the Tour de France was known as the 'red lantern' – *lanterne rouge* – a term borrowed from the railways; the final train carriage had once carried one on the back. In 1957, describing the slowest rider slumped over his bike after completing a stage, he wrote, 'Nobody took any notice of him – and he took no notice of anyone. It wasn't the *lanterne rouge* in front of me; it was an old lady. When I spoke to him, he returned from far away, surprised to find himself where he was.' Blondin's accounts were filled with literary and historical references, and he worked hard to make sure the language was never dull. Borrowing the term for stage-race cyclists – '*forçats de la route*', 'convicts of the road' – he coined one for the band of writers accompanying them: '*forçats de Larousse*'.

If he made a mistake, even near the bottom of the squared paper, Blondin would tear up the page and start again. When he was satisfied, he handed the pages to a junior staffer who would hang around the hotel picking up reports from other writers and pass them to one of the telex operators. His poetic style was passed down to the next generations of *L'Équipe* reporters. One would begin learning his trade in the basement of the office, cutting out the telexes and distributing them to the newsroom.[19]

Sales of *L'Équipe* hovered around 200,000, declining sharply after the Tour de France. Although the paper was not losing money, Goddet was not exactly flush with cash. He had lost much of his wealth when the assets of *L'Auto* were seized. The laundry list of items placed under state control included his shares in the Parc des Princes and Velodrome d'Hiver, as well as a portfolio of shares and bonds that spanned everything from real estate to mining and included one particularly exotic investment – a bond that paid out twice a year from the state Government of Brazil's Amazon region.[20]

Deprived of these assets, Goddet had borrowed from friends and financiers to start *L'Équipe*, and then gone further into debt after the Government ruled he had to buy back the assets of *L'Auto*. He agreed to pay a total of 130 million francs, a hefty price to take back control of what his family had worked hard over half a century to build and maintain. Perhaps wary of

---

19 Philippe Brunel profile by James Startt: https://pelotonmagazine.com/features/aerogramme-day-17-philippe-brunel/

20 Copy of seized *L'Auto* holdings obtained by author from French national archives

revisiting his war effort, he said publicly it was a reasonable price but it left his finances in a perilous state.

His accounts were like his love life — chaotic. By the age of fifty, he was gearing up for his third marriage. His second was to a singer called Odette Etienne. She and her sister had a hit called 'Faire le Tour de France', a cheerful harmony about the desire of winning the race for every Frenchman with a bicycle. At twenty-four, she was perhaps too much to handle; they separated after five years. The divorce added another creditor to his balance sheet; he now had to make even more alimony payments.

However, one day in December 1954, a new moneymaking opportunity arose. Goddet's football journalists became excited about a plan for something called the 'European Cup of L'Équipe', a competition that would pit European football's royalty against each other in midweek matches under floodlights. The idea had come from a football correspondent on a trip to England to cover a friendly match between Wolverhampton Wanderers and Honvéd, the champions of England and Hungary.

On a Monday night, the journalist took his place at Molineux stadium outside Birmingham with 55,000 spectators. On a muddy pitch, Wolves rallied from a two-goal deficit to win 3-2. The correspondent normally telephoned his match report through to Paris by phone without taking notes, but missed the deadline for the next morning's newspaper and instead relayed his article the following day after reading the *Daily Mail*'s account that declared Wolves 'champions of the world'. At the bottom of his story, he took objection, citing Real Madrid and AC Milan as contenders to that title. To settle the debate, an international club championship should be launched.

It looked like a throwaway line but his colleagues in Paris ran with his idea and were now working on an outline for the competition. Under their six-page plan, competing clubs would get 90 per cent of the match-day income and 5 per cent each would go to the organiser (*L'Équipe*) and the national football association where each match was played. Away teams would get $1,000 each to cover their costs. Goddet liked the idea – the competition would increase sales of the newspaper on a Wednesday and Thursday when there was not much sport to draw in readers. But, already stretched financially, he did not want to take on the risk of bankrolling the European Cup of *L'Équipe*. He asked his pals at *Gazzetta dello Sport*, along with *Marca* in Madrid and *A Bola* in Lisbon, to share the costs.

Goddet also wrote to football's global and European governing bodies asking for support. FIFA replied it was an 'extremely interesting' concept but its statutes (article 38, to be precise) meant it could not organise a club competition. With snow falling at the Gare du Nord station, two *L'Équipe* journalists boarded a draughty train for a thirty-hour ride to Vienna to speak to UEFA officials at their first congress. Seated in a red armchair in his hotel suite, England's Stanley Rous received the pair with a warm smile and disappointing news – UEFA was not in the business of organising club competitions.[21]

Undeterred, Goddet invited eighteen European club representatives to Paris for a weekend meeting in a private room at the Ambassadeur hotel near the *L'Équipe* office. A group of middle-aged men wearing woollen suits, some with thinning hair swept back with Brylcreem, talked through a typed

---

21 *L'Équipe: 50 ans de coupes d'Europe*, 2005

one-page agenda. Among them was a former player and coach called Santiago Bernabéu, the Real Madrid president. He sat next to his young treasurer, working out the numbers on the proposed competition.

On Saturday night, Goddet took the group for after-dinner drinks to see Les Bluebell Girls cabaret act. The following day, the clubs agreed to *L'Équipe*'s proposed terms – a sixteen-team knockout cup, with the final at the Parc des Princes. The clubs would split organisation costs and take their own gate receipts. The newspaper would provide the trophy. Goddet had found a way out of taking on the risk of bankrolling the competition, a decision that in hindsight was not a good one. Alas, Monsieur Jacques was never smart with money; even a minority stake today in the European Cup, now the Champions League, could have made future generations of his family billionaires.

With the European Cup now going ahead, with or without its co-operation, UEFA finally agreed take over the organisation and the costs. A few months later, Alfredo di Stefano led Real Madrid out on to the pitch against Reims in the final. Advertising hoardings showed off the logo of *Le Parisien Libéré*. Real won 4-3 and lifted the cup made by a local silversmith with the *L'Équipe* logo on the base. When he handed Bernabéu the trophy, Goddet said, 'Take good care of it . . . it's a love child.' The newspaper had successfully launched, almost overnight, the biggest club competition in world football.

With Di Stefano bossing the pitch, Real Madrid won the next four editions of the European Cup. Off the pitch, the influence of Goddet on the competition faded fast. UEFA soon took the final from Paris to Madrid, and made a new trophy, removing the *L'Équipe* logo.

Nevertheless *L'Équipe* and its veteran editor continued to enjoy considerable international prestige. Goddet dined with government officials and diplomats, and was on first-name terms with the most powerful sports administrators. But his affable public persona hid longstanding money woes; because of the long shadow of his war record and his lack of business acumen, his finances were becoming ever more shaky. He needed a bailout.

When Goddet wanted to talk business, he would venture over to Amaury's patch, sometimes lunching with him at Fouquet's. One day in 1965, he trekked over to the Champs Élysées with a momentous proposal – he asked Amaury if he was interested in acquiring *L'Équipe*.

Goddet offered a 51 per cent controlling stake in the paper, but Amaury made clear that he wanted all the shares if they were to have a deal. He soon got his way, buying out not only Goddet's 70 per cent stake but the holdings of two of his associates. As part of the takeover, Amaury promised to keep Goddet, who was approaching sixty, in the editor's chair as long as he wanted. He would be carried out of the newspaper office in his coffin, Amaury joked. 'Jacques,' he said, 'you will only leave your home feet first.'[22]

The takeover allowed Goddet to clear all his debts. Publicly, little changed. He continued to toil on the next day's paper from the same Montmartre street where he had worked since the 1930s. But the family business had fallen out of his hands; he had relinquished all of his family jewels and Amaury now owned the Tour de France outright. To sort out its finances,

22 Goddet: *L'Équipée belle,* 1991

Amaury appointed René Laure, a straight-backed army general, as *L'Équipe*'s managing director. As they reviewed the incomings and outgoings, Amaury remarked that he could not understand why sports reporters were getting paid more than soldiers.

To trim expenses, he tried to merge *L'Équipe* with the sports desk of *Le Parisien Libéré*, but the army man managed to stop the move. Amaury also sought to reduce the number of pages. When the union of journalists threw up a roadblock to his cost-cutting, Amaury flew into a rage, blaming Goddet's lifestyle for the financial mess he had left behind. 'He has got us into this situation,' Amaury roared, 'because he was stupid enough to marry the wenches who seduced him.'

4

Rivalry

On the Tour de France, 1960s

As Amaury wrestled with the finances of *L'Équipe*, he was conscious of the downward pressure on his bottom line of organising the Tour de France. Because *Le Parisien Libéré* and *L'Équipe* together bankrolled the expenses of some 120 riders, it was now he alone who picked up the bill. This included the cost of all their meals, with a quart of red wine at breakfast and dinner. In a sign of how the 'open bar' culture was ingrained in the sport at the time, in Louis Malle's documentary *Vive Le Tour!* there is a shot of half a dozen riders jumping off their bikes midway through a stage and dashing into a café. They clack across the empty terrace in delicate leather shoes with a pedal-aligning metal groove on the underside. Inside, a barmaid hurriedly hands them beer bottles from the fridge. They scamper away without paying, leaving Amaury facing yet another invoice.

The amount of prize money was also a burden for Amaury, having climbed steadily in the 1950s.[1] The publicity caravan, the oddball rally of cars and trucks, still covered a portion of the

---

1 Prize money research by Jean-François Mignot viewed at https://bikeraceinfo. com/tdf/tdf-prizes.html

costs and mayors across France helped out by paying a hosting fee in return for the travelling circus stopping in their towns. However, with no ticket sales possible – apart from the last-day hurrah in the Parc des Princes – the race was always in the red. In 1953, for example, the owners had to write off a 12-million-franc loss as marketing expenses. The Tour de France was one of the few Amaury assets that consistently lost money and, after taking over sole ownership, he began to put pressure on his personal envoy at the race, Félix Lévitan, to look at ways for the race to break even.

Having started out shadowing Goddet, Lévitan, the chief sports reporter of *Le Parisien Libéré*, had gradually become more influential. While they put on a united front, the two Tour de France executives never really got along.

Lévitan felt out of place in the posh social circles frequented by his colleague. As part of a privileged upbringing, Goddet had attended a small boarding school run by a former army captain and his wife on a bend on the River Thames near Oxford. Cows grazed in fields, and boys could choose from cricket, rowing, fencing and fishing. He got around on a drop-handle-bar French racing bicycle, a gift from his father. After school, he joined his dad's newspaper, where he was given the honour of being the only French journalist to cover the 1932 Los Angeles Olympics. He sent back breaking news by telex, and longer reports by airmail.[2]

Lévitan was raised on the other side of the river from Goddet in rue de Frémicourt. It was part of a southern neighbourhood where working-class graft was everywhere. In these streets,

2 Goddet, *ibid*

butchers hauled carcasses straight from the abattoir on to wooden carts, dairy delivery men lined up tin pails on the pavement and vegetable sellers competed to hawk their produce while it was still fresh. Lévitan was the youngest son of a cobbler who had his shop at the heart of this activity. His father made galoshes by soaking old shoe rubber overnight in basins of water in the backroom. The next day, he would shape the rubber into water-proof shoes. The taxi drivers who took their vehicles for repairs at a garage next door liked them because they kept out the cold.[3]

Even in this humble part of town, newspaper stalls were everywhere, as abundant as grocers. Parisians craved news almost as much as food and Lévitan found himself immersed in the press business at the age of fifteen. He worked for a news agency as a telephonist filing copy to the news desk for journalists covering races at the Velodrome d'Hiver. A year later, he would have his own first cycling story published and, at twenty-one, he covered the Tour de France for *L'Intransigeant*, an evening newspaper. He rode pillion on the back of a motorbike over potholed mountain roads that were no more than gravel tracks. His job included filing the reports by phone or telegram at the end of each stage for the more senior journalists.

On one Alpine stage, he waited atop the Col de Galibier to check the time difference between the riders trekking up on two-gear steel bikes. On the other side of the mountain, there was a treacherous descent. Race director Henri Desgrange wanted to make sure journalists didn't get in the way – and that the evening papers did not scoop *L'Auto*, which did not come

---

3 Radio France: Félix Lévitan interview, 12/7/1976

out until the morning. He ordered Lévitan and his peers to let the riders pass. But the young man was determined to file his report in time for the evening edition and a furious argument ensued.[4]

Many years later, Lévitan would buy an apartment on rue du Renard, on the smart side of town near Notre-Dame cathedral. Yet throughout much of his working life, his jealousy of Goddet seemed to consume him. When Goddet received the Légion d'Honneur for services to France, he would wear the small scarlet rosette on his jacket lapel for official functions, taking it with him to the 1960 Rome Olympics. It was a discreet act of boasting, but Lévitan craved the state accolade, too. Soon after Goddet acquired a Ferrari, Lévitan bought a Jaguar sports car; he could not read English, so he attached stickers to gauges and levers with the French words for 'choke', 'heater' and 'windscreen wipers'. After the *L'Équipe* editor sought to become mayor of Saint Tropez, where he had a holiday home, Lévitan engineered the position for himself in Auffargis, south-west of Paris, where he had his second home.

Eventually, Lévitan, like Goddet, bought a home on the Côte d'Azur, too, acquiring an apartment on the seafront at Cannes. 'Why is he obsessed with following my shadow?' Goddet asked a confidant. 'I know he also wants my place in the Tour de France race director's car.'[5]

In the early 1960s, the tension between Lévitan and Goddet overheated. Acting on Amaury's brief to cut costs, Lévitan pushed to bring back teams funded by sponsors in the place of

4 Lévitan did not make it down the mountain in time to Grenoble to get his report into the evening edition that day
5 Marchand, *ibid*

national teams from western Europe and regional French teams. Under Lévitan's plan, the sponsors would underwrite the costs of the riders, relieving the pressure on Amaury's financial position. As a sporting romantic, Goddet did not like the idea and got into a long-running and bitter argument with his nemesis. He had always defended the national-team format as the purest version of sport. He saw the Tour de France as like the Olympics and World Cup, a global event where sporting values and prestige trumped business. Pelé's canary-yellow Brazil shirt was not cluttered by a sponsor's name at the 1958 World Cup, nor was Muhammad Ali's white singlet when he won a gold medal at the 1960 Games.

Amaury did not take much interest in sporting heritage himself. The only time he got really worked up about sport was when the French rugby team was playing. One weekend, he called Goddet in a fury when the French narrowly missed out on winning the Five Nations in a 6-4 loss to Ireland. The tournament came down to the final kick but, on a windy day in Dublin, the moustachioed French kicker screwed his penalty wide. Amaury blamed the English referee for letting the heavy Irish scrum kill the game and called Goddet to make sure L'Équipe castigated the official in the next day's paper.[6]

Amaury viewed the friction between Goddet and Lévitan with a certain sadism, letting it drag out for more than a year before coming down on the side of Lévitan. In 1962, the race returned to the format of privately funded teams. With the boom times over for bike makers, it opened up the space on the front of riders' jerseys to a wider variety of retail businesses,

6 David Garcia: *La Face Cachée de L'Équipe,* 2008

everything from Italian coffee machines (Faema) to French wine (Margnat) and Belgian beer (Wiels). Often the teams would be named after up to three companies in order to increase their budget, making the leaderboard messy. Jacques Anquetil, the first winner in this new epoch, raced for a team called Saint-Raphael-Helyett-Hutchinson that was funded by the makers of an apéritif, bicycles and tyres.

Almost overnight, the Tour de France riders had become marketing frontmen for dozens of corporations. Still fuming about the change after Anquetil's win, Goddet said, 'Riders have essentially become advertising hoardings.'

But now it was Amaury, not him, who called the shots. The return of private teams pared back *le patron's* financial losses and, in a more subtle change, empowered Lévitan to come out of Goddet's shadow.

The infighting between the organisers did not damage the spectacle. To most people, the teams – whether national or corporate – were merely a vehicle for cycling's biggest stars and they were now able to watch the climax of each stage live on television. Now the final climb of each day was filmed by cameramen riding on the back of motorcycles, bringing in-the-moment excitement to millions of people crowded around televisions in bars and living rooms. The close-up images public television was able to capture showed the furrowed brows and straining muscles of the cyclists as they fought to outdo each other. None of these battles was more captivating than the climax of the 1964 race when Anquetil appeared to be losing his three-year grip on the Tour de France.

With a couple of days left, he looked spent as he weaved from side to side on the road encircling the extinct volcano

Puy-de-Dôme. Unable to contain Raymond Poulidor as the road became steeper and narrower, Anquetil leant into his rival's shoulder. They rode shoulder to shoulder for a few moments, inseparable, like two exhausted boxers clinging to each other and unable to muster the strength for a knockout blow. Then Poulidor broke free and raced ahead to the summit, cutting the champion's advantage to 14 seconds.

It was a duel everyone was talking about across France. Anquetil was the blonde, blue-eyed champion from Normandy who was a godsend for the gossips: he had seduced his doctor's wife, and apparently more than one dancer while on military service in Algeria. Brown-haired Poulidor, tanned and muscular, was the housewives' choice: the son of a farmer from rural France, he was polite and humble. The more Anquetil dominated the race, the more his rival became popular.

The next day, Anquetil was able to defend his lead and his title but France had already fallen for the gentle charms of Poulidor, who took advantage of his popularity to draw premium appearance fees and endorsement contracts. "The more unlucky I was," he said, "the more the public liked me, and the more cash I earned."

Some of the other cyclists in this new era were only too happy to take on this secondary role as marketeers for the benefit of the new teams that employed them. Among them, Tom Simpson. He donned a bowler hat and carried an umbrella to play the role of a City gent for press photographers while wearing bike maker Gitane's kit. Never mind that he was the son of a coalminer from Nottingham.

One of the other potential keys to success for riders, apart from elevating their media profile, was doping. From the early days of the race, riders had consumed a concoction of stimulants from whisky to speed and painkillers. It was an open secret. Anquetil freely admitted to using drugs in his pursuit of success, while Simpson tragically died while struggling up Mount Ventoux, his heart stopping after taking amphetamines in an effort to win a better contract.

While Simpson's death sparked an outpouring of grief in 1967, the push for change only went so far. A few days later when a *L'Équipe* journalist wrote an article suggesting the Tour de France should be shortened to two weeks to protect the health of cyclists, there was hell to pay. For posing a threat to the race's business model, he got into so much trouble that he felt his job was on the line.

It would be decades before the race had a deeper reckoning with drugs.

5

Revolution

Paris, 1970s

Away from running his businesses, Émilien Amaury's refuge was the countryside. He bought a high-walled house called La Clairière (The Clearing) near the village of Vineuil-Saint-Firmin, north of Paris. It was close to the Chantilly forest where he was stationed with the Spahi horseback regiment during a two-year stint as a soldier in his youth. The house's wooden balconies and window frames were painted light blue and, set against the pinkish bricks of the pastel exterior, under blue summer skies it gave the mansion a Mediterranean air.

It was at this rural escape that he and his wife lived with their children Francine and Philippe. From the windows, looking out past the garden they could see the dense forest. In the cellar, there were reputed to be thousands of bottles of wine. In the gardens, there was a coop of hens that provided the family with fresh eggs. Completing the homely lifestyle were two dogs, Falk and Tournet, who were said only to obey the master of the house.

The area was a horseracing centre like Newmarket, drawing trainers and stable lads from across the English Channel to work for wealthy owners such as the Aga Khan. At the centre of the hub was Chantilly racecourse, home to the Gallic version of the Derby and Oaks races. Every morning, trainers took out thoroughbreds on wide sandy paths that cut through the forest beneath the green foliage of overhanging trees. Amaury owned three horses that he kept at a private stable and liked to take them out for an early-morning ride to clear his head, sometimes sharing the sandy tracks with champion jockeys. At the weekend, he took his daughter Francine for riding lessons.

On Sundays, the Amaury family attended mass at the village church. Inside the adjoining chapel was a stained-glass window paid for by Amaury depicting Saint François de Sales, the patron saint of journalists.

In his Champs Élysées office, life was by no means tranquil. Amaury was no longer the daring young Resistance hero making a name for himself in the newspaper business. His career had peaked and, now in middle age, it was bottoming out. He was struggling to prop up his business empire whose profits were being eroded by heavy costs and competition from radio and television.

Nor was he the darling of the Government anymore. He had fallen out with Charles de Gaulle, who had by now returned for a second stint as President. Amaury was incensed by the General's declaration that the people of Algeria, then ruled from Paris, should have the right to their own autonomy. It was a decision that gnawed at Amaury. In his late teens, he had served with the Spahis in north Africa, learning to fire a rifle, ride a horse and bivouac in the desert. He rejoined the same regiment at the start of the Second World War and, on special occasions, wore on the left lapel of his suit two medals won during France's brief warfare. He was deeply disappointed that

De Gaulle should even consider giving up the lands he defended as a young man.

In his increasingly right-wing weekly *Carrefour*, Amaury railed against De Gaulle for being so liberal. As other newspapers condemned bombings in Paris by groups opposed to Algerian independence, Amaury ordered his *Le Parisien Libéré* editors to remain silent about the terrorism in his increasingly downmarket daily. The militancy over Algeria reached a new level in August 1962 when military officers tried to assassinate De Gaulle as he travelled in a black Citroën DS saloon towards Paris: the car was peppered with machine-gun fire but the general escaped unharmed.

Among younger generations, respect for Amaury and his Resistance peers was declining fast as memories of the war faded. He, in turn, was becoming increasingly embittered about life away from his countryside retreat. On the evening of Monday, 6 May 1968, rioting students rampaged in and around the rue de Rennes where Amaury had lived with his young family before and after the war. They dug up cobblestones to hurl at police, overturned cars and buses, slashing their tyres and setting them on fire. Over previous days, they had rioted in the Latin Quarter, the district where he had dined and watched movies with his wife. Police responded with tear-gas grenades and handed out beatings with wooden batons that the *Guardian*'s correspondent said were sometimes of a 'sickening ferocity'.[1]

The street outside Amaury's long-time home resembled a battlefield; there were burnt-out cars and buses. Most older men and women were too scared to leave their homes, shuttering

---

1 The *Guardian* article 7/5/68 (reproduced 6/4/2018)

their blinds, although some came on to the street to argue with the students. For Amaury, more fanatical than ever about order and authority as he approached his sixtieth birthday, it would have been a shocking sight to behold.

Inspired by the uprising, millions of workers joined a nation-wide protest. Among them were the union men of *Le Parisien Libéré*. The movement was a pushback against the post-war establishment that Amaury was part of. According to an American correspondent in Paris who witnessed the scenes, one of the key messages of the crowds was that 'a glorious record in the Resistance no longer justified its holder laying down the law.'[2]

As the world changed around him, Amaury gradually morphed into a 'paranoid' ageing man, who turned to fortune tellers and faith healers for guidance, according to his biographer. He became a 'fragile man of marble'.[3] Sometimes, his newspapers reflected his increasingly bizarre views. He was known to bark orders down the phone line to the newsroom from his country house. In one article, perhaps on his insistence, *Le Parisien Libéré* reported that some of the ringleaders of the 1968 student rioting on the Paris pavements were foreign militias who took their inspiration for insurrection from the leftist fighters waging war in the swamplands of Vietnam.

When, one day, Jacques Marchand, a representative of the newsroom at *L'Équipe*, arrived at 114 Champs Élysées for a meeting, Amaury looked him up and down with a suspicious

---

2 Daniel Singer: *Prelude to Revolution, France in May 1968*
3 Vadepied, *ibid*

air before fixing on a design on his scarlet tie. Suddenly, Amaury lunged at Marchand, grabbing him by the collar.

'How dare you provoke me?' Amaury said. He had spotted what he thought was a Communist hammer and sickle on the tie.

Marchand, shaken up, explained it was nothing of the sort. It was the motif of a bicycle. The tie was a gift from the British Cycling Federation. He was a cycling reporter, not a revolutionary.[4]

Typically only upstanding men with short hair and a military background commanded Amaury's respect. Squinting at new acquaintances because of failing eyesight, Amaury would seek out their jacket buttonhole to see if they, too, were decorated. At his first meeting with a recently hired news editor at the same newspaper, he eyed him suspiciously and said, 'I hope you are not flaky.' Depending on his mood, he would go on to address him by his first name, surname or – if really angry – his job title: '*Monsieur directeur de la rédaction*'.

Amaury's demeanour would terrify staff. Senior executives called to La Clairière for weekend meetings nervously gathered in his bureau as he sat with his dogs by his side. The staff shifted nervously in their seats, anxious to get on with the hounds and keep their master calm.[5]

Le Parisien Libéré was hamstrung by outdated printing presses and a labour-intensive production process. A move downmarket to compete with *France Soir* had only served to give it a more trashy air that, privately, Amaury was ashamed of. By 1974, even with more sensational headlines and gossipy stories,

4 Jacques Marchand: article in *L'Équipe Raconte L'Équipe*
5 Edouard Seidler: *Sport à La Une,* 1986

it was making an annual loss of 16 million francs. As Amaury sought ways to win back readers, he experimented with two versions – the traditional broadsheet and a new tabloid. But standing in his way to modernise production was *le Livre*, the print union. If he cut one of the editions, workers would be made redundant.

This impasse was partly his own fault. After the war, he had helped draft a Government directive that meant that the union allocated blue-collar workers to dozens of newspapers in Paris on a daily basis. The idea of sharing production costs was to open up the market and pare back the pre-war dominance of media magnates. However, the directive had handed power to workers, who now answered only to one man – the print union boss. Roger Lancry had long hair, played saxophone in a jazz band and drove a snail-shaped Citroën 4CV. He could shut down the *Le Parisien Libéré* printworks with a flick of a switch.

In a mark of his influence, Lancry was invited to a sumptuous breakfast in the Ritz hotel suite of Robert Maxwell when the owner of the UK's *Daily Mirror* was planning to launch a French tabloid.[6] Some of the blue-collar newspaper workers earned more than journalists and one or two of them would turn up for work at the wheel of a Mercedes, the same marque of car that Amaury drove. Sometimes, they were permitted to knock off work after five hours. The union had passed down militancy from father to son, even spreading their solidarity abroad. They sent shiploads of paper pilfered from *Le Figaro* to Cuba to print Fidel Castro's propaganda sheet *Granma* – two large fishing boats

---

6 Roger Lancry: *La Saga de la Presse – D'Émilien Amaury à Robert Hersant*, 1993

were quietly sent from Le Havre to Havana until the scheme was uncovered by the newspaper's management.

Amaury was determined to break Lancry's grip on his business. He ordered new presses from the United States that did not need laborious page-by-page typesetting. Then he began to trim costs, reducing the number of copy editors by a quarter. In response, the union suspended publication of his newspapers. Amaury ratcheted up the tension by announcing plans to jettison the broadsheet edition.

The following year, Amaury made good with his threat, shutting the old presses and laying off 650 staff. Gathering his men, Lancry called the fight with Amaury an all-or-nothing contest. Lose to him and the other newspaper owners would defy them. In the winter of 1975, the union went on strike, occupied the premises of *Le Parisien Libéré* and hunkered down.

As Amaury tried to restart production at a new plant in the suburb of Saint-Ouen, Lancry oversaw guerrilla tactics. The union men put up roadblocks outside the plant to stop trucks carrying the paper. When they were able to get their hands on bundles of freshly printed newspapers, they hurled them into the Seine. On the streets, they fly-posted a Western-style 'Wanted' picture of Amaury in dark glasses, which he wore to protect his cornea damaged by ageing. 'This man has deprived 650 workers of their jobs,' the poster said. Some workers even trekked to shout slogans against him outside his countryside home, where his faithful dogs kept them at bay.

Amaury fought back, hiring private delivery firms and security guards at the new plant. The conflict became increasingly ugly and the roads outside a battlefield; one striking worker was blinded by tear-gas thrown by police.

At the start of the summer, a bomb that police believed was intended to harm a senior *Le Parisien Libéré* journalist was left at the home of a reporter with the same name from news wire Agence France-Presse. Lancry said that the print union had nothing to do with the attack. The union was robust in pursuing its objectives, but it was not a criminal organisation, he said. The AFP journalist died from his injuries.

At the height of the battle, Amaury was blockaded into a building by print union workers. As he was finally escorted out by bodyguards amid jeers, he turned to Lancry, glared at him and said through gritted teeth, 'I will never negotiate with you.'[7]

* * *

Amaury's battle with blue-collar staff was into its second year when, on a crisp April morning, hundreds of print union workers rose before dawn across Paris and, in a convoy of buses, converged on country roads around Chantilly near La Clairière.

This time, their target was the Amaury-owned cycling race Paris–Roubaix that was known as the 'Hell of the North'. The course, across bone-shaking stretches of cobblestones, was often accompanied by freezing cold and rain. A fall on the jagged, slippery slabs of stone could mean a smashed cheekbone, or broken collarbone.

It was the highest-profile one-day cycling race in France, part of the portfolio of events *L'Équipe* had inherited from *L'Auto*, and brought in a sponsorship contract from Banque National de

---

7 Lancry, *ibid*

Paris. The riders who finished the seven-hour slog – and many didn't – were often so caked in mud that they were unrecognisable at the finish. Tradition dictated that they showered off the dried layers of mud in a spartan stone changing room.

After breakfasting on medium-rare steak and pasta, the cyclists left their hotels and pedalled leisurely out of the main square of Chantilly at 9.20 a.m. They passed the Château de Chantilly, whose previous owners included the aristocrat Henri d'Orléans and the English bank Coutts, which looked after the Queen's money.

In the genteel surroundings, it was an easy start in the so-called neutral zone for the 153 riders, who included Eddy Merckx, known as 'the Cannibal' for his voracious appetite for victory. Merckx was the insatiable king of the road, winning five Tours de France, three editions of Paris–Roubaix and a multitude of other major races.

He had first won the Tour in 1969 at age 24, pummelling the rest of the competition with a winning margin of more than 17 minutes, and then kept winning at an extraordinary rate. At the Tour, his unerring domination in the yellow jersey led a middle-aged Frenchman, frustrated by the marauding Belgian, to punch him in the stomach. In the summer of 1975, chasing a sixth victory in seven years, Merckx finally cracked. In a frantic attempt to make up time, he broke his jaw when he collided with another rider. Vomiting and spitting out blood, he carried on, against the doctor's advice. When a journalist asked him later why he had persevered, his answer was simple: 'It's not in my character to give up.' He had the same bloody-minded determination on the bike that Amaury possessed in his working life.

Émilien Amaury leant on his Resistance pals in Charles de Gaulle's provisional government to build a newspaper empire from zero. Here, aged 38, he works the phones at his Champs Élysées office. (*Keystone-France/Getty images*)

The *L'Équipe* office in Rue Faubourg Montmartre was a Paris landmark for decades, receiving visits from sports stars including Marcel Cerdan (here arriving by car), Sugar Ray Robinson and Pelé. (*Presse Sports*)

With 'a pockmarked face like a bitter apple, big ears and a little nervous body' the manual worker Jean Robic was no pin-up but became an overnight star in winning the 1947 Tour de France.
(Stringer/Getty Images)

Italians Fausto Coppi (left) and Gino Bartali battle it out in the Alps at the 1949 Tour de France. Bartali won that day's stage to take the lead only for Coppi to overhaul his advantage the next day. *(Presse Sports)*

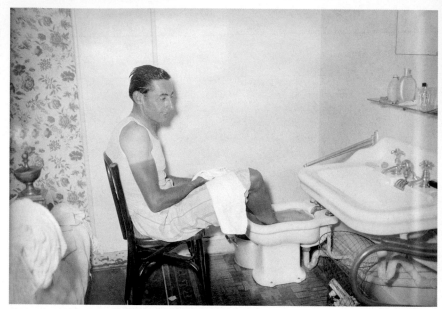

Fausto Coppi soothes his feet in a hotel room in Les Sables d'Olonne after a stage of the 1949 Tour de France. Paint peeling from the skirting board shows how unglamorous life on the road could be. *(Presse Sports)*

Looking like a film star, Fausto Coppi receives flowers from singer Line Renaud after winning the 1949 Tour. The sash on the bouquet promotes wool maker *Laines Sofil*, the yellow-jersey sponsor. *(Presse Sports)*

Charles de Gaulle – in a double-breasted suit – watches Tour de France riders go by in a crowd of spectators near his country home in Colombey-les-Deux-Églises. *(Hulton Archive/Getty Images)*

In safari get-up, the Tour's showman director Jacques Goddet jokes with deputy Felix Lévitan and Jacques Anquetil in 1962. Lévitan coveted Goddet's role and eventually wrested power from him. *(Presse Sports)*

In the first Tour de France finish on the Champs Élysées President Valéry Giscard d'Estaing helps Bernard Thévenet into the yellow jersey. Émilien Amaury (in dark glasses) and Felix Lévitan look on. *(Michel Ginfray/Getty Images)*

Émilien Amaury arrives at the Élysées Palace for a reception with President Valéry Giscard d'Estaing to mark the end of the 1975 Tour de France. *(Presse Sports)*

Members of the print union drink beers and smoke in the canteen after shutting down the printing press and occupying the offices of *Le Parisien Libéré* to protest cuts announced by Emilien Amaury. *(Gery Gerard/Getty Images)*

Striking workers, protesting job cuts at *Le Parisien Libéré*, littered a stretch of the Champs Élysées outside Émilien Amaury's office with copies of the newspaper in 1976. *(Getty Images)*

Philippe Amaury (left), his wife Marie-Odile – wearing a fur coat – and sister Francine watch as a priest bows before the coffin carrying the body of Émilien Amaury following his death in a horse-riding accident. *(Michel Artault/Getty Images)*

With an eye on marketing the Tour de France in the US, Felix Lévitan and wife Geneviève welcome Dustin Hoffmann (centre) to the 1984 race. The actor was researching a proposed cycling movie that was later canned. *(Landrain/Presse Sports)*

On this cold April morning, as the cyclists chatted amongst themselves on the way to the start line they heard shouting further up the countryside lane. The road was blocked by hundreds of noisy union officials in flat caps and donkey jackets. Shouting 'AMAURY . . . SCUMBAG!' they chucked newspapers into the air and on to the windscreens of race organisers.[8]

They left a narrow passage for the cyclists. As Merckx passed, they slapped a red 'Solidarity with *Le Parisien Libéré* workers' sticker on the back of his russet-coloured Molten team jersey. It was a good-natured gesture – protestors and riders had no gripe with each other – and police carrying rifles and batons did not intervene. However, with the road strewn with newsprint, the race start was delayed by more than an hour, a small psychological victory for the union men.

Lancry's pressure was taking its toll on Amaury. His newspaper was losing thousands of readers every week and there was no end in sight to this war of attrition; the strikers, supported by a fighting fund of donations from their peers on other newspapers, were as united as ever.

Two days after the race, Amaury was driving his Mercedes 450SE along the same country lanes with plenty to worry about. He was a couple of miles away from home, near the pretty country town of Senlis where his wife was from, and he knew the rural roads around there well. Narrow tarmacked roads cut through wheat fields, with overhanging trees on either side obstructing the view, and making bends potentially treacherous.

---

8 Scene from *A Sunday in Hell,* a 1976 documentary by Jørgen Leth

Perhaps tired and impatient, he put his foot on the accelerator. He was travelling at 50 kilometres per hour, according to his own estimate, when he lost concentration. His car veered across the road, slamming into the side of an oncoming Renault 5 hatchback.

At the wheel was a twenty-eight-year-old woman but it was her friend in the passenger seat who was more seriously hurt. As the two dazed drivers tried to recall to police what had just happened, an ambulance arrived on the scene, brought out a stretcher and rushed the victim to hospital. Berthe Leclercq never recovered, dying from her injuries six months later at age forty-three. Amaury was tried for manslaughter at a local court, adding another layer of trauma to his already stressful life. The newspaper baron did not attend the hearing because, his lawyer told the court, he feared it could become another target for a union protest.

The state prosecutor agreed with Amaury's lawyer, saying he was guilty of only a 'small lapse of concentration' and asked for his driving licence to be suspended. At a hearing a few weeks before Christmas, he was ordered to pay the modest amount of 76,650 francs (£9,000 today), to Leclercq's family. Amaury did not make any public comment.[9]

With the court case adding to his anxiety, the last thing Amaury needed was disruption extending into his other business interests. When his faithful Tour de France race director Félix Lévitan, who was by now aged sixty-five, called to suggest training a younger man to become race director, Amaury told him, 'I don't want to hear anything about

9 *Le Monde*: 3/12/76 and 10/12/76

succession plans right now.'[10] The Tour was one of the few parts of his empire that was untouched so far by the turmoil engulfing him.

In fact, the Tour was more prestigious than ever. The previous year, the Government had lifted the race's official credentials to new heights by agreeing to Lévitan's request to allow it to finish on the Champs Élysées for the first time. It was a major statement – closing the avenue usually only happened on Bastille Day – and huge crowds came out to cheer the cyclists. One journalist called the final day of that year's race the biggest popular fête in the centre of Paris since the Liberation.

Amid the fanfare, French President Valéry Giscard d'Estaing sat alongside Amaury at the finish line, a show of support for the embattled newspaper baron. The president helped Merckx's conqueror Bernard Thévenet into the yellow jersey on the podium, while D'Estaing's wife congratulated the winner. Amaury stood a step back, just out of the limelight. Sealing the bond with the state was a memento that Thévenet received from the president, a handmade porcelain bowl.

With Amaury as its owner, the Tour de France was a target for protestors the following year. During the seventh stage, near Nancy, a group of union men began to litter the route with unread copies of *Le Parisien Libéré*. Cyclists at the head of the race had to dismount and wheel their bikes over a road covered four inches deep with newsprint, according to one account. Upset at this disruption to the national fête spectators at the roadside rushed to clear up the papers, allowing the race to carry on virtually unaffected. One of the bystanders drove to

---

10 Author interview with Xavier Louy, Lévitan's deputy

Lévitan's hotel that evening to proudly recount their good deed. Messing with Paris–Roubaix, it seemed, was one thing, but interrupting the Tour de France was a step too far for the French public.[11]

Conscious of the Tour's status in France, union officials dialled down protests, handing out leaflets explaining their grievances to race spectators instead. On another stage, they broke into a VIP enclosure, but did no more than seize the microphone of a television journalist and begin commentating in a playful manner. In what was a long and sometimes boring race, a bit of humour did not go amiss in the travelling circus. At one point Dutch cyclist Gerben Karstens – known as Karst the Clown – picked up a traffic cone while riding and placed it on his head, to loud cheers.

On the final day in Paris, prepared for an attack, black-uniformed riot police were positioned along the route. The union men decided against disrupting the Champs Élysées finale, although they took a few hundred more francs off Amaury's in-the-red balance sheet by littering the avenue outside his office at number 114 with some more of his unsold newspapers.[12]

11 Radio France: Félix Lévitan interview, 12/7/1976
12 Lancry, *ibid*

6

Death

Piste des Lions, Chantilly, 2 January 1977

A t around 8.00 a.m., the wheels of Émilien Amaury's car crunched across the gravel drive of La Clairière as he drove out on to the open road towards the stables at Chantilly. There was frost on the fields and the roads were empty. A day earlier, New Year's Day, he had taken out one of his six horses, called Chouan d'Ive, and had told the stable lad to prepare him again for the next day. When he arrived this time, the young man had fed and groomed the nine-year-old gelding. However, he informed Monsieur Amaury that the horse was nervous, perhaps because of the particularly cold morning air.

In an effort to calm him down, he had taken him for a short canter in the forest. Amaury had experienced no problems the previous day and climbed on to the restless thoroughbred and made for the forest and its wide sandy paths.

Amaury led him around the forest for about twenty minutes, by which time Chouan d'Ive still had not shaken his ugly mood. In a moment of restlessness, Amaury was unseated from the saddle. Cursing under his breath, Amaury remounted with the help of two early-morning walkers and continued in the direction of the Piste des Lions, a 3-mile-long straight. It was here on a spectacular wide track flanked by overhanging trees that jockeys prepared for some of the biggest flat races of the season. They would gallop through the forest at speeds of up to 40 miles per hour. Amaury liked the adrenalin of riding fast, even if, at the age of sixty-seven, he was not as athletic as he once was.

But just as they accelerated from a canter to a gallop, the horse reared up, hurling Amaury from the stirrups headfirst into a tree trunk. A few minutes later, at 10.30 a.m., he was found unconscious, slumped at the foot of the tree. A passer-by raised the alarm. Amaury was taken by car to the jockey hospital at Chantilly racetrack. From there, he was transferred to the emergency unit of a Paris hospital suffering from serious head and spine injuries. Doctors said he had no hope of surviving and, at 4.30 p.m. the same day, he was taken back to the family home La Clairière, from where he had set off only a few hours earlier. His daughter Francine, who was in her forties but still lived with him, was floored. Her mother had died three years earlier.

Now she was all alone in the big house. Émilien had adored his daughter, a literature graduate. At his office, he would proudly show off her two-tome history of *Le Petit Parisien* newspaper that started out as a university thesis. He had financed its publication. Later, Francine had taken on a series of mid-level roles in the family business. Once, she accompanied Eddy Merckx to a reception at the *L'Équipe* office after one of his Tour de France wins, standing primly before the window with him and his wife as crowds massed on the street outside. But her life was underpinned by countryside pursuits, walking the dogs and riding the horses. To mark their mutual affection, Amaury had ceded about 25 per cent of his shares in *Le Parisien Libéré* to his daughter over the last four years of his life. Émilien was less generous to his son, an introverted young man who had decided to study law. According to one account, he spent just fifteen minutes at Philippe's wedding to Marie-Odile Kuhn, the middle-class daughter of a pharmacist from Strasbourg.

At 6.30 p.m., a press release carried by *Agence France-Presse* announced that Émilien Amaury was dead. Such was the animosity between Amaury and the print union, his senior management at *Le Parisien Libéré* assumed it was murder. Police from the local Chantilly police station began enquiries, phoning the print union leader Roger Lancry to find out if he had an alibi. He was two hours away at his country home, enjoying a Christmas-period break. 'Thanks for checking up on me,' Lancry said.[1]

There was little sympathy for the dead press baron after his bloody two-year battle with the print union. The next morning, left-wing newspaper *Libération* ran the front-page headline, 'AMAURY'S HORSE ESCAPES UNHURT FROM AN ACCIDENT', a cruel and deliberate shrug at the passing of the press baron. A few days later, satirical magazine *Charlie Hebdo* ran a caricature of him lying in a coffin, a menacing bulldog face, strong chin, slicked-back hair and boxer's nose. 'A Bastard Dies', the caption read. A horseshoe, the symbol of luck, covered his eyes.

On this Monday morning, as newspapers carried the story of Amaury's death, Francine slipped out of the house with

---

1 Lancry, *ibid*

Jean Sangnier, her father's lifelong friend. They went by car to the Credit du Nord bank on the small high street of Chantilly. It was a ten-minute drive. Francine had brought the key to open her father's safe and allow them both access to a private room adjacent to the entrance. Inside, they found the compartment stacked with dossiers and official documents detailing his equity in twenty-seven companies. There were also some rolls of banknotes. One unconfirmed report said there were tens of millions of francs tucked away there. But, after sifting through the papers carefully, they discovered that there was no Will.[2]

Francine was anxious to know how her father's business would be divided up and whether she would get his La Clairière estate and Champs Élysées office, not to mention his other assets worth an estimated 65 million francs,[3] including the prime money-makers *Le Parisien Libéré* and the *Marie-France* magazine. At home, Francine continued her search for the Will, uncovering a white envelope in a drawer that looked promising. On the front, in green ink, was written 'This is my Will' and on the back the initials 'E.A.' Inside, there was a letter dated 29 May 1968.

A nervous flyer, Amaury had apparently written the letter in his study at home before boarding a light aircraft to Strasbourg to look at a new printing press. It was written before his wife's death and outlined what should happen to his wealth if the plane crashed. Francine would take his place as president and

2 Vadepied, *ibid*
3 *Le Monde*: 'Le testament d'Émilien Amaury', 14/6/1980. According to Insee, France's National Institute of Statistics and Economic Studies, 65 million francs in 1997 was worth the equivalent of about €40 million in today's money.

general director of *Le Parisien Libéré* and manage the portfolio of twenty-seven companies with her mother. Her brother Philippe, the letter continued, 'having wanted to make his life outside the family, should continue his law studies and receive from his mother and sister the means to live comfortably, without passing 250,000 francs per month'.[4] After this snub to his son, Amaury signed off the letter with a hug to his faithful dogs Falk and Tournet.

Francine presented the green-ink letter to a notary to validate.

She and her brother stood side by side at the front of the tiny old village church for the funeral. It was an icy day; the slate roof was covered with snow, and there was no heating inside. The cold seeped in through the low sandstone arches and grey stone floor. The pale light struggled to penetrate the stained-glass windows. Everyone kept their coats on. As the coffin was brought in, the siblings got up from their rickety wooden seats. The casket was draped in a large French flag, freshly laundered and pressed. Resting on top, displayed on a velvet cushion, were half a dozen medals Amaury had been awarded. Standing alongside were serving soldiers from the Spahi regiment. Next to them were frail-looking, white-haired Resistance members wearing berets and carrying flags bearing the Cross of Lorraine emblem that was adopted by Charles de Gaulle during the war.

Afterwards, at the nearby cemetery of Saint Pierre de Chantilly, three gendarmes stood guard at the burial, perhaps wary that the print union might deliver a final show of defiance.

---

4 Vadepied, *ibid*

In the biting cold, Philippe stood next to his wife Marie-Odile, who was dressed in a black fur coat and fussy high heels. Francine was on her own, a few steps away, looking tired and wan as her father's coffin was lowered into the ground.[5]

On French television, a debate was already swirling around what Amaury's death meant for the print workers on strike for the last two years. In an interview, Claude Bellanger, the founding *Le Parisien Libéré* editor, who was now its managing director, said Francine would replace her father as chief executive, if she wanted. But she was short on management experience and agreed that he should continue to manage the day-to-day operation of the newspaper. The following day, he announced he would continue the fight against the print workers.

Bellanger was not as personally invested in the fight as Amaury and, a few weeks later, he saw no other viable option than to open negotiations with the print union. He even agreed not to publish the newspaper on the day of a general strike that year, a decision Amaury would have reviled. This conciliatory behaviour upset Francine, who said he was acting contrary to the wishes of her father. Finally, one summer morning after all-night negotiations fuelled by Camembert sandwiches, Bellanger reached a peace deal – all 650 laid-off workers would be offered a new job or early retirement.

By now, Philippe Amaury had gone to court to seek his share of the family fortune. He disputed that the letter his sister had found in their father's office was actually his Will. His lawyer even suggested it might be doctored. A judge called on handwriting

---

5 Description of funeral and burial based on black-and-white Getty Images archive photos

experts to scrutinise the missive. Philippe's lawyer made much of the fact that the letter had no signature, and the solitary 'E.A.' initial seemed to be scant authorisation given he had scattered less-important documents with his initials.

Surely this piece of paper was not enough to assign one of France's biggest fortunes?

Part II

Squeezing the LeMond: the Tour de France in the Television Era

7

Succession

Saint-Ouen, 1983

After months, then years, of legal back and forth, the judge ruling on the case of *Philippe Amaury v Francine Amaury* decided that the green-ink letter presented by the defendant did not constitute a Will, partly for one simple fact – there was no signature. The family assets, the judge ruled, should be therefore split 50/50 between the two siblings. In a further setback for Francine, he said the 25 per cent stake in *Le Parisien Libéré* given to her by her father before his death was not binding because the divestment was also not witnessed by a notary.

Finally, there was clarity. But then Francine lodged an appeal, kicking off another round of hearings. Several more months passed. More legal bills were racked up. After she had exhausted her final chance of victory in the courts, she agreed to a deal. By now, six years had passed since their father's death. Under the agreement, Philippe would get *Le Parisien Libéré,* the cornerstone of the empire, plus *L'Équipe* and the Tour de France. She would take the old advertising business and two women's magazines – *Marie-France* and *Points de Vue* – plus a cash makeweight worth millions of francs[1], money which Philippe had raised by selling 25 per cent of his newly acquired assets to an investor.

A new era was here, and it looked completely different. France's newest press baron did not resemble his father in any way. Philippe Amaury wore thick-rimmed black glasses and a shapeless, double-breasted grey overcoat over his suit. The dome of his head was bald. Even in his thirties, he looked and dressed as if he was much older. There would be no office on the Champs Élysées, no lunches in Fouquet's and no hobnobbing with the French political élite. Philippe moved into the *Le Parisien Libéré* office in the drab north-west suburb of Saint-Ouen.

Saint-Ouen is an industrial sprawl at the end of metro line 4. Bordering a ring road, it was home to a flea market, a warren of antique stalls at the foot of a grey skyline of modern office blocks. The redbrick *Le Parisien* office was across five floors. Philippe drove into the car park at the back, going up to his office via his own private lift, and did not cross paths with many staff. Because of his reclusive nature, he was little known by most of his 1,000 employees. He did not address staff meetings. It was said that if he went through the main reception, he would need to show an identification badge to prove that he worked there. In an undated black-and-white picture, he stands alone in his vast office, looking a little lost. He stares out into the distance

---

1 Francine went on to forge a disastrous alliance with Belgian publisher Maurice Brébart, shackling herself with his heavy debts. She ploughed 50 million francs into their joint venture *Editions du Hennin* in return for 75 per cent of the business, but the company could not keep up with payments, leaving her inheritance rapidly losing value. She soon sold *Marie-France* to Bauer, a German media company, and *Points de Vue* to businessman Jimmy Goldsmith. After that, Francine largely disappeared from public life.

through a large window. Next to him, there is a pile of newspapers neatly stacked on his desk.

Philippe lunched on his own behind a pillar in a middle-class restaurant called Le Coq de la Maison Blanche, which, in those days, had a Michelin star and a set menu but was cheap enough for even those who were careful with their money. One day, when one new staff member saw him reading the newspaper while eating, he went over for a chat. Amaury muttered a few words, before returning to his paper. When the employee recounted his experience, he was told, 'Don't even think about saying hello . . . everybody leaves him alone.'[2]

Across town in historic Paris, the other pillar of his publishing empire, *L'Équipe,* was still propping up the same Montmartre hill alongside ageing theatres, nightclubs and restaurants. Classic cafés with zinc bars, shops selling fur coats and posh hats were being replaced by a hotchpotch of convenience stores and restaurants catering to a younger clientele; each morning, the smell of cooking from a Chinese restaurant wafted through the window. Amid the changing scenery, the building remained very old school. A concierge still washed the cobblestone courtyard each morning with a mop and bucket of water.

Inside, over three floors, seventy-five journalists worked amid a warren of corridors and wooden staircases. The office was gradually being modernised. Editor Jacques Goddet's art-deco office was given an upgrade – black lacquer wall panelling was replaced with pinewood. Desktop computers had started to replace typewriters. After the war, staff had used a pulley to

2 David Garcia: *La Face Cachée de L'Équipe,* 2008

heave post and equipment to the upper floors, but now there was a lift. The clubby world of the sports press was alien to Philippe and he would have felt like a rabbit caught in a trap in the *L'Équipe* building. He rarely visited.

On quiet Friday afternoons, Philippe would slip out of *Le Parisien* office. With his wife's golf clubs in the boot of her modest Fiat Tipo hatchback, they would drive to the edge of town and spend the afternoon playing eighteen holes. It was a chance to discuss business strategy. The husband-and-wife team hired a couple of smart executives from the advertising industry to lead the day-to-day management of the business. Philippe would delegate them to speak at the traditional New Year's champagne toast to a couple of hundred staff. He was too shy to do it himself.

Jean-Luc Lagardère was the investor who had acquired 25 per cent of Philippe's business. For now, he was a passive share-holder, but he had designs on a takeover if the shy press baron could not turn it around. He had the first right of refusal if Philippe wanted to make another equity sale to raise additional finance.

A dashing entrepreneur, Lagardère had become something of a French society icon by successfully leading a military arms company. Dubbed 'Tarzan' by his staff for his work ethic – he held 7.45 a.m. meetings with them on the factory floor – he was the polar opposite of the introverted Philippe, who could not summon the courage to speak to his own employees. Alongside making missiles, Lagardère had used his company's expertise to design a Formula One car that Jackie Stewart drove to the 1969 title. Occasionally, he took a weekend off, hopped in a plane and went to Courcheval to go skiing with the French

President, Giscard d'Estaing.[3] Philippe, who was more than a decade younger, shunned the bright lights and Parisian society to spend time with his family at home.

Lagardère had recently acquired Hachette, the doyen of French publishing that opened the first news-stand in Paris outside the Gare de L'Est in 1852, and this part of the business – now called Relay – owned stores at stations and airports across Europe and north America. He also owned the women's magazines *Elle* and *Paris-Match*. But he was an entrepreneur by nature and was always looking for deals; he wanted to pick off Philippe's new assets.

Philippe was determined to make a go of it on his own, however. With his inner circle he set about recovering the circulation of *Le Parisien Libéré* that had plummeted to barely 300,000 copies. During his father's ownership, the red-top newspaper, like the *Sun* in London, had moved downmarket with a right-wing populist bias to compete with *France Soir*, and its mix of crime, sport and gossip gave it the moniker 'the newspaper of the concierges', the doormen who flicked through its pages in the halls of smarter apartment buildings. A typical front page had a racy picture of the fourth wife of Greek shipping magnate Stavros Niarkos in leather hot pants, leather waistcoat and no bra. Philippe's verdict was diplomatic: '*Le Parisien* was a great newspaper. Later, it became less good.'

By now, the French had abandoned not just *Le Parisien*, but the press in general. The age of the average newspaper reader was sixty-nine. (That compared to fifty-two in the rest of

3 Vincent Nouzille & Alexandra Schwartzbrod: *L'acrobate, Jean-Luc Lagardère ou les armes du pouvoir*, 1998

Europe.) Now television dominated and Parisians no longer relied on the vendors at the city's bottle-green news kiosks to provide them with information. 'Before, when there was an event we went on to the street to read about it,' one veteran reporter said. 'Now we go home to see it.' The Government gave out subsidies and tax breaks worth 5 billion francs per year to prop up newspapers, but increasingly once-wealthy press barons considered the business model to be unsustainable.

However, every day Amaury turned up to work looking for ways to prove them wrong. In a design makeover, Amaury removed 'Libéré' from the title after forty-two years and replaced the red masthead with a more conservative blue. Inspired by regional American newspapers, *Le Parisien* cut out naked flesh and targeted middle-class households, with a dozen hyperlocal editions in and around Paris. It was not a title for the intellectuals; it never claimed such pretensions. Instead, it focused on a mix of local news and practical information such as movie times and chemist opening hours.

As Amaury got to know the press business, he discovered just how wasteful it was to flood every district of the capital with newsprint every morning. *Le Parisien* destroyed about 150,000 unread copies each day, about one in five produced.[4] The pulped papers were seen as just part of the business; daily sales depended on the vagaries of each person's daily routine. In more wastage, at the end of every night, staff threw out a pile of single-use aluminium sheets used to print that morning's edition. They were dumped, with a clatter, on to the back of a scrap metal truck waiting at the back door.

Challenging these inefficiencies, Amaury's team increased

---

4 Clyde Thogmartin: *The National Daily Press of France*, 1998

household deliveries to almost 20 per cent of sales – a higher ratio than any other major newspaper in France. He collected an extra €500,000 a year by selling the aluminium plates to local factories. Finally, he invested in more economical regional presses outside Marseille, Nantes, Lyon and Toulouse, which each needed only seventeen production staff to make a regional edition called *Aujourd'hui*.

Readership of *Le Parisien* rose steadily to about 450,000. Meanwhile, sales of *France Soir*, with its page-two picture of a topless model, plummeted to below 100,000. Philippe's methodical route to progress in the brash 1980s of hairspray and shoulder pads did not change him. There was no rock-'n'-roll lifestyle, no sports car, no boasting in the media. 'I am no Citizen Kane,' he said in a rare interview. His biggest ambition was to fly by Concorde to New York. But he did not afford himself time for such a luxury. There were more challenges ahead that he faced, one day at a time.

The newspaper industry was about to face a new problem. At the time, the French Government was convinced it needed to supercharge the tech industry to keep pace with the United States, whose standard bearer in this growing sphere was a company called International Business Machines Corp. In 1982, in an attempt to compete with IBM's might, the Government began distributing millions of free beige desktop computers with a flip-down keyboard. People could use these to dial up via their home phone line to a video text network known as Minitel. The project, a precursor to the Internet, meant millions of French were online before their American counterparts. They could dial up the platform to search the phone directory, order pizza and check their bank balance.

This state initiative was bad news for *Le Parisien*, which faced losing readers who bought the paper to check the weekend weather forecast, scan ads for jobs, apartments and second-hand cars. From now on, readers could do all of this on Minitel. Newspaper owners led a public-relations offensive, warning state control of information was a threat to democracy. In a compromise, the Government agreed to give newspapers free access to a channel (3615) on Minitel where they could make money by posting ads, along with providing real-time information such as traffic reports and sports scores. *Le Parisien* became part of a twelve-month pilot.

The outcome was not exactly as expected. Before long, Parisians began to see posters of sexy women on billboards alongside the number 3615. Wearing a silk negligée that rode up her tanned thigh, a brunette with luxurious hair cascading down her back looked out at them seductively. The text next to her said: '*Between women and men, in complete privacy, live, 24 hours per day*'. For *Le Parisien* and other newspapers, this was a means to lure customers to the most lucrative part of Minitel, the adult chat rooms that lured bored teenage boys and male office workers.

After the first three minutes gratis, *Le Parisien* received 80 centimes for every minute someone stayed online. Scrambling to tap this new demand for real-time news, information and lascivious chat, Amaury's newspaper employed sixty full-time staff on the project, and watched revenue steadily grow. Some newspapers paid students to keep the clients online as long as possible with titillating typed messages.[5] To save the blushes of

---

5 Denis Perier: *Le Dossier Noir du Minitel Rose*, 1988

users, the charges would not be itemised on the next month's phone bill.

It was something of a contradiction; even as Amaury made his newspaper more respectable, he received a cash windfall from these so-called pink messages that helped make the newspaper profitable again. In 1987, the new owner of *Le Parisien* was among private companies to share in $240 million of revenue from Minitel.[6]

As Amaury restored the fortunes of *Le Parisien*, he sent one of the two young executives he had hired across town to run the rule over another pillar of his new empire.

★ ★ ★

On the first floor of the *L'Équipe* office, the Société du Tour de France had appropriated its own office behind a door with a frosted-glass window; this was the domain of Félix Lévitan.

When Émilien Amaury bought out Jacques Goddet's shares in the Tour de France, Lévitan became the race's managing director, overseeing Merckx's reign and then the emergence of a French superstar, Bernard Hinault. Ever since, he had given his nemesis a weekly update about preparations throughout the winter months. But he kept some of the most important stuff to himself. When asked about the division of power between him and Goddet, Lévitan said, 'It's easy. I'm in charge.'

For years, Lévitan had a simple mandate from Amaury – the Tour de France had to break even so his newspapers could reap the spin-offs from extra newspaper sales. *L'Équipe* sold an extra 100,000 copies per day during the three-week race which,

---

6 Perier, *ibid*

totted up over three weeks, amounted to about 2.5 million francs in extra revenue.[7] Right up until his death, *le patron* had trusted Lévitan to take care of the race. Now he was gone, Lévitan had lost his compass a little. He barely knew Émilien's son Philippe, who had shown little interest in the development of the family's sports assets. But, after all these years, he was still in the groove. It felt as though he was obeying Émilien's orders from beyond the grave. Philippe would let him get on with it for a few years yet.

Even in his late sixties, Lévitan was as trim and dapper as ever. In his office, he would lunch at his desk on a ham sandwich and glass of water. He could also be as fierce as ever as he prowled around his territory. On the Tour de France, when he walked into the press room, the chatter and clack-clack of typewriters subsided and reporters looked up anxiously to see who might be in trouble this time.

As light drizzle fell in the Dutch university town of Leiden at the start of the 1978 race, Lévitan saw the local promoter had sold advertising space in the hall where the 110 riders would soon roll down the ramp for the opening time trial. Lévitan paced around, muttering to himself. He had not given permission for this. It would dilute the value of the fees paid by the official race sponsors outside. He angrily ordered the adverts to be taken down.

As the start time neared, a few French riders told him that the narrow, rain-soaked route, partly over cobbles, was slippery, and asked for the short stage to be cancelled. There was no such request from the Dutch cyclists, who led a home sweep of the

---

7 Then the equivalent of about £250,000 (GBP)

top four places. As the winner Jan Raas slumped on his handle-bars after a 6-minute, 39-second dash around town, Lévitan announced, with an air of vindictiveness some put down to the unauthorised advertising, that the times would not count because of the wet conditions. The Dutchman would not don the yellow jersey. The next day, a local newspaper described Lévitan as the 'Tour Dictator'.[8]

Lévitan shrugged it off. 'If you're a public figure,' he said, 'you need to have a crocodile's skin.'

By now, it was becoming more difficult for Lévitan to balance the Tour de France's books. The costs were approaching 8 million francs. To increase sponsorship money, he created a jersey for the top climber whose polka-dot design was bank-rolled by chocolatier Poulain, and a white jersey for the top young rider financed by industrial giant Alfa-Laval. A men's underwear maker was among a plethora of other minor spon-sors, putting its name to a daily prize for the most elegant performer. To look after this expanding array of brands, he employed a capable Parisian – his daughter. Claudy Lévitan was said by one colleague to be, after her father, the best-paid employee of the Société du Tour de France.

These minor deals were helpful, but they were not game changers. The Tour de France was by no means an economic behemoth: it remained a national festival with a cast of riders from western Europe. Less than two percent of the field were from outside the Old Continent. Bernard Hinault, the domi-nant rider of the early 1980s, was a huge star in France but little

---

8 *Account based on NOS* documentary *'De valse start van de Tour de France' (2011)* and article in *De Trouw* newspaper, 1/7/2015

known in most parts of the world. Goddet had his own ideas about how to give the race a financial boost. He called for a global edition of the Tour every four years – like the World Cup and Olympics. The quadrennial race, he wrote in a front-page editorial in *L'Équipe*, would have stages spread around the world. It would, he told readers, win the sport of cycling new fans and create 'tremendous economic interest'.

Lévitan was withering in his response, not least because Goddet was interfering with his position as race director. There were 'insurmountable complications' with his idea, he said, including time zones and flight stopovers. 'Playing at ocean-hopping would be fantastically costly and fantastically pointless,' Lévitan wrote. There was no need to embellish the Tour de France: it was beautiful as it was. 'Listen, when a work of art is of high quality, it stands on its own . . . so a painting by Salvador Dali, for example, does not need an elaborate frame to enhance it.'

The Tour de France 'will one day go' to the US or Japan for a couple of opening stages but nothing more, Lévitan said. He fired off a twenty-page complaint to Philippe Amaury about Goddet's insubordination. The shy new boss presumably felt a little awkward being asked to intervene in a spat between two old men who should have known better than to quarrel in public.

Lévitan looked at other ways to take the Tour de France global, focusing on the Tour de l'Avenir – the Tour of the Future – as a stepping stone for nations outside cycling's heartland. This approach had already had some success. When Alfonso Florez won the week-long race in 1980 with a Colombian team, he came home from Paris to Bogotá to receive a rapturous welcome at a velodrome owned by drugs baron Pablo Escobar. Three years later, Colombia entered the Tour de France for a voyage into the unknown – an unprecedented tilt at the yellow jersey. The attempt captured the imagination of the Latin American country. In a playful reference to Los Conquistadores that had once pillaged its continent for gold, one of the team sponsors billed the modern-day adventure as 'La Conquista de Europa'.

With skinny frames, dark skins from hours in the tropical sun, and nicknames such as *El jardinerito* (the little gardener) or *El flaco* (the skinny one), the Colombians added a new layer of exoticism. They came with an army of excitable radio journalists who gave French star Laurent Fignon his own nickname – *Filet Mignon*. The radiomen recorded their breathless commentary on to tape, added advertising jingles, amassed a pile of one-franc coins and then played the audio down a public phone line to Bogotá.

With Colombian sports fans hooked, Lévitan stalked the halls of the annual general assembly of cycling's ruling body offering to cover the cost of plane tickets for dozens of foreign cyclists to the Tour de l'Avenir. The dawn of a new age of long-distance travel meant it was not a prerequisite for riders competing in French races to be an overnight train ride away. He invited federations from Morocco, Turkey, Venezuela, Costa Rica, Ireland, Mexico, Finland and Japan.

The Japanese took the plunge. However, their riders, more familiar with the short-course, track-cycling *keirin* races, were not used to riding wheel to wheel on open roads. The team assembled by the National Cycling Federation overlooked basic rules, such as consuming calories as they burned energy on the bike, and struggled to keep up. Only two of the seven-man team finished. After taking reams of photos and reams of notes, the team's coaches flew home and went back to the drawing board. Meanwhile, Japanese television didn't seem to quite know what to make of the peculiar world of road cycling, packaging Tour de France highlights with a feature on the making of *foie gras*.

Lévitan's biggest target was the United States, and he had begun working with an entrepreneur to try and crack the American market. Philippe Riquois was a tall urbane globetrotter who shuttled across the Atlantic, assisting French companies expand into the US. As it stood, the Tour was not bringing in any big money from broadcasting; even the French public broadcaster forked out next to nothing. But Riquois reckoned deep-pocketed US television networks would be willing to pay. After all, the market price to air the 1976 summer Olympics in Montréal had recently risen to a whopping $25 million.

Riquois enlisted the help of a sports marketing firm based on New York's Park Avenue. Capital Sports was run by two former college athletes – from baseball and American football. They had heard of the Tour de France but it seemed to them perhaps a bit too quirky, a bit too oddball for the US market: in their eyes, it was akin to other unusual European spectacles like bullfighting in Spain. The American media did not cover the race with the same gravitas as in France. A *New York Times* freelancer in Nice filed entertaining dispatches. Under the headline 'ANQUETIL WINS THE TOUR DE FRANCE AND EUROPE YAWNS', he described the cautious French champion as riding like an insurance agent. On this side of the Atlantic, Le Tour was hardly considered prime-time sport. Still, in a booming market, there was room for even niche sports. A few years later, US sports giant IMG began production out of its London studios on a

syndicated weekly sports show called *Transworld Sport* that
included *kabaddi*, a mixture of rugby and wrestling popular in
India.

When Jonathan Boyer became the first American to make
the Tour de France start list in 1981, the interest level went up
a tick. Boyer had a home near Lake Annecy in France, allowing
him to train in the Alps, learn to speak fluent French and
become an insider in the world of pro cycling. He had been
hired by the Renault team to mentor a promising nineteen-
year-old rookie called Greg LeMond. That year, LeMond was
considered too young and inexperienced to start the Tour. So,
as a *domestique,* Boyer would serve French star Hinault, bringing
him water bottles and riding in front of him to shield him from
the wind. NBC decided to send a four-man production crew to
France to track Boyer's progress. For the rights, the network
agreed to pay $100,000 to air a thirty-minute segment over four
weekends. It wasn't anywhere near the $25 million Olympics
deal, but it was a start.

From Park Avenue, Capital Sports sent a young staffer to Nice
for the start of that year's race to assist NBC.[9] He arrived on the
Côte d'Azur, where he was dazzled by the shimmering
Mediterranean, and the colourful array of brands on show at the
Tour. Even for the employee of a marketing company which had
embossed winter Olympics mascot Racoon Roni on everything
from enamel pins to glass ashtrays and belt buckles, the convoy of
bikes and cars was astonishing. There were logos everywhere.
Crammed on to Hinault's bike and kit there were seven on display:

---

9 The staffer was Robert Ingraham, then aged twenty-seven. This segment is
largely based on author's interview and email exchanges with Ingraham.

Renault cars; TF1 television; Elf petroleum; Miko ice creams; Gitane bicycles; *Le Coq Sportif* clothing; and *L'Équipe*.

Even when all the space on the yellow jersey and other team kit was taken, it was still possible to grab some of the limelight. A few years earlier, Pernod had arranged for Eddy Merckx to wear number 51 on his jersey to promote Pastis 51, an anise apéritif. For cheeky marketing stunts, however, nobody trumped Guy Merlin, a real-estate developer. He persuaded Lévitan to start and end several stages of the Tour de France in the 1980s at a fictitious beachside town called Merlin-Plage that did not exist except in the pages of a glossy sales brochure. It was the name of his new holiday resort, where he was selling 100,000-franc apartments.

The young American sports marketeer, while surprised by the naked commercialism at the Tour de France, soon got a feel for his job. His mandate was to help provide the best possible access for NBC. Speaking through an interpreter, he secured permission for a cameraman to ride pillion on a motorbike alongside the peloton to film Boyer. It was a privilege usually reserved only for the host broadcaster. Tradition dictated national champions wore their country's colours during the season. Boyer, however, was fitted out in a Stars-and-Stripes jersey, even though officially he was not American champion. After bending the rules for Pernod and Merlin, Lévitan had no problem adjusting them for NBC.

The American television production team wanted to show everything – images of their man slogging his way up the switchbacks of the snow-topped Alpe d'Huez, having his thighs kneaded by a masseur in his hotel room, and tucking into a steaming evening meal of chicken and mash. Occasionally,

Hinault's team shooed the NBC crew away but they did a good job cramming three weeks of action into four half-hour segments. A senior American sportscaster, fresh from covering John McEnroe's Wimbledon victory, talked over the videotape to add gravitas. Asked if the Tour would catch on back home, Boyer said, 'The fire is lit.'

He was right. The following year, CBS outbid NBC, paying twice as much, and a staff journalist at the *New York Times* went to the race, receiving red-carpet treatment including a chauffeur-driven car. At one point, his veteran driver, who seemed to know everyone, pulled alongside to chat with Hinault as he rode on one low-key flat stage. Hinault turned, smiled and proceeded to lean on the open car window and explain that day's race tactics to the astonishment of the journalist in the back seat. 'It was like watching a baseball game from the New York Yankees dug-out, and asking the star hitter how the game was going.'[10]

As the race pulled into Paris, Riquois and his American business partners celebrated how their bet was taking off with a sumptuous dinner under glass chandeliers at the Hôtel de Crillon, finishing with a dessert of raspberries and cream. CBS and the *New York Times* were big noises in the media, they all agreed. They decided to parlay their $120,000 cut of the two-year CBS deal into starting a race of their own to keep the momentum going. It would be called the Tour of America.

The following spring, Lévitan persuaded several teams to travel to the United States for the three-day race to contest $100,000 of prize money. Fifty-five European riders took part

---

10 Author interview with former *New York Times* columnist George Vecsey

along with twenty on North American squads. Riquois appointed himself race director, hiring Lévitan as a consultant. (Lévitan's $20,000 fee went to the Société du Tour de France.) The *New York Times* told readers that it was a transcendental moment for the sport, like the US baseball team visiting Japan in 1934.

As the peloton rode past the rolling landscape of Virginia, with picket-fenced houses, Riquois stood in the open–top race director's car at the front of the field, imperiously swatting away curious bystanders encroaching on to the road. One onlooker said the tall Frenchman looked like a field marshal. The race finished in the capital by the White House just as cherry blossoms had come into bloom.

While the race looked good, there was not much substance to the initial enthusiasm. Riquois had failed to attract US dollars; the main sponsor was French car manufacturer Renault. While French company executives shrugged about chit-chat that riders were doping – it was nothing new – American companies were wary of being associated with drugs. 'There was constant apprehension about this thing lurking in the shadow,' said a Capital Sports executive.[11] 'It was the great unspoken.' As a result, sponsors stayed away, the Tour of America ended with an $839,000 loss, and was discontinued.

Ever the optimist, Riquois shrugged off the disappointment; he saw dollar signs elsewhere that would soon make up the deficit. As Boyer had said, the fire was lit in the United States. In 1984, not one but two Americans cyclists stood on the Tour de France podium – a man and a woman.

11 Ingraham, *ibid*

With an eye on the US market, Lévitan had introduced a women's Tour de France, to keep pace with the Olympic Games, which that summer in Los Angeles had women's cycling races for the first time. At the inaugural Le Tour de France Féminin, thirty-six riders rode the last forty miles or so of the men's stage, providing a curtain-raiser for waiting crowds. Laurent Fignon, the defending men's champion, was among those in the conservative French cycling establishment who were less than welcoming, saying he would prefer to watch women pursuing other endeavours. But the women's event was a hit, partly thanks to Marianne Martin, from Boulder, Colorado.

The *New York Times* published a picture of Martin winning a stage in the Alps on its back page. The image shows the twenty-six-year-old raising one arm into the air with an expression of surprised delight. A British photographer covering the race noticed that the women riders, competing for a tiny fraction of the pool of prize money, appeared to be having a whole lot more fun than the men. French crowds cheered them on enthusiastically. Martin won the race outright and stood on the Champs Élysées alongside Fignon. Both of them wore the yellow jersey.

Also standing on the podium was Greg LeMond, who finished third overall in the men's race and, at the age of twenty-three, wore the white jersey as best young rider. Finishing among the top three of 170 riders was a tremendous achievement for someone competing in the race for the first time. No wonder the Tour of America flop was shrugged off as inconsequential by Riquois. In Martin and LeMond, here was a fresh-faced pair of Americans who would really put cycling on the radar in US sports.

At around this time, Mark McCormack, whose Cleveland-based IMG agency had represented sports stars including

Muhammad Ali and Bjorn Borg, was among those to become interested in how the internationalisation of the French race was gathering pace. McCormack spoke French and was familiar with the old-fashioned ways of Europe. In a VIP box at the French Open, he met Goddet and made an enquiry about buying the Tour de France.[12] His invitation was quickly declined.

With the race's commercial outlook brightening, Lévitan negotiated a clause with domestic public television under which Société du Tour de France could sell the live images it produced to foreign broadcasters. It meant they would not have to incur the considerable expense of sending a production crew like NBC; they could just take the host broadcaster's feed, and talk over it from the comfort of a studio.

Following small but landmark agreements on this basis in Japan with Fuji TV, and Colombia with Radio Cadena Nacional, Riquois struck a deal in the UK with Channel 4. Broadcasting from London, Channel 4 host Richard Keys presented a 'bike racing for dummies' edition by discussing everything from gear-changing ('it looks very complicated') to water bottles ('the riders drink as they go along') – and thanks to slickly edited highlights, the coverage in the UK was soon pulling in each day more than 1 million viewers. There was surely now no doubt the Tour de France was going global?

During the summer of 1984, Lévitan, on behalf of Société du Tour de France, signed a contract with Riquois under which the businessman could deduct the previous year's Tour of America loss as expenses, offsetting them against the

---

12 Louy interview, *ibid*

international promotion of the Tour de France. Both men were keen to put the flop behind them and concentrate on the promise that lay ahead.

By most accounts, Lévitan did not explain the arrangement clearly either to Philippe Amaury or his most senior executives. For two and a half years, the contract went unexamined in a locked drawer of Lévitan's desk in the *L'Equipe* office, one more secret hidden among the warren of rooms and creaking wooden staircases.

The following summer Riquois was watching the race in a huddle with a group of Tour de France executives. While technically these execs were supposed to be neutral, there was little doubt they favoured a home winner – they were a patriotic lot and besides, a French champion had always raised everyone's spirits. Hinault was sometimes difficult to love because of his pugnacious character, but there was no doubt he was a tremendous competitor and a national hero. At one point, Hinault, who was comfortably the race leader, crashed and lay on the ground for several minutes, receiving medical care.

The right side of his face covered in blood, he eventually rode gingerly to the finish line. While the group of Tour de France execs groaned, one of them glanced over and saw that Riquois had a glint in his eye.[13] If Hinault abandoned, his teammate LeMond would be in the lead. He was already anticipating the commercial spin-offs of an American man riding down the Champs Élysées in the yellow jersey.

---

13 Louy interview

8

Scandal

Montmartre, 1985

At 8.30 a.m. on an October morning, an elegant woman wearing a scarlet shawl strode across the courtyard in front of the *L'Équipe* building, her high heels click-clacking on the cobblestones. Marie-Madeleine Schillinger had become one of the few women bankers in 1960s France after attending business school. More recently she had just set up her own public relations and advisory firm and her clients included Morgan Stanley and the broadcaster RTL. Normally, her work took her to the smart eighth *arrondisement* or the sleek skyscrapers of La Défense business district, but today she was in a more downmarket corner of the city. Her trip to Montmartre was to enquire about obtaining the Tour de France rights for Chinese state television. After announcing herself at reception, she entered the office of Société du Tour de France on the first floor. She was greeted by Lévitan's deputy, Xavier Louy, a friendly young man who apologized for the smell of cooking wafting up from a Chinese restaurant.[1]

Neither Lévitan nor Philippe Riquois was there. By then in his seventies and semi-retired, Lévitan had begun to spend most

---

1 Author interview with Xavier Louy

of the week in his apartment in Cannes where the weather was more clement. As for jet-setting Riquois, who knew where he was? He could be in Paris, Miami or New York.

With both executives absent, Louy was unable to help his guest much, but he offered Schillinger a coffee and they chatted about the economics of professional cycling. She was eager for inside information. In his previous job, Louy had worked in the office of the Prime Minister and was responsible for closing public roads during the Tour de France. That's how he had got to know Lévitan. His job at the Société du Tour de France was more unconventional; one of his tasks each year was to persuade the Soviet Union Cycling Federation to bring an amateur team to the week-long Tour de l'Avenir race by handing over an envelope of cash. 'With a bit of money,' he said, 'we worked things out.'

Even in faraway lands, the Tour was catching people's attention. Certainly, the arrival of LeMond on the scene was a trigger for more interest. The previous year, Dustin Hoffman had turned up when the race reached the Pyrenees to research a role in a planned movie based on a 1973 fictional book, *The Yellow Jersey*. Hoffmann accompanied Lévitan in car number 1 which preceded the riders. In an interview with the *New York Times*, the actor said the human drama in the film would make up for people's lack of knowledge of the French race. 'Even if you make a film about Eskimos, it should say something to other people,' he said.[2]

At their morning meeting, the conversation flowed between Louy and Schillinger. He felt she was a classy lady: she was taken

---

2 *New York Times*, 'Dustin Hoffman's Tour de France', 14/7/1984

by his warm smile. In fact, they got on so well they would eventually begin a romance, and two years later they would marry. During their courtship, they talked more about the Tour de France's peculiar business model. The finances were a bit untidy, like the under-the-table cash deal with the Soviet Union, and the role of Riquois was somewhat of a mystery.

Schillinger went looking for more information about the race's cash flow. That was not so easy because the financial accounts were not published at the time. However, using her business contacts, she managed to obtain a copy of the agreement signed by Lévitan two years earlier in which Société du Tour de France wrote off the 1983 Tour of America's losses of nearly $1 million. She showed it to Louy. He was astonished – it was a contract that he had never seen before.

After ruminating for several days, Louy decided to write a note to his boss. He found it easier than broaching the subject with him in person. Everyone knew that Lévitan could be prickly. The note set out how he was unhappy with the increasingly important role of Riquois in the Société du Tour de France, even though he was not an executive or even an employee of the organization. When Louy phoned a couple of days after sending the note, Lévitan hung up, without saying a word.

For the rest of the week, Lévitan would not take his calls. Eventually, when they met in person, he explained drily that he could no longer work with him. Feeling like an outcast, Louy went to the office of Jean-Pierre Courcol, the managing director of *L'Équipe*, and the man Philippe Amaury had sent to modernise the newspaper.

Embarrassed by his predicament, Louy explained to Courcol how his relationship with Lévitan had broken down over the

mysterious contract. He asked if he could switch to another part
of the business.

After taking notes of all the details of the bust-up, Courcol
said he would see what he could do.

For a while, Louy heard nothing back.

Then, on a March morning, Lévitan arrived at his office on
the first floor to find a court official waiting at the door with a
search warrant. The man took an inventory of everything in his
drawers, and asked Lévitan to open his safe. His personal posses-
sions were stacked in boxes in the corridor. Five business
contracts were taken away for examination.

It was, Lévitan said, similar to when he was detained by the
Nazis in a round-up of Jews during the war. Three years into
the German occupation, he had been interned in one of 200
individual cells in a military prison in Paris. From his cell
window, he saw other prisoners being led away one by one to
be shot.

Now, when he least expected, Lévitan felt his world crumbling around him.

A few days later, on a Saturday, the dull winter weather known
as *la grisaille* cast a heavy leaden sky over the zinc and slate rooftops of Paris. Amid the gloom, the warmth of spring was a
distant prospect as Lévitan was summoned back from sunny
Cannes. When he arrived, he found Philippe Amaury waiting
for him at the *L'Équipe* offices, along with Courcol and a second
senior sharp-suited executive. At least there was a familiar face
– his old nemesis Jacques Goddet.

The proud seventy-five-year-old man facing the inevitable
inquisition had a single trusted ally in the room, his lawyer Jean-
Jacques Bertrand.

'It was like a trial,' Bertrand said.[3] 'It was terrible for Lévitan, he was very upset.'

To make matters worse, his wife Geneviève was seriously ill in Cannes, and he was fretting over her fragile health. After a dry *bonjour*, Courcol confirmed they had asked the police to investigate the relationship between Lévitan and Riquois. Lévitan, throwing up his hands, said that the board had signed off on the contract, writing off almost $1 million, and there was no question of him having done anything wrong. He did not have a stake in any venture with Riquois, and had always acted in the best interests of the Amaury family. Philippe Amaury looked on, barely saying anything.

Lévitan sought out Goddet to vouch for him. They had worked together for forty years, through good times and bad. The *L'Équipe* editor knew how hard Lévitan had toiled, defending the business interests of the Amaurys. But Goddet offered no help. He said he had no knowledge of the contract uncovered by Schillinger. Courcol tried to reach a settlement but Lévitan insisted he had done nothing wrong. He refused to step down from his post. They would have to fire him instead, and see each other in court.

The Société du Tour de France issued a short media release to announce that Lévitan had left his role. As rumours swirled, he called a news conference. Still a card-carrying journalist in his old age, Lévitan addressed the crowd of reporters as 'dear colleagues'.

'Material possessions are not important to me,' Lévitan said, his voice cracking up. 'But I will fight to the death for

---

3 This segment is based on author's interview with Jean-Jacques Bertrand, Lévitan's lawyer

moral capital because I intend to live in peace for the rest of my life.'

Lévitan, in his defence, laid out what he had achieved since leading the Tour de France, furnishing more detail than he would normally share with journalists. After arranging a money-spinning start in Berlin later that year, the race was on course for a record 14 million franc profit.[4] There was no question of him having profited personally, he told them. All he owned was his Cannes apartment, a modest country home in Auffargis, a café and a mobile home at a campsite.

Amaury responded the following day by saying Lévitan had no mandate to negotiate commercial deals in the United States, and his lawyers filed a claim for misappropriation of funds. Lévitan was fired, Amaury said, after 'twisting logic and account-ing'. His lawyers wrote to Riquois to say he considered the television deals he had negotiated with CBS and Channel 4 in London null and void. 'We prefer that the television rights are sold within the company,' Amaury said.

Lévitan, meanwhile, sulked in Cannes. The apartment he shared with his wife overlooking the palm-tree-lined Promenade de la Croisette was decorated with kitsch marble eggs, bright bowls and shiny porcelain. With the blinds drawn to shield the living room from the sun that July, he watched the television images of riders gathering in Berlin ahead of the Grand Départ that he had arranged and which would bring the Amaury family 3 million Deutschmarks.

His daughter Claudy, who had kept her job with the Tour de France and was in Berlin, reported back to her father how he

---

4 About £1.4 million (GBP) at the time

was missed by race insiders. As the race was about to get under way, cyclists posed for photographs in front of the Berlin Wall. With the start bordering the Eastern bloc, it seemed the Tour de France had come a long way from its roots. Amid the chatter of a new frontier, *Le Figaro* noted that Lévitan had been erased from the official race guide as though he was 'a disgraced Soviet official'. Normally, Lévitan prided himself on conserving the secrets of his profession but, upset by his treatment, he threw himself into writing his memoir that would tell the 'real' story of the Tour de France.

Courcol had taken charge of the meeting that sealed Lévitan's fate.[5] Courcol was an athletic, well-dressed young executive who was keen to blow out the cobwebs at *L'Équipe* and had arrived 'like a bomb' at the office, according to one staffer.[6] He removed the wooden partitions that separated pokey lock-and-key offices to create an open-plan newsroom; he modernised the broadsheet newspaper with a cleaner, more colourful design; and he poured resources into a glossy weekend magazine in order to attract more advertising revenue from the hawkers of fashion brands, cars and beach holidays. Among the target audience were upwardly mobile readers in their thirties and forties. In the words of a future editor, *L'Équipe* was on the way to becoming 'the Club Med of the mind', an entertaining break from the daily grind of work.[7]

As a young man, Courcol was a tennis player, his sporting

---

5 Interview with Bertrand. According to Courcol, it was Philippe Amaury that had ordered Lévitan's abrupt dismissal, saying: "It's not a question of negotiating, I'm kicking him out." (Source: *L'Équipe Raconte Le Tour de France*)
6 Edouard Seidler: *Sport à La Une,* 1986
7 Jerome Bureau quoted in *Le Monde,* 24/2/96

career straddling the dawn of the professional era, when players began to receive bigger pay cheques. He once led Arthur Ashe two sets to one on the clay courts of the French Open, before capitulating to the American star. However, middle-ranking journeymen like him could not expect to become rich from the sport. After nine years on the circuit, and before he turned thirty, he left tennis to pursue a career in advertising. Following a successful stint at Havas, now he was the rising star in the Amaury family business.

Over lunch one day, Courcol told colleagues he was not emotionally attached to the rich history of the newspaper but liked the challenge of making it more dynamic. The daily newsroom editorial meetings bored him. He was more interested in design and finding ways to increase advertising revenue. Before long, he oversaw the relocation from Montmartre to modern offices in Issy-les-Moulineux, a one-time industrial suburb off the Paris ring road that was transforming itself into a media hub.

When staff moved into the new office, his ever-expanding marketing department took up a whole floor above the newsroom. Meanwhile, thousands of black-and-white photos and negatives, some dating back half a century, were left to languish in cardboard boxes in a corner of one of the three tiers of the underground car park.[8] They included rare 1930s images of Marcel Cerdan in the boxing ring.

When he suggested creating a historic photo archive, the picture editor was told, 'Nice idea, but is that going to help us sell any more papers?'

★ ★ ★

---

8 Seidler, *ibid*

As a boy racing on the amateur circuit in the US, Greg LeMond had read up on the European cycling scene in French magazines and soon realised that, to follow the money in this sport, he would have to move to the Old Continent, following a little-used career path for American athletes. In 1979, he taped some dollar bill signs from a newspaper ad to the handlebars of his racing bike and began chasing his goal.[9]

His first contract with the Renault team in France was worth a measly $18,000 – less than what he brought in as an amateur in the US. The team allocated him and his young wife a home in Nantes that had no furniture, heating or hot water. The weather in the Breton town was awful. But he was following the money, chasing it down even. By the start of his first Tour de France in 1984, he was on a salary of $125,000. He was the surprise of the race, beating the great Bernard Hinault to the top of the twenty-one-switchback climb atop the Alpe d'Huez by 14 seconds.

Hinault had also started out on a tiny salary and worked his way up the pay grades. By the time of LeMond's arrival on the scene, Hinault had four Tour de France wins to his name and a fearless reputation among his peers. As a Tour novice, he had faced up to the race 'dictator' Lévitan over the lack of rest riders were getting following a 5 a.m. start. At the 1984 Paris–Nice race he brawled with shipyard workers who blocked the route, throwing punches like a bar-room brawler. He was nicknamed 'the Badger' because he would not let go in a fight.

LeMond was altogether a gentler soul, who had started to

9 Daniel de Visé: *The Comeback – Greg LeMond, the True King of American Cycling, and a Legendary Tour de France,* 2018

attract admiring glances because of his talent. After outpacing Hinault up the Alpe d'Huez, he was relaxing in his twelfth-floor hotel room with a spectacular view of the mountain top. As he lay on his bed reflecting how everything was happening so fast, there was a knock on the door. LeMond opened it to find a beautiful brown-haired Frenchwoman wearing motorcycle leathers standing before him.[10]

She asked him if he knew who Bernard Tapie was. He did. Tapie was a flashy French entrepreneur, who loved the media spotlight. LeMond agreed to meet him and rode on the back of the woman's motorbike to the hotel where he was staying in the same ski resort.

In his hotel room, Tapie told the young American of his plans. He had acquired a French company that made the quick-release fitting that clipped boots to skis. The company, *Look*, which he had acquired for one franc, was losing money on its ski business but had developed a similar product that could clip the shoes of cyclists to their pedals.

The snug fit was more aerodynamic, ensuring less energy generated by pedalling was lost than with the traditional leather toe straps used by almost everyone in the sport. Tapie had started a cycling team to promote the new device and some of his other business interests including La Vie Claire, a chain of health-food shops.

That winter, in a typically flamboyant manner, he had launched the squad at the Crazy Horse cabaret club at an event with a tiger and two women models wearing the team maillot,

---

10 Richard Moore, *Slaying the Badger: Greg LeMond, Bernard Hinault and the Greatest Tour de France*, 2012

the design of which was based on an Yves Saint Laurent cocktail dress.

Together, Tapie confided to LeMond, they would make the 'medieval and introverted' world of professional cycling like Formula One, the cutting-edge of technology.[11] If he came on board and joined the team, Greg was promised a share of *Look* royalties in the United States.

On behalf of his son, LeMond's father negotiated a three-year salary with the entrepreneur that rose to $300,000 per annum. With a flourish, Tapie proclaimed that LeMond had signed cycling's first $1 million contract. The American's father, a real-estate developer from Nevada, was as determined chasing dollars and francs as his son on the bike. He also bargained into the deal eight first-class airline tickets, two Renault cars and free fuel.[12]

The size of the contract ruffled a few feathers among the old-school in French cycling. Tradition held that riders were from humble rural stock, not business-savvy globetrotters. Tapie also signed Hinault, calling him a softie at the negotiating table compared to the LeMonds. It's possible that, even as four-time champion, he was not earning much more than the young American.

After his crash at the 1985 Tour de France that had sent a shiver of anticipation through the body of Riquois about the prospect of an American victory, Hinault found himself reeling.

---

11 *L'Équipe: Bernard Tapie, un révolutionnaire dans le cyclisme*, 3/10/21. Many of the companies Tapie took over he failed to revive. However, the Look clip-in, clip-out pedal device took off, and was quickly copied. He sold the company for 260 million francs in 1989, making an impressive profit on his 1-franc investment. Even today, Look maintains a design similar to the defunct cycling team's colours.
12 De Visé, *ibid*

His Ray Bans had rammed into his face, breaking his nose, and over the next few days he could only breathe through his mouth. He was faltering badly. However, when LeMond asked their team director for permission to chase the yellow jersey, he was denied that liberty.

With the frustrated LeMond on a leash, Hinault hung on for his fifth victory. In return for his loyalty, he promised to help the American to win next time. Twelve months later, everything appeared on course for that outcome, but after they crossed the line together in apparent harmony on a mountain stage, Hinault unexpectedly changed tack, proclaiming: 'The Tour is not finished.' After surviving a stressful few final days, LeMond eventually prevailed. On July 28, 1986, in the bottom right-hand corner of the *New York Times* front page, there was a surprising headline: 'IN PARIS, AN AMERICAN WINS TOUR DE FRANCE'.

As the race opened up to the world, a young executive from cognac maker Martell took over Lévitan's job as Tour de France director.

Jean-Francois Naquet-Radiguet boasted that amid the parched earth of Venezuela he had managed to produce the amber liquor, normally made from white grapes grown in the chalky soil of Aquitaine. Just like back home in southwest France, copper stills distilled the wine, with the liquor left to age for two years in charred oak barrels. The wealthy Cadillac-driving classes of Venezuela enriched by the oil industry had developed a taste for Scotch whisky and French brandy over the local throat-burning rum. They enjoyed the bouquet of vanilla and dried fruit of cognac, and the fact they could afford to buy a $1,000 bottle of the stuff drunk in the Old Continent.

'Everyone told us we would never get the project off the

ground, but we did,' Naquet-Radiguet said.[13] 'And the cognac was good.'

As part of its marketing budget, the cognac maker sponsored an amateur cycling team in Venezuela – Club Brandy Martell.

With a master's degree from Harvard, Naquet-Radiguet arrived at the helm of the Tour de France speaking five languages, plus the business argot he used freely, like '*le marketing*' and '*le branding*'. Within weeks of becoming the first non-journalist to take the job, he was calling the eighty-five-year-old Tour de France a product. After Lévitan's reign, this was an abrupt change for many in the parochial world of French cycling where everyone knew each other. Lévitan was so old-school he sometimes used the pre-1960 valuation of the French franc. Uncomfortable with '*le sponsoring*', he preferred another word '*parrainage*', derived from Latin.

The Tour was, if truth be told, a little stuck in the past thanks to the centime-pinching newspaperman who had run it well past retirement age. Naquet-Radiguet scoffed at the Tour de France's gaudy caravan that handed out trashy trinkets like keyrings, candy and cheap hats to spectators. He grimaced at the tatty podium ceremony, on a portable stand that looked like it was part of an infant-school nativity play. And he was disappointed that sponsors who paid generously to have their names associated with the race had nowhere to entertain their guests before each stage other than the local café.

At the 1987 race, without LeMond – recovering after almost dying in a hunting accident – and Hinault – who had retired the previous winter – there was a chance for other cyclists to take

---

13 *Le Monde*, 4/7/87

the limelight. On a brutal stage in the Alps with *hors-catégorie* climbs – ascents so steep they were unclassified – Stephen Roche of Ireland battled so hard to stay in contention with Spanish leader Pedro Delgado that he needed to be administered oxygen when he reached the summit. He then had a hospital check-up to make sure he was all right. By the final stages of the race, with a couple of thousand miles in their legs, riders looked unhealthily emaciated.

Roche overhauled Delgado in the time trial to take a forty-second lead going into the final day. However, Naquet-Radiguet was amazed to see, Delgado did not challenge the Irishman on the last stage. He had already congratulated him the day before, saying 'I have had 4,500 kilometres in which to win the jersey, and I couldn't do it.' For most of the twenty-fifth and final day, he slow-pedalled in the middle of the peloton. Because he was not a cycling fan, Naquet-Radiguet was only vaguely familiar with the tradition that riders did not compete for places on the ceremonial ride to the Champs Élysées. For him, this killed the television spectacle.

He started making plans to brush up the Tour's game. 'I went into a stuffy environment and opened the windows and doors,' he said.[14]

There were those in the French cycling establishment who did not take kindly to this Harvard alum telling them that they had been getting things wrong. 'I was pretty good on TV,' he said. 'But some people thought I was stepping on their toes.'

A few weeks after Roche's win, Naquet-Radiguet and Louy

14 Daniel Friebe: *The Cognac Salesman and the Conman* (Chapter in *Cycling Anthology, Volume 5,* 2014)

– who had returned as deputy race director – travelled to the Austrian Grand Prix, amid the Styrian mountains.[15] Formula One motor racing was embracing the future, and they wanted to find out more. The horseshoe-shaped circuit was set among fields of yellow buttercups and green woodland. Fans had pitched tents on the slopes. As the pair arrived, the mountains echoed to the deafening roar of engines, and they could smell the whiff of petrol and danger. During the season, carbon-fibre monocoques built for speed over durability routinely burst into flames, and the death of drivers was common.

As racers put their live on the line, Bernie Ecclestone, a former second-hand car salesman from south London, was introducing a new business model. For decades, motor racing in Europe had been the preserve of national automobile clubs overseen by exotically named aristocrats and royals, the privileged few who had the time and money to smash up expensive racing cars for a hobby. This côterie of gentlemen had formed what would become known as the Fédération Internationale de l'Automobile in 1904 to set the international rules for racing. Ever since, the FIA had operated from a mansion overlooking Place de la Concorde.

When Ecclestone arrived in Formula One as a driver and then team owner in the 1950s, the impoverished British racing fraternity had taken over from the aristocrats as the main racers on the circuit. They were mostly broke. They scraped a living by mortgaging their homes, building single-seat cars in draughty warehouses and doing deals for spare parts from public phone

---

15 This segment is based on author's interview with Xavier Louy, deputy Tour de France director

boxes. Acting for the British team bosses, Ecclestone first bartered for more prize money from the European noblemen that ran the FIA. He then made a play to manage Formula One's commercial rights.

It was a clash between teams and organisers that professional cycling would experience sporadically over the next 40 years.

Standing in Ecclestone's way was French federation boss Jean-Marie Balestre, a former motor-racing journalist on *L'Auto* newspaper. Unusually among his peers, he did not have an aristocratic title or royal lineage. With a square jaw and stern expression, he was a tough negotiator. On one of his first encounters with him, Balestre tried to intimidate Ecclestone, who had led a series of successful strikes by UK teams to improve their conditions over the previous four years. Just as the broad-shouldered Frenchman sought to put him in his place over his latest demands for more prize money, five-foot-two Ecclestone rose from his seat and began adjusting paintings on the wall. Balestre, becoming angrier by the second, snapped the pencil he was holding.[16]

Finally, Ecclestone came out on top when Balestre, by now a senior FIA official, in 1981 agreed to cede him the commercial rights to Formula One on the grounds he was a capable operator.

Ecclestone bundled the television rights to more than a dozen races, giving them the same format and start time, and sold the package to public broadcasters like the BBC and RAI to ensure the widest possible exposure. At the same time, he stripped out the mini sponsor deals that circuits had bartered, replacing them

---

16 Max Mosley autobiography, *Formula One and Beyond*, 2015

with global deals with multinational companies like Marlboro cigarettes, Olivetti computers and Pirelli tyres, all keen on catching the eyeballs of millions.

In a world where television was replacing newspapers as the main medium for news and entertainment, this approach seemed sensible to Naquet-Radiguet. If only, he mused, it was possible to align all the sport's diverse transnational interests. Somebody would probably need to knock some heads together, just as Ecclestone had done. The Londoner saw himself as the only sheriff, running Formula One without a deputy. He used a brick-sized satellite phone to make sure local race-owners were aligned.

By the time the Tour de France men visited, the revenue, profit and cash reserves of Ecclestone's operating company were rising exponentially. He was on the way to turning Formula One into a billion-dollar business. When technology advanced and he switched to a pocket-sized mobile phone, he picked the ringtone from the soundtrack of *The Good, The Bad and the Ugly*.

Amid the ear-splitting roar of the engines in Austria, Naquet-Radiguet and his Tour de France aide marvelled at their surroundings. The paddock zone where team staff and guests mingled was no longer the domain of greasy mechanics in overalls, foldaway picnic tables and flasks of tea. Now it was a VIP enclave with waitresses serving champagne and canapés to the clients of sponsors.

Four years earlier, a former Marlboro public relations executive had started running this corporate hospitality venture for Ecclestone, borrowing the idea from Wimbledon. Guests enjoyed first-class service, a few metres from the pit lane, and they rubbed shoulders with daredevil drivers like Niki Lauda, who had cheated death in a 1976 fireball crash. (Lauda, who was so badly burnt he was read the last rites by a priest, returned to racing six weeks later.)

Ecclestone made sure to add a sprinkling of extra stardust by inviting celebrities from movies, pop music and fashion to races. Everything was immaculately arranged. In a pressed white shirt and black slacks, Ecclestone paced up and down the paddock, and was known to 'go berserk' if a sign was out of place. In this Formula One paddock, as the din of racing cars subsided before the race itself, the Tour de France men chatted with the motor-racing correspondent from *Le Parisien* about how they would like cycling to follow Formula One and become part of a global championship.

Aligning cycle races into a year-round soap opera with a cast of colourful characters would be tricky; the most prestigious foreign two-wheel races were owned by sports newspapers like Italy's *Gazzetta dello Sport* and Belgium's *Sportwereld* that were focused on their national markets. That could wait for another day. But, in the short term, the Tour de France could at least emulate Formula One's corporate hospitality. At the time, cycling did nothing for sponsors such as Banque Nationale de Paris before each stage. There was a messy free-for-all with fans, race officials and journalists jostling for space around the riders as they rode from hotel to start line. With nowhere else to wait, cyclists sat on the bonnets of their team cars as they waited for the off.

As Formula One's travelling circus packed up their equipment, Naquet-Radiguet and Louy returned to Paris to draw up plans about how to make their own version of the Formula One paddock. The following summer, a mobile VIP enclosure known as the Tour de France Village appeared at the start of each stage. Sponsors could invite guests to a breakfast of fruit, *pain au chocolat* and café, while they soaked up the ambiance, chatted to team staff and watched riders prepare for the stage start.

The concept was an instant hit. Companies chartered flights from Paris to take guests down for a day out in the mountains. Within four years, there was a waiting list of firms eager to pay the 400,000-franc (£40,000) entry fee, and the village was bringing in some £1.5 million a year from corporate hospitality to the Amaury family.

After corporate hospitality, Naquet-Radiguet turned his attention to television. At the time, newspapers sales were already declining and the trickle of cash from broadcast rights was by no means abundant. There was a scattering of dollars from the US, UK, Japan and a few other territories, nothing more. However, the new boss saw an opportunity in the deregulation of the French television market.

In 1987, state-run TF1 was spun off as a private channel to compete with another new station, La Cinq. For the first time, this deregulated market created the possibility of an auction for the rights to air the Tour de France with public broadcaster Antenne 2. Based on the daily audience of millions of viewers, it was reasonable to assume that the race rights were worth something in France.

Naquet-Radiguet opened negotiations with TF1 about paying market rates based on the race's home audience. La Cinq, which was part-owned by Silvio Berlusconi, also began exploring the possibility of acquiring the rights.[17] Some said Berlusconi

17 Louy, *ibid*

was taking the level of French television downmarket; critics called the new channel 'Coca-Cola TV'. And so the Tour de France executives started looking for a decent amount of money from the brash Italian magnate to switch to the new channel.

Philippe Amaury felt uneasy about removing the Tour de France from state television, which had aired the race for almost forty years. Public television was a faithful companion. It had been there to film riders lapping the Parc des Princes velodrome for the first brief live broadcast of the race in 1948; it had been there to take grainy footage of stages in the Alps, transported back on the overnight train to Paris to be shown the next day in cinemas. And now, as loyal as ever, it was there to beam hours of live colour images into millions of French living rooms.

Philippe was worried about damaging this historic bond with the state. Every year, he relied on the Government to close off public roads and provide police assistance to enable the race to take place. He took a dim view of the behind-the-scenes talks with privately owned television channels and, partly as a result of this, Naquet-Radiguet lost his job after barely a year.

He left a legacy, nevertheless. As well as instigating the money-spinning Tour de France village, his idea to start an auction for the broadcast rights resulted in public television agreeing to pay a more reasonable sum. Meanwhile, the plans to spice up the final day led, two years later, to the most gripping finale in the race's history.

LeMond had recovered from a near-death experience on a turkey shoot when his brother-in-law mistakenly shot him, leaving 60 pellets lodged in his body. Absent from the race for two years, he found himself up against Laurent Fignon, the bespectacled pony-tailed Frenchman known as the Professor. In a time trial, with millions watching on television, they duelled for the Tour de France.

It was a box-office finish. Some 300,000 people lined the route from Versailles to Paris. LeMond, wearing an aerodynamic yellow helmet, flew over the course. After crossing the line he stopped and turned to watch Fignon's time ticking on, a crowd quickly forming around him. The Frenchman, his blonde pony-tail loose, was sluggish. LeMond held his head in astonishment. He had won by 8 seconds.

Many in the private sector complemented Naquet-Radiguet for taking a bold step into the future of entertainment. He quickly moved on, taking a job with perhaps more scope for innovation by becoming commercial director of TF1. Meanwhile his push for change was too radical for Amaury and the old-fashioned French cycling establishment – the next year they went back to the last-day ceremonial ride into Paris.

9

Threat

On the Tour de France, 1998

At Cannes airport, an eighty-six-year-old man waited in the terminal by the only runway. He was wiry and suntanned and wore a suit. When he got to his feet, he walked slowly, with the aid of a walking stick. The last eleven years had been lonely, much of it confined to his apartment on La Croisette, the avenue lined with palm trees hugging the bay. After a lifetime of frenetic activity, the silence in his life was a shock. 'You don't know what it's like when the phone stops ringing,' he said.

Some of his old friends from cycling called him on his birthday, but others stopped talking to him. For half a century his working life had consumed him until, one grey winter day in 1987, it had all ended. But on this bright summer morning, he had a rare visitor – an executive of the Amaury family sports business. He had come to take Félix Lévitan back to the Tour de France. The old man boarded the private jet and strapped himself in.

In the courts, after a decade of back and forth, Lévitan had cleared his name. An appeal court judge found no evidence that he had acted improperly in writing off the losses of the Tour of America. He agreed to an out-of-court settlement, paving the way for this day, his return to the race that he had known first as a newspaper reporter in the 1920s.

After he was fired as Tour de France director, he worked on his memoir, secured a publishing deal and sent the manuscript to his lawyer to review. But then Lévitan had second thoughts. He decided to put a stop to publication, wiring his advance back to the publisher. His secrets remained behind lock and key in his lawyer's basement in rue Richard Lenoir, near Place de Bastille.[1]

As the small jet climbed into the air and began cruising at 30,000 feet, Lévitan gazed down from his window seat and saw the jagged rocks of the Alps sprinkled with snow. Without much difficulty, he was able to pick out the Col du Galibier. As a twenty-one-year-old reporter, he had crossed that mountain pass on the back of a motorbike while covering his first Tour de France and got into an argument with the race director Henri Desgrange when he refused to wait for the race cavalcade to go past him. All those years ago, he was an ambitious young man in a hurry and he had a deadline. On the same Alpine pass, as a race director years later, he witnessed arch-rivals Fausto Coppi and Gino Bartali share a water bottle in a momentary pause in their duel. The moment was witnessed by only a couple of other people but it was captured by a photographer on a motorbike and helped burnish the Tour de France's legend. Ah, so many memories.

Lévitan's companion on this day was the man who had taken his place as the top business executive of the Tour de France. A

---

1 According to his lawyer Jean Jacques Bertrand, the unpublished manuscript is 'somewhere in the basement' of his office. The author asked Bertrand for permission to see it but, after the death of Lévitan's daughter a few years earlier, there was no one he felt who could give him the mandate to share the document.

former Olympic champion skier, Jean-Claude Killy had been hired to lead the family's new holding company, Amaury Sport Organisation. In this new era, the business and sporting sides of the Tour's management were now separate. Killy led from the background while Jean-Marie Leblanc, as race director, dealt with events on the ground. Leblanc's role was partly diplomatic, to keep all the factions in the travelling circus happy. After a career as a rider, he had a stint covering the sport as a *L'Équipe* reporter. He was an insider, and popular to boot. Killy, meanwhile, was more at home schmoozing in boardrooms.

Killy was raised in Val d'Isère, where his father ran a ski shop. As a teenager, he played truant from school to ski, and eventually left education aged fifteen. It became second nature for him to hurtle down the piste at 60 miles per hour. At the 1968 Olympics in Grenoble, in the space of a week, he won three gold medals. At the time, his day job was earning 760 francs a month as a Customs official three miles from the family home on the Italian border. He had dashing looks – a chiselled jaw, white teeth and a healthy glow – and a helping of French insouciance. At his first meeting with IMG founder Mark McCormack in Switzerland, he ordered wine. When the Cleveland lawyer raised an eyebrow about the wisdom of an élite athlete drinking alcohol, the young skier shot back, 'Would you rather I drank milk and skied like an American?'[2]

Without McCormack, Killy might have ended up with a minor salary upgrade and a job working in marketing for the local tourism office in Val d'Isère. In the end, he became rich beyond his dreams. In the course of three years, Killy appeared

---

2 *Sports Illustrated*: 'A Man and His Kingdom', 12/2/1990

on the cover of *Sports Illustrated* magazine three times. Thanks to McCormack's tireless deal-making, the Frenchman became one of the world's richest athletes, signing a flurry of endorsement contracts from Chevrolet to Coca-Cola and American Airlines. He left Val d'Isère to live in Switzerland, buying a house by Lake Geneva. He loved the art of making money, almost as much as racing, and the trappings that it afforded – private jets, five-star hotels, Rolex watches. At the peak of his career as a corporate pitchman, he said, 'Now I can have anything I want.'

Killy's switch to company man buried much of his youthful *joie de vivre* from public view, according to the journalist Hunter S. Thompson, who interviewed the Frenchman for a 1970 magazine profile in some soulless settings surrounded by public-relations executives for Chevrolet.[3] Now, Thompson wrote, everything for Killy was about *le fric*. 'His time and priorities are parcelled out according to their dollar/publicity value.' At one point, Killy estimated he had 100 business deals. In one of his most lucrative, he took a 35 per cent stake in an upscale winter sports clothing company. After changing its name to Killy, his cachet helped to power the retailer's annual sales to more than €100 million.

By middle age, Killy had given up on even casual weekend skiing because he did not like being slower than anyone else on the slopes. Now he kept fit by cycling and still weighed barely 70 kilos, the same as in his heyday. He continued to be a regular in blue-chip company boardrooms, including Coca-Cola and Rolex.

---

3 *Scanlan's Monthly*: 'The Temptations of Jean-Claude Killy' by Hunter S. Thompson, March 1970

His long list of business contacts was one of the reasons why he was hired by Philippe Amaury. To the new role, he brought with him his partner in his successful ski clothing business. Together they made an effective duo. The Olympic champion, who left school with barely any qualifications, was the charmer, with a seductive voice and twinkle in his eye. His partner, Alain Krzentowski, or KRZ, was a Paris business-school graduate from a middle-class family. He would become the organiser, a key figure in the growth of the new Amaury project that, like KRZ, soon developed an acronym of its own – ASO.

The new company extended its sports portfolio wider. Amid a boom in personal fitness, it acquired the Paris Marathon from the town hall led by mayor Jacques Chirac. The marathon was turning into a mass-participation road race, harnessing the ambitions of both elite runners and weekend warriors. The family business also took over the Dakar rally, a mythical car and motorbike rally through the Sahara Desert that was dreamed up by a petrol-head adventurer called Thierry Sabine. With the help of broadcast partner France Télévisions, Amaury executives improved the coverage of the money-losing race, showing spectacular helicopter views of bikes and cars travelling over sand dunes, and attracting new sponsors. The number of entrants rose six-fold.

On the Tour de France, more had changed since Lévitan's sacking. The Tour Féminin he instigated was discontinued. The extra financial burden included the cost of keeping helicopters up in the air for an extra couple of hours to cover the women's race – it was deemed too expensive. After the 1989 edition, the race was scrapped. And so the only women in the limelight were the models hired by sponsor Crédit Lyonnais bank to present the day's race leader with the yellow jersey.

With women marginalised, all the focus was on the men's race, and bringing in more television and advertising income. As the sports rights market heated up, Killy and KRZ had been able to double the fee the state-owned broadcaster paid to air the Tour de France and extend the foreign reach to 170 countries. The more widely the race was shown, the more they could command from sponsors.

Much of Lévitan's legacy remained. There was still the polka-dot jersey and finale on the Champs Élysées, both of which he had instigated. Foreign television deals continued to be sold under the agreement he had negotiated giving France Télévisions exclusive rights at home and ASO the freedom to sell them abroad.

Greg LeMond had begun a trend of focusing all his efforts on the race because it was the one event that could make him rich and famous back home, where all the other cycling races paled into insignificance. Every year, more American TV and newspaper journalists came to the Tour to follow his progress. It was, more than ever, the mecca of road racing and, even to the casual sports fan in the Anglophone world, it was transitioning from an obscure event to a fixture on the global sports calendar, along-side Wimbledon and the Monaco Grand Prix.

The more LeMond performed well at the Tour de France, the more he and the race became well known around the world. In 1990, the year after his third race win in five years, LeMond had become one of the top thirty best-paid athletes in the world with an estimated $4 million in salary and endorsements. He was earning almost as much Diego Maradona, and half as much as Michael Jordan and Jack Nicklaus.[4] Helped by the wider exposure LeMond gave the race, the number of sponsors from outside France continued to grow steadily until they made up almost half of all major deals. In 1996, Nike paid for its swoosh to be on the yellow jersey, replacing the cockerel of French brand Le Coq Sportif.

This internationalisation of the race was exactly Lévitan's plan all those years ago, and he could reflect with some pride on the part he had played in the transformation. However, the rise in the Tour de France broadcast revenue was steady rather than stratospheric. And it was not only because Amaury felt more comfortable with state television. As the market opened up to new private channels, there were several barriers to entry to screening Le Grand Boucle, the Big Loop around France. French legislation required the main stages of the race had to be on free-to-air television, effectively ruling out interest from subscription channels like Canal+. Meanwhile, free-to-air television stations like Berlusconi's La Cinq that relied on advertising income were put off by the production costs involved with following the race around France as well as the 5.00 p.m. finishes that were long before the prime-time evening slots.

In other sports, television revenues were flowing in much faster. Airing midweek European football matches played under floodlights was a much simpler way to win market share. In football, Canal+ had begun to offer serious money to broadcast live games. Up until now the state broadcast had paid virtually nothing. During this period, Bordeaux football club president Claude Bez barred a state television crew from its European

---

4 *Forbes* magazine, 20/9/1990

Cup game at home to Athletic Bilbao to free up space for a broadcaster that would actually pay him. An accountant with a bushy handlebar moustache, Bez said he was not running a charity. He needed cash to buy star players and keep fans happy. His situation was simple. 'With money, you are the best president,' Bez said. 'Without money, you are an idiot.'

While the 60 million francs paid by state television to air the Tour de France was still a comparatively small amount, it was growing at a fair clip and did not escape the attention of the teams. When the Spaniard who ran the ONCE squad, including the Tour de France contender Laurent Jalabert, found out about the extra television money that was accruing in the Amaury family's bank account, he and his peers decided to negotiate a share. If teams in football were being rewarded with broadcast money, why shouldn't they? The Spaniard, Manolo Saiz, and other cycling team managers appointed a Swiss marketeer to barter them a share of Tour de France television rights. They agreed the Swiss broker would get 30 per cent of whatever he could negotiate.

But Saiz was no Bernie Ecclestone. It was a poorly thought-out plan, and it lasted barely twenty-four hours. The man they had nominated to represent them worked for IMG, which still had a contract with Killy. Even before a formal representation contract was signed, an order arrived from head office in Cleveland to shut down the arrangement. According to one account, Killy had intervened.[5] Instead of sharing the race's new profits among the teams and athletes, the former skier's job was to look after the Amaury family's bottom line. 'You can say what

5 Bruno Roussel: *Tour de Vices*, 2001

you want,' Killy would say on at least one occasion as ASO boss, according to a colleague,[6] 'but I only care about *le fric* [the cash].'

That was a refrain that Lévitan could identify with.

On this July 1998 morning, the private jet carrying him and Killy was heading to Ireland, and the start of the Tour de France. Two hours into the flight, it began its descent over the Irish Sea. On landing, they took a taxi to Dublin Castle, where journalists were preparing curtain-raising stories about the race in a temporary press room. Lévitan was stunned to see such a substantial media presence; there were 1,200 accredited reporters and scores of television trucks parked outside, led by France Télévisions' small army of vehicles. 'The size of it all,' he marvelled.

As a stern race director, he had silenced reporters when he walked in, such was his fearsome reputation – the Tour Dictator. Now he was a smiling old man returning to make peace with the race, and reminisce about old times. 'There is no grudge anymore,' he told a Dutch journalist. He sat down to chat with Bernard Hinault who was now working as a race ambassador. They talked and talked some more. There was more than enough time to catch up. The race was to start the following day. The Grand Départ was the culmination of a year of planning and logistics, and, while there were plenty of nerves ahead of the opening day, Lévitan did not have a care in the world. He was on holiday, as free as a bird. Killy had agreed to drop him back at Cannes airport in three days' time.

By 7.00 a.m. the next morning, Lévitan's return to the race

---

6 *Le Monde Diplomatique*, July 2009: This quote in an article by David Garcia is attributed to Killy by Jean-Pierre Carenso, the former race director.

was about to be overshadowed. ASO staff were still sleeping at the 500-room Burlington Hotel when Killy was called to the suite of a colleague, along with race director Leblanc and Bruno Roussel, manager of leading French team Festina. The three men sat around a small table, still not fully awake. On the table, room service had delivered a pot of steaming coffee. Just as Roussel had poured himself some and was about to stir in a spoonful of sugar, Killy said, 'OK, Bruno . . . what's going on?'

Two days earlier, Roussel explained, he was packing his bags before leaving for Dublin when he received a phone call from his deputy to inform him that police had arrested the team *soigneur* Willy Voet on the French–Belgian border at 6.45 a.m. In the boot of his Festina-emblazoned Fiat Marea, they found cooler bags containing 238 ampoules of erythropoietin (EPO), 82 shots of human growth hormone, 60 testosterone doses as well as amphetamines, corticoids and blood thinners. Because the *soigneur*'s phone was switched off, Roussel had not managed to speak with him. The rest of the team had caught the ferry without him.[7]

'Shit, Bruno, why could you not have warned us before?' Killy said.

Roussel thought that it could turn out to be a minor *contretemps* and, he ventured, the *soigneur* might be released with a warning.

In fact, Voet was in a foul-smelling police cell in Lille, waiting for a court appearance.

In the press room, the media soon found out. After receiving a tip from a police source in Lille, a Reuters correspondent filed

---

7 Roussel, *ibid*

a six-paragraph story about an employee of the Festina team being taken into custody. As the news hit the wire, journalists swarmed around the Reuters man asking for more details.

The cycling was now a sideshow to the big story, and Englishman Chris Boardman's victory on the opening day time trial through the streets of Dublin was pushed to the bottom of the news agenda. That evening, Willy Voet's arrest was leading the television news in France.

There was no obvious precedent at the Tour de France, and therefore no indication of what might happen next. Over the years, individual cyclists had received minor reprimands for taking stimulants but this was different – police appeared to have uncovered systematic and sophisticated doping.

As the news spread, the swarm of reporters moved to Leblanc. He tried to calm down the frenzy, saying it would be wrong to ban the Festina team for what could be an isolated incident. The next day, he tried to lighten the mood by telling journalists he had supped a pint of Guinness with his lunch, and encouraged them to sample the dark Irish bitter and the local whisky.

★ ★ ★

The Tour de France was in turmoil. Panic had spread among dozens of drug-using cyclists on different teams. Some flushed EPO down the toilet in their hotel rooms or disposed of unused $50 vials by dropping them into empty Coke cans and crushing them with the sole of their shoe. The race's convoy of cars disembarked from a Stena Line ferry and rolled into the Breton port of Roscoff. When five vehicles bearing the *L'Équipe* logo descended, bystanders hammered on the roof and spat at the windows.

In Brittany, a hotbed of cycling, the Tour de France was under assault. Nowhere was the race more beloved, nowhere were fans more upset about it being defiled. Fans threw urine on to one of the dozen *L'Équipe* journalists covering the race. Insults flew in every direction. 'We were the witnesses of a world disintegrating,' one said. To protect themselves, they removed the newspaper's logo from the side of their cars. Reporting on the bike race became secondary to the drugs scandal. When Festina team manager Bruno Roussel opened the curtains of his hotel room, he saw forty journalists staring back at him.

Less than a mile from the finish line of a stage to Cholet a couple of days later, Roussel was on the phone to his lawyer when a police motorcyclist pulled up to him and gestured for him to follow. He was expecting this moment. He had just enough time to take a pullover from the back of the team car, throw it over his shoulders, mumble something to journalists and disappear with police into a battered blue Peugeot hatchback.

At the local police station, Roussel did not collaborate at first but, after a sleepless night on a wooden bench, he called his lawyer, his wife and teenage daughter before confessing everything. 'I cracked like a dam flooding,' he said.[8] He admitted the team was involved in systematic doping, and had pooled income to spend on the drugs. The team *soigneur* who had been caught red-handed had not been acting on his own.

'This changes things,' said Killy, with typical *sang-froid*. His job had just become a whole lot more complicated. For the

---

8 Roussel, *ibid*

foreseeable future, he would spend his days on the phone and in meetings trying to protect the most precious asset in the family business from irreparable damage.

At the end of that week, and still with no coherent plan on how to calm the controversy, Killy had an invitation he could not turn down – dinner with Jacques Chirac. The French President and his wife Bernadette owned a seventeenth-century château as a summer getaway near Corrèze, where a stage would finish the next day, a Saturday.

On arriving at the weather-beaten château topped by gothic spires, Killy spent much of the time hovering in the corridor on a landline phone talking to Leblanc, the race director. At one point, Bernadette Chirac, looking anxious, went over to ask whether the race would be suspended. In a sign of the cosy relationship between the state and the Tour de France, she and her husband were due to appear on the podium the next day to congratulate the stage winner. The vexed discussions continued. President Chirac was more relaxed than his wife: he was in a summer holiday mood and had no responsibility for the mounting scandal that was being overseen by sports minister Marie-George Buffet, a Communist party member in the coalition Government.

With short blonde hair and blue eyes, she was a smoker who last played sport at her *lycée* in a Paris suburb more than thirty years earlier. She didn't fit in with the clubby nature of French sport dominated by men. In her role, she was responsible for doping controls and even handing down bans, and was only just getting to know the depth of hostility generated when an outsider like her interfered. A few weeks earlier, she had ordered the drug testing of the French football team at their World Cup preparation camp in the ski resort of Tignes and the sports media was so hostile about the disruption that she considered leaving the role. Now she was braced for more hatred. Prime Minister Lionel Jospin, the Socialist party leader who had appointed her, told her, 'Now it's started, you have to take responsibility.'

Buffet was not there that evening, but among the guests at the Chirac château was ninety-three-year-old Jacques Goddet, who had arrived with his third wife Rosine carrying an Armagnac from 1932, the year of the President's birth. Delighted with the gift, Chirac opened the Armagnac after dinner for a snifter. It was late in the evening after Madame Chirac had retired to bed that Leblanc arrived. He was served a plate of charcuterie and salad, while the President poured him a glass of red. Leblanc explained that they had decided to expel the Festina team, but the race would go on.[9]

The following afternoon, Leblanc met the Festina riders in the back room of a modest *tabac*. He told them they had no option but to pull the entire team out of the race. It was damage limitation as he tried to keep the show on the road. The riders eventually agreed. The next week, Festina riders were led in handcuffs to the cells at Lyon police station. The arrest, shown on television, provoked a sit-down protest by the rest of the peloton on a road in the foothills of the Pyrenees.

The scandal was lurching from one grim storyline to another. A few days later, the Dutch team TVM's riders were questioned until midnight on the eve of an Alpine stage and the peloton

---

9 The scene inside the Chirac family château was recounted 20 years later in the newspaper *Libération* (4/7/2018)

slowed to a halt again. It looked like the race was falling apart. In an editorial, *Le Monde* called for the Tour de France to be abandoned, even 'if it will bury our childhood dreams with it'. Leblanc visibly aged, according to one witness, as almost a century of history looked as though it might come to an end on his watch.

As the front man for the Amaury family enterprise, Leblanc was desperately trying to keep the show on the road. Every day there seemed to be a new twist in the scandal. The ONCE team was one of four Spanish squads to pull out, ordering staff to load up the bikes. The Spanish sports newspaper's staff also left the race, accusing the French of being ungracious hosts. Even on the inside of the Tour de France circus, it was almost impossible to follow what was happening in real time. Every day, Leblanc had to ask journalists to keep him up to date with each new development.

There were bad vibes everywhere. Italian teams finger-pointed at French authorities; a French team manager turned his back on journalists from *Le Monde*; making use of cardboard hands given out to promote a sponsor, spectators ripped off all the fingers bar one to show cyclists the middle finger.

Halfway through the race, amid the maelstrom, Killy flew to a Coca-Cola board meeting in Atlanta.[10] His role as a non-executive director earned him $200,000 per year in consultancy fees plus first-class travel and hotel perks, putting him on a par with top executives. Presumably he was asked: 'What in the hell is going on over in France?' Coca-Cola was paying 30 million francs to have its logo appear along the course of the tainted race.

---

10 De Mondenard, Jean-Pierre: *La Grande Imposture*, 2009

At one point, Leblanc received a note from the Interior Ministry that said the police investigation into doping would continue but would not specifically target riders. In a bluff to try and keep the race going, he turned this scrap of information into an official statement. Eventually, the race made it to Paris but fewer than half of the riders who started the race arrived at the finishing line on the Champs Élysées.

On his return to the race, Killy put on a bullish front about the future of the Tour de France. 'You can't destroy a myth,' he said. But, privately, the Amaury executives were scrambling for ideas to put a line under the scandal, which threatened to come with a financial hit as the companies that bankrolled the event considered their options. Leblanc floated the idea of returning to national teams for the first time in thirty-six years in an effort to change this dangerous dynamic. Perhaps the commercially minded team backers were part of the problem?

Long after the Tour de France had finished, the exorcism of French cycling continued to play out in front of an investigating judge. That autumn, the manager of Française des Jeux, one of the French teams, was among those pulled in for questioning at Lille police station.

Marc Madiot was a minor celebrity in France. As a rider, he had become only the second French winner in thirty years of Paris–Roubaix. In fact, he had won it twice in his career. Years later, he would tell how riders of his era took amphetamines they bought from the chemist to help them keep pedalling during criteriums, the money-spinning unofficial races that came in quick succession after the Tour de France. It was almost fashionable at the time to take speed. Jack Kerouac downed amphetamines while writing *On the Road*, and philosopher Jean

Paul Sartre swallowed them to increase productivity. 'We didn't feel like we were cheating,' Madiot said. 'We were like students drinking coffee to stay up all night before exams.'[11] Even when a rider tested positive for a prohibited substance in the 1970s and 1980s there was a minimum kerfuffle: a fine, a time sanction and a warning that a ban would follow next time. If he was not in contention for the race lead, newspapers treated it not as major news but as a banality, on a par with a traffic offence.

At Lille police station, Madiot decided to treat his time in detention as a mental test like riding Paris–Roubaix. When he won in 1985, his plan was simple enough – to stay calm amid the cacophony of cheering crowds, horns of team cars and revving motorbikes, and not to become riled by other riders jostling for the best position. It was all about *la tête* and *les jambes*, the head and legs. He rode straight down the middle of the country lanes, avoiding the edges slathered in mud. As the cyclists slogged through the frigid north-east of France, some crashed, breaking bike frames and collarbones. Others simply gave up, too cold and dispirited to continue.

Madiot rode on at the front of the race, relentlessly working the pedals of his steel bike. He was caked in mud from his white Renault cotton cap to his shoes. After seven hours in the saddle, the mud had dried out, turning grey. As his rivals lost their mental battles, he ploughed on alone at the front.

In the police station, like in television dramas, there was a good cop, bad cop duo firing questions at him. One was kind, the other aggressive. They were trying to make him crack. After

---

11 Marc Madiot: *Parlons Vélo*, 2015. Madiot said that he never took amphetamines in official races.

three hours, he was shown to a cell and slept on a concrete ledge under a blanket that smelt of urine.

Waking him at 6.00 a.m., the cell guard showed him the local newspaper *La Voix du Nord*, which carried an article about his arrest. That morning, the questions continued. Perhaps he would be weaker and more vulnerable after a night gathering his thoughts in captivity. Madiot maintained that he had nothing to hide. He kept calm. He told the two detectives that he could not discount doping by individual riders but, he repeated, there was no systematic doping on the Française des Jeux team.

He stuck resolutely to the same line. The policemen took a break, leaving the room to discuss what to do. For a few minutes, Madiot was all alone in the interview room with his thoughts. Eventually, the officers came back. They decided they did not have enough evidence for him to go before the investigating judge. It was still early in the morning, so they invited him to have breakfast with them.

He accepted a beer, and walked free.[12]

<hr />

12 Madiot, *ibid*

10

La France

Renazé, Mayenne

Adecade before his arrest, Marc Madiot had begun the 1987 Tour de France wearing the *tricolore* jersey as national champion. It was the year of Lévitan's sacking, the Berlin race start and the Roche–Delgado duel for victory. Madiot was in the prime of his career, one of a small group of standout riders in a nation that took professional cycling seriously and treated riders with reverence. A few days after the start in one of Europe's biggest cities, the race would stop by the small village where he was born and raised, the son of a farmer.

With a population of 2,000, Renazé in the landlocked Mayenne region was by far the smallest stage finish at that year's race. One of France's least populated *départements*, Mayenne is a peaceful rural idyll that borders Normandy and Brittany and gets little fanfare in tourism guide books. The River Mayenne flows south for 120 miles, cutting through fields and past small towns before emptying into the Loire.

For the Tour de France to pass through their home town would be a proud moment, not only for Marc but also his younger brother Yvon who raced on the same Système U team.

Both young men would be the talk of French television commentators that day, not to mention all the locals in the three-bar town. It was special days like these that helped to foster a sense of national unity in *la France profonde*. For many, the transformation of sleepy towns like Renazé was the essence of the great race.

As teenagers, the brothers had worked on the family farm, milking cows, making cider from apples and collecting hay bales. On Saturdays, after getting up at 4.00 a.m. to milk his cows, their father would haul their racing bikes on to the roof rack of the family Peugeot 404 and drive them to junior races. His wife made rice cakes for the boys to refuel with. Neither followed their father into farming, but Marc drew parallels with the path they chose. 'Cycling is 98 per cent suffering, 2 per cent pleasure . . . and the life of a farmer is like that,' he said. 'The only moments of pleasure are the birth of animals, a good crop of wheat.'

At the time, many French dairy farmers were struggling. In the early 1980s, the European Community had introduced a complex system of milk quotas, subsidies and levies that tangled them in red tape and put pressure on their finances. Farmers grew angry with Jacques Delors, European Commission President. They accused him of making their life a misery by trying to standardise milk production from Brussels. A former French finance minister, Delors wanted to turn parochialism into European strength to compete against the US's powerhouse economy. He used tennis to try and make his point that Europe had to sharpen up its game. 'Have you ever seen John McEnroe prepare for a big tournament by hitting balls against the wall of his country house?'

The Delors administration paid the Amaury family business to promote the single European market by extending the route of the Tour de l'Avenir from France to other European countries, with a finish in Brussels. In his eyes, cycling was not just a rural French pastime passed down through generations but an example of European unity. One team, for example, sponsored by Carrera Jeans, had riders from Belgium, Denmark, Italy, Ireland and Switzerland pulling for each other at races.

In another Delors–Amaury tie-up, Tour de France riders would have on their race numbers, alongside the French flag, the European symbol of a circle of yellow stars on blue background. Early in the 1987 race, Madiot spotted the small emblem that was not much bigger than a postage stamp. Each day, before pinning the number 65 to his shirt, he took out a pair of scissors and cut off the mini European flag. 'I wanted to support the farmers,' he said. 'I was on their side.'

A *L'Équipe* journalist noticed and wrote a story about this small act of rebellion. When Delors found out, he came to see Madiot before one of the stages the following week. 'You can't do that,' he told him.[1] The farmer's son ignored him, continuing with his ritual before each stage. 'There is nobody who can oblige me to wear the European flag,' Madiot said. 'If I changed, I would not be respecting my father.'

As the peloton headed to Renazé, Madiot wanted a stage victory in his *tricolore* jersey (shorn of the European flag). For miles around, on a hot summer day, the fields near the town were packed with the cars of hundreds of day-trippers. Spectators

---

1 Author interview with Madiot

four-deep lined the main road into town. For the *Ouest-France* newspaper, which Madiot Senior scanned each day for the prices of livestock and cattle feed, his two sons Marc and Yvon were the story that day. Marc planned to attack six miles out from the town square – the same square where he met his friends as a teenager, and where his mother went to market for fruit and vegetables.

In the end, neither brother managed to get into the five-man breakaway group. It was a Dutchman who sprinted to victory. No matter for the Madiots – you lost more than you won. 98 per cent suffering, 2 per cent pleasure.

Still in their cycling kit, the brothers appeared on a television chat show after the stage to reminisce about their childhood. Gilbert Montangné, one of France's most popular singers, capped the festival atmosphere with a free concert that evening. The blind crooner wore dark glasses as he sang and played the piano. For the locals in sleepy Renazé, it was a bit like the Super Bowl teams pitching up in a tiny town in America's mid-west, along with Stevie Wonder. The locals would talk about their day in the spotlight for years to come.

More than the Tour de France, Madiot's career would be forever marked by Paris–Roubaix; four years later, he won the race again. At the age of thirty-five, he broke his leg on the cobblestone course, ending his career. He went back to Renazé and took a job in one of the village's three bars for a couple of years. And when national lottery company Française des Jeux decided to bankroll a new team, it appointed him team manager. He then moved to Paris. For a proud farmer's son, the city had its attractions but he was not fond of the litter, pollution and noise and often yearned for home. He took regular trips back and modernised the stone farmhouse where he was brought up. He loved the idea of sleeping in the house where he had slumbered as a child all those years ago.

Française des Jeux had its roots in a lottery created to help soldiers injured during the First World War, and wanted to use the team to burnish its patriotic credentials. The team set up in the company's headquarters on the outskirts of the capital. Madiot took a single symbolic share, and was given an identity badge like all the other lottery staff in order to get past the entry barrier into the office.

The marketing plan was for *blanc, bleu et rouge* to run through the team. Two-thirds of the first squad was French, with three of them wearing the *tricolore* jersey as national champions of the road race, time trial and cyclo-cross championship. It was akin to a French national team.

Often, the team was on the road at as many as three different races at the same time, but all the French riders came together each year for the national championship. As Madiot addressed them just before the start, he worked himself up into a frenzy. His monologue referenced *la patrie, la Marseillaise* and what it meant to be French. One of the team's riders said, 'At that moment, we feel this energy uniting us.'

Initially, the lottery company signed a three-year agreement to bankroll Madiot's team, with an option to extend. But within eighteen months, its future was thrown into doubt by the Festina scandal. Management wondered whether it made sense to tie the brand to what was now a besmirched sport, and began canvassing opinion about whether to pull out. The future looked bleak for the new team. Madiot said, 'We had both feet in the shit.'

Française des Jeux was not the only company reviewing its involvement in professional cycling. Crédit Lyonnais, a Tour de France sponsor since 1981, deliberated over pulling 35 million francs in funding. A top executive said he would be prouder to finance the renovation of French schools than bankroll a race fuelled by doping. One by one, team managers were hauled in to questioning by the judge investigating the Festina affair. It was a make-or-break moment for the sport. 'We knew that cycling could disappear in France,' Madiot said. 'It was a question of life and death.'

In an informal pact between French teams, sponsors and race organisers, each one agreed to work together to cleanse the sport. They all decided that there was too much at stake to walk away. The Tour de France, they concurred, was a French institution, too important to disappear. The race was embedded in the fabric of the country, whether you liked cycling or not.

Besides, the race now had another valuable purpose – it had become a tourism advert for *La Belle France*.

The state broadcaster now used a 360-degree drone normally used for military reconnaissance to linger on snow-capped peaks, peaceful farmland with hay bales, and historic châteaux. Around the world, viewers with no interest in cycling tuned in to enjoy the scenery. The host broadcaster even prepared notes for foreign counterparts about landmarks on the route. The images, lasting about 100 hours each July, were worth tens of millions of euros, if not hundreds of millions to the French tourism industry.

To be sure, it was an expensive business shooting all of this; a chartered aeroplane circled some 8,000 metres above the cyclists in order to bounce off signals to the studio from television cameras mounted on motorbikes and helicopters. But the marriage between state-run France Télévisions and Amaury Sport Organisation was as strong as ever, tied up in long-term deals that typically lasted five years or more. The public broadcaster gradually increased its investment in the race, upping its daily coverage to five hours from two, and adding a behind-the-scenes magazine programme before the evening news.

There were some other interesting spin-offs as well. On a May evening in 1995, the production team that worked at the Tour de France sent a light aircraft above Paris in the same way they would do when covering a stage of the race. On the streets below, a cameraman, riding pillion on a motorbike, captured footage of Jacques Chirac and his wife being driven through the streets in a Citroën CX Prestige moments after he had won a presidential run-off against Lionel Jospin. For thirteen minutes, France Télévisions had the first live images of the President Elect as he sat back contentedly on the leather seat, his hand resting on the open car window. Staff in the studio clapped, cheered and slapped each other on the back; none of the private channels could compete.[2] It was all thanks to the Le Tour.

In the end, the bond between the state and the Tour de France proved too profound to be broken by the Festina affair. The race continued to enjoy the privilege of ending on the Champs Élysées, the Tour de France directors continued to be on familiar terms with the President of the Republic, and Chirac carried

2 Marc Endeweld: *France Télévisions, Off the Record – Histoires secretes d'une tele publique sous influences*, 2010

on the tradition of giving a handmade porcelain bowl to the winner of the yellow jersey.

As their country united behind the Tour de France, Marc and his brother Yvon, who was responsible for recruitment on the Française des Jeux team, became more committed than ever to defending the race against cheating and began to ask cyclists for their medical records and blood parameters before hiring them.

For French riders, there was a powerful incentive to stay on the right side of the law. If they cheated, they knew they could end up in handcuffs. This threat was much more remote for the foreign riders who lived and trained abroad. In Spain, for example, doping was not a criminal offence like in France. When they began talks with the manager of Floyd Landis – a young American cyclist based in Girona – the Madiots asked to examine his physiological data as well. They were told that the strict Mennonite religion of Landis precluded him from doping, but they insisted on seeing his records anyway. According to Marc, they did not hear back.

Thanks to the support of sponsors and public television, the Amaury family's income was barely dented in the year of the Festina affair. In a minor financial setback, sales of Amaury's *Vélo* magazine fell by 6 per cent. But that was easily offset by the effect of the national football team winning the World Cup the same year. That boosted advertising sales of *L'Équipe* by 21 per cent as companies queued up to align themselves with the history-making team.[3] Even after all that had happened at the 1998 race, Amaury Sport Organisation ended the year with a respectable 11-million-euro profit. But it was difficult

---

3 ASO published accounts for 1998 accessed online by author

to know at this stage whether the backing of the state and corporate France was enough to put the scandal behind them. ASO's year-end financial report noted the worrying events of that year's race and how they might yet impact on the family firm's bottom line. Who knew what the next Tour de France would bring?

★ ★ ★

A rider on one of the French teams was fully aware of the advantage of injecting $50 vials of EPO into his veins. In the thin air of the mountains, it would produce oxygen-carrying red blood cells to give you extra stamina when you most needed it. It could make the difference between an ordinary result and a podium finish, an extraordinary return on investment that could be worth hundreds of thousands of euros in bonuses and improved contract terms. A couple of years earlier, just as he was starting his career, he had seen the then leader of a race eating a Magnum ice cream while out on a post-dinner stroll after a gruelling mountain stage as riders trailing him lay exhausted on their hotel beds. That image would stay imprinted in his memory.

But when news of the Festina team bust reached him at the start of the previous year's race in Ireland, he resolved to destroy the clear-liquid vials hidden in the crushed ice inside his thermos. He did not want the stress of carrying that around France, anticipating a knock on his hotel-room door by a *gendarme* at any moment. He quietly disposed of the contents. As nervous chatter buzzed around his teammates about the French police investigation, he was relaxed. Now, nobody could touch him. Instead of tuning in for news updates when he got to his room after each stage, he turned on MTV. 'I was like, hey, I've got nothing on me,' he said. 'What's going to happen?'[4]

It helped that this cyclist barely spoke French. At the Cofidis team's breakfast table, he did not understand the gossip of his teammates about the arrest and searches of other team cars. On the start line of each stage, amid the noise of revving motorbike engines and jeering of fans, the twenty-six-year-old American called Bobby Julich put on some wraparound dark glasses and stared straight ahead.

At the end of the first week, Julich was joint-second overall after a fine time trial, and was looking strong in the mountains, too. Two weeks later, as the race limped into Paris, he crossed the finish line in third place in the general classification behind two other men who had dabbled with the dark side of the sport. Julich was the first American since LeMond to finish on the podium.

Julich now had to make a life decision in the prime of his career. He had a year left on his contract with Cofidis and brought his fiancée Angela to live with him in a rented flat he used as his training base near Nice on the south coast of France. When she asked him about doping, he told her everything and promised to stop. It was too dangerous to carry on. Besides, he figured that most other riders would take the same view. Instead of stocking his fridge with EPO vials that winter, he began looking for other ways to improve his performance. He ordered a $6,000 hypoxic tent to stimulate his body's production of oxygen-carrying red blood cells while sleeping. It was legal

4 Alasdair Fotheringham, *The End of the Road: The Festina Affair and the Tour that Almost Wrecked Cycling*, 2016

under anti-doping rules, but not ideal; it was difficult to sleep comfortably inside a sealed tent in your own bedroom.[5]

He also bought himself a $4,000 power meter to wire up to his bike for training sessions. The power meter was the size of a pager you could fit in the palm of your hand, and was becoming more common among riders. During downtime, they would chat about their maximum power-output numbers, and how long they could sustain them. These were the magic numbers that could track your fitness during the winter. 'I'm a 420 right now,' one might say. This referred to the watts he could generate, heart pounding, at full power for twenty minutes.

Julich knew, from his indoor testing with the US Olympic team, that he could sustain about 425 watts for about twenty minutes. On the mild winter days on the Côte d'Azur, he set about trying to crank up his performance. Each day he would try to increase his pain threshold by the smallest of margins. 'As long as I hit the numbers, I am going to win the Tour de France, or at least finish on the podium again,' Julich said. 'I set myself a goal of 450 watts. I would pin it in front of me and push myself.'

On six- or seven-hour training rides, he pursued the magic number – 450. When the weather was poor, he watched a tape of his third-place finish for inspiration, and chased the number on his home trainer. Even though he was now the top-ranked rider on the team, Cofidis did not provide him with a coach or someone to help monitor his training programme.

The French team was considered a bit of a 'mom and pop' organisation by North American riders. At the time, rather than turning to science and data, the team's managers trusted in the

---

5 Author interview with Bobby Julich

instincts that had served them and the generations before them. They did not bother to look into nutrition either. Rather than supplying riders with energy drinks, they squirted lime cordial into their water bottles. Instead of energy gels, they stuffed their feed bags with croissants, and tartines lathered with jam and cream.

A couple of years earlier, another American had signed with Cofidis at the same time as Julich.

Lance Armstrong had arrived at the Tour de France with the Motorola team in 1993 as a brash Texan with an eye for pretty blondes – and a short temper. When a reporter for *L'Équipe* knocked on his hotel-room door that year, he found the 21-year-old American watching Lucky Luke cartoons on television. 'You don't know anything about cycling,' Armstrong told the journalist, castigating him and his paper for not writing an article about Motorola's surprise third place in a team trial four days earlier.[6]

The next year Armstrong moved into a villa by Lake Como with a couple of north American teammates and their girl-friends as they further immersed themselves in the rhythms of the European cycling season. He agreed to join Cofidis in 1996 but diagnosed with testicular cancer before racing began, he could not compete and the team cancelled the second year of his reported $2 million deal.

Now cancer-free, Armstrong lived down the road from Julich but their careers had diverged. Julich stayed with the French team; Armstrong signed with a new team backed by the US Postal Service.

---

6 Christophe Wyrzykowski in *L'Équipe Raconte Le Tour de France*

Armstrong hired a coach to monitor his training programme. Dr Michele Ferrari carried a set of bathroom scales around in his camper van to weigh his client before and after each session. Making regular trips to Nice from Italy in this mobile clinic, he tracked Armstrong's weight and power data over days and weeks to plot a graph charting his progress. He had identified the power-to-weight ratio as the most important number to analyse – Armstrong's power threshold (approaching 500 watts) divided by his weight (somewhere between 70 and 75 kilos). Armstrong was trying to chase a magic number of 6.7. This was more sophisticated sports science than Julich's.

On a June morning two weeks before the Tour de France, Armstrong struck out from his home along the coast past Monaco to the foot of the 927-metre Col de Madone. He had come to gauge if he was hitting the right numbers. Some eighteen months earlier, he had set a time of 36 minutes up to the summit. This time, he flew up the narrow, winding road in 30 minutes, 47 seconds – an unofficial record for the ascent. Armstrong was ready.

Julich, however, was not. He felt drained. An allergy to the olive trees on the coastal hills had messed with his immune system, and he had begun to realise that the hypoxic tent he slept in at night was starving him of oxygen and making him feel weak. Yet, without any expert advice like Armstrong's on training and rest, he continued to keep pushing himself. 'Two weeks before the Tour, I realised I was in trouble,' Julich recalled.[7] 'I was a shell of my best.' By 'training like a robot', he

---

7 Author interview with Bobby Julich

had exhausted himself. The $10,000 investment on a hypoxic tent and power meter had not paid off.

Julich did not let on to the media about his lack of form and, on the eve of the 1999 Tour de France, he was still considered one of the favourites. When his and Armstrong's Litespeed time-trial bikes arrived at the same workshop for a tune-up before a minor race in the US, mechanics considered Julich's to be the higher priority. At the Tour de France, Julich had the number 1 pinned to his team jersey as the top finisher in the race from the previous year. (The defending champion Marco Pantani was excluded, and runner-up Jan Ullrich was injured.)

The race began with a gentle 4.2-mile time trial, but it was already enough for Armstrong to show his form. He powered into the lead by setting the fastest time. Julich was 28 seconds off the pace. As Julich struggled, Armstrong felt both light and strong; he was at peak fitness thanks to the scientific precision of his coach and training regime.

In a time trial a week later, Julich crashed, breaking his elbow and several ribs. He sat on the side of the road to receive medical treatment as his fellow American flew past. Armstrong went on to win his first Tour de France that year. There was no sign of a decrease in power at the front of the race; the average race speed rose to a record 25 miles per hour. It would not be until the following year that a test for stamina-enhancing EPO was introduced. Six years later, retroactive testing uncovered the drug in urine samples taken from Armstrong after the prologue and five more stages.

With his crew-cut hair, sunglasses and determined air, Armstrong had a military air. Tour de France historian Jacques

Augendre compared his US Postal team to the '*force de frappe des marines*', the strike force of the American marines.

Against this firepower, Julich and his French teammates were helpless because they did not dare take EPO anymore. The divide between the dopers and non-dopers would come to be described with a euphemism – '*ciclisme à deux vitesses*', two-speed cycling. As some riders near the top of the general classification cheated their way to supremacy, the French tended to ride clean, and more slowly. They slogged away in vain, saints to martyrdom with no hope of winning their national race. Most of their suffering was in silence. There was an *omertà*, a tacit silence, jealously guarded because money and careers were on the line. Members of the Amaury family business suspected that the race was the victim of widespread cheating, but – like the French riders – they felt helpless.

The best-known of the martyrs was Christophe Bassons. He was on the Festina team when the drug bust turned the Tour de France upside down but, according to witness statements by his teammates, the twenty-four-year-old was the only rider on the team who had steadfastly refused to dope. He had even turned down the offer of a salary rise to stay true to his principles. This had made him something of cult hero in the French media. He became known as 'Mr Clean', the man who had stood up on his own to the temptation of cheating. As he screened possible Française des Jeux hires, Marc Madiot had no reason to worry when it came to this young gentleman. He signed him to a one-year contract.

While riding for Madiot's team in the 1999 Tour de France, Bassons penned a column in *Le Parisien* about life inside the peloton. In one article, he wrote that Armstrong's sudden rise to the top of the sport after recovering from cancer had 'shocked' other riders. This comment soon became part of the gossip on the road. Other riders cursed him for breaking the code of silence. When he tried a solo breakaway, they closed him down and quickly caught him like a group of schoolyard bullies. Armstrong grabbed the Frenchman by the shoulder and, according to Bassons, told him that, 'what I was saying was bad for cycling, that I must not say it'. He says Armstrong finished his tirade by saying, 'Fuck you!'

As Armstrong crushed the opposition, the leading Française des Jeux riders finished that race well outside the top ten, almost half an hour behind the Texan. During the next six years that Armstrong won the race, the French team's top-performing rider would finish 76th, 66th, 19th, 78th, 16th and 29th. Madiot was so vexed by the unfairness of it all, year after year, that he could hardly control himself in team manager meetings when sitting across from the gloating US Postal team manager Johan Bruyneel. 'There was hatred among the team managers,' another team leader said. 'It was very intense.' On one occasion, spittle from Madiot's mouth flew across the room as he tore into Bruyneel, pounding his fist on the table in front of him.[8] The Belgian shrugged laconically; how come all these French guys were becoming so puritanical now?

Armstrong soon abandoned his home in France, moving across the Spanish border to Girona. In Spain, according to a German rider, you could tape EPO syringes to your windscreen, drive down the road and nobody would care. Riders on one Spanish team would take a cocktail of drugs each week to

---

8 Author interview with team manager who witnessed the scene

fine-tune their wattage output. Testosterone injections aided muscle fatigue in tired legs, while EPO jabs boosted stamina. If a drug tester happened to come knocking, there was a magical red powder known as Polvos de Madre Celestina that could save the day; by dissolving it into your urine sample, you destroyed the evidence.

The stain of doping had hardened the attitude of the Amaury family firm. The Tour's first prize, which had increased eight times between 1980 and 1995, was now pegged firmly at €400,000.[9] Why would they reward the riders if they felt they were cheating? Pushing back with bureaucracy, the French also delayed paying the money to winning riders until the following year, once all the drug testing results had come in, and after the lucre was stripped of income tax. Amid the continuing desecration of their race by outsiders the Government and ASO become ever more aligned to the French teams and riders, the perennial losers in their own race. They were all united in support of their travelling national fête – and hatred of foreign cheats.

Along with the frustration of the ever-increasing winless period, something else gnawed at Madiot. Bicycle racing was as French as the Eiffel Tower, Edith Piaf and the baguette. But he felt national influence fading in what he considered to be a French sport. As recently as the mid-'90s when Armstrong arrived in the sport, there were barely any native English speakers among the riders and the lexicon of the sport was predominantly French with words like *soigneur, domestique, bidon, musette, peloton* and *commissaire*. In 1994, an English journalist was jeered at a Tour de France press conference for asking a question in the

---

9 https://bikeraceinfo.com/tdf/tdf-prizes.html

language of Shakespeare and Dickens. The rider rolled his eyes at the nerve of the questioner – and answered in French.

But now, English was creeping into the sport as the world became more globalised. One third of foreign teams were gradually changing the sport's language and traditions. By the turn of the century less than 20 per cent of the field was French. The Tour de France now had an English language website, English-speaking press liaison staff and the race radio that communicated with team managers was now in both French and English. Teams from Belgium to the Netherlands began to use English, not French or Dutch, as the common language. Years later, this creeping anglicisation would reach deepest France. On the eve of a provincial race in Cholet, not far from Madiot's family home, the British race commissaire started addressing a meeting in English. Madiot began to seethe. When the official messed up the pronunciation of Française des Jeux, he exploded with rage. 'We were in a town hall in France so we should have been speaking in French,' he said later. 'If I was in a town hall in England, I would speak English.'

Madiot actually had a soft spot for American culture. He wore cowboy boots and, when on holiday in the United States, he went to see Nascar races. He and his brother had even raced for a US team, negotiating their salaries with the 7-Eleven team manager through a translator, scribbling down numbers on a scrap of paper in a Paris café.[10] A deal was soon done and the next season they both rode for the team. For the brothers, *le fric* was *le fric* whether it was paid in dollars or francs.

---

10 Author interview with James Startt, an American journalist based in Paris who acted as the impromptu translator in the café

Where Madiot drew the line was when these Americans threatened French interests and traditions.

Many of his compatriots felt the same way and cheered when, in the summer of 1999, José Bové, a pipe-smoking sheep farmer with a handlebar moustache, smashed up an under-construction McDonald's in southern France to protest a trade spat that caused the United States to impose heavy duties on Roquefort. Some of the cheese was made from milk produced on Bové's farm. Some 40,000 people turned out to support him as he became an icon of the anti-globalisation movement. His bail was paid by farmers' groups and activists, and he turned up to sentencing – he was given three months in prison – wearing sandals. One French news weekly said on its front cover: 'Should we canonise José Bové?'

Both ASO and Madiot viewed with suspicion the increasing influence of the Union Cycliste Internationale (UCI), the Switzerland-based ruling body whose ambitious Dutch president was excited by how Armstrong was making cycling a bigger draw outside France, and looked to build a calendar of events outside cycling's European heartland. This would become an existential threat to small regional races in France like the poetically named Les Boucles de la Mayenne, 'The Bends of the River Mayenne', whose route meandered through the Madiot family's local region.

Everyone in French cycling knew where these small races fitted into the sport's ecosystem but the ruling body had a global perspective and was working hard to market the sport in the New World. In 1984, the UCI had introduced a points ranking system to make the season more structured and easier to follow for an American audience unfamiliar with the sport's traditions.

The new system meant that Madiot earned himself a number of points the second time he won Paris–Roubaix as a rider. This did not necessarily please him. 'I don't give a fuck about points,' he shouted in an interview years later. 'When you win Paris–Roubaix, it's not about points.'

As cycling team meetings became more fractious, amid arguments about doping and how to develop the sport, American team manager Jonathan Vaughters witnessed a series of meltdowns by Madiot as he expressed 'his hatred for anything that threatened the *patrimoine de France*'. His voice would become louder, his face redder, until he finally flew off the handle altogether. 'Holy shit that boy can go off,' Vaughters said.[11] 'By the end of one of his diabolical monologues, you felt like Napoleon had risen from his tomb and was marching towards Waterloo once again.'

11 Jonathan Vaughters: *One Way Ticket – Nine Lives on Two Wheels,* 2019

Scoop

Issy-les-Moulineux, 2005

Away from the increasingly fractious Tour de France, its owners lived comfortably but without ostentation. Philippe Amaury and his wife Marie-Odile owned a modest apartment in a smart neighbourhood of Paris and a country retreat in Chantilly that was much smaller than the sprawling La Clairière mansion of his childhood. The lady of the house liked to dress well, but without breaking the bank. She drove a sensible French car, a Peugeot 308, around the local roads in stark contrast to the Mercedes limousine that her late father-in-law had thrown around the country lanes.

Marie-Odile Kuhn was brought up in a middle-class family in Strasbourg near the French border with Germany, the only girl among a family of four boys. Her father was an optician and her mother president of a regional family association – the Association des Familles du Bas-Rhin – which had been founded after the war to protect the conservative tradition of French families. After graduating with a degree in English literature and a Master's in journalism at Strasbourg University, she set off for the French capital in 1968, the year of the Paris uprising, beginning a career in advertising at Young & Rubicam making ads aimed at middle-class families. One glossy magazine ad she helped produce for the cooking-oil producer Lesieur shows a bride at a boozy wedding reception about to tuck into a silver plate of deep-fried *pommes dauphine*.

She was comfortable enough in Paris but she was proud of her roots and liked to speak the German-influenced local dialect of Alsace whenever she got the chance, addressing fellow Alsatians with the greeting, '*Wie geht's*?' She found some Parisians a little snooty – her husband aside, of course – and it irked her when they boasted about their schooling, especially those who had gone to places like the Sciences Po, whose alumni included François Mitterrand and Jacques Chirac. She felt that her university in Strasbourg was just as good.

At home, she and Philippe brought up their children Jean-Étienne and Aurore just like any other middle-class parents. At work, she and Philippe had an office on different floors of *Le Parisien*'s office building in the suburb of Saint-Ouen and sometimes did not cross paths during the working day. 'We were sufficiently independent not to bother each other,' she said. But there was plenty of time to discuss strategy on the golf course, or at home over the dinner table.

As the couple guided *Le Parisien* into the twenty-first century, average daily sales were still rising, if slowly. They ticked a little closer to half a million every year, partly thanks to the regional edition *Aujourd'hui*. But they were both cautious by nature, and watched anxiously as other newspapers around them began to implode in the advent of the Internet era. They had struck lucky with the arrival of Minitel in the mid-1980s but the inexorable rise of free online news was changing consumer habits quickly, and it was becoming increasingly difficult to break even.

When the usually cautious Philippe was persuaded to diversify by buying a technology theme park, it was a rare foray into a new sector. More than 2 million visitors came to visit Futuroscope's 3-D cinemas, play video games and learn about the wonders of the Internet, but visitor numbers had peaked by the time of his acquisition and the park near Poitiers lost at least €26 million in two years. Vexed by the widening financial black hole, Philippe swiftly sold the venue and parted company with his top aide Jean-Pierre Courcol.

Philippe was spooked by the mistake and became even more careful not to overstretch the family's finances. Rather than take interest-bearing loans to invest, he set aside profits to bolster reserves. These increasingly came courtesy of the Tour de France. In a three-year period over the turn of the millennium, the family paid themselves dividends totalling €30 million courtesy of Amaury Sport Organisation.[1] Sport only accounted for 18 per cent of the family business, but it was far more profitable than newspapers. Sticking with what they knew best, the family focused on expanding sports events including *L'Étape*, a one-day amateur race based on a stage of the Tour de France.

At the race itself, there was a one-man monopoly: Lance Armstrong. Scientific research showed that during the transformation of the young cartoon-watching jock to supreme athlete he had, by stripping fat from his quarter-back frame, increased his power-to-body weight ratio by 18 per cent. And all this after overcoming advanced cancer, chemotherapy and dark thoughts about death. His comeback to win the 1999 race acted as an

---

1 ASO financial accounts accessed online by author. By now, Killy had left ASO after receiving a $7 million golden handshake.

effective antidote to the Festina scandal, at least on the surface. It was a tale of the ages that cut through to major American television networks, bringing plenty of new coverage for the Tour de France. But even as this compelling new narrative covered up the race's tainted image, there was one potential problem that continued to nag within ASO. Those in the know suspected the story was too good to be true.

All kinds of gossip circulated among riders. There was talk of Armstrong using a hospital room in Nice for blood transfusions to boost his red blood cell count and artificially lift his stamina. One of the team mechanics had a girlfriend who was a nurse and suspected something. Maybe it was true, maybe complete nonsense. Rumours like this filtered through to the small group of reporters who covered cycling for *L'Équipe*.

For decades, journalists had found the lines between working for the daily sports newspaper and the Tour de France were blurred. Often, the bottom line was that you worked for both. Each part of the Amaury business was supposed to complement the other. The crossover between the two businesses meant *L'Équipe* reporters had their own annexe in the press room or the first row of seats reserved. They were the creators of the race's in-house paper and often enjoyed the inside line on what was going on behind the scenes, although for obvious reasons they could not write up everything they saw.

One of the *L'Équipe* journalists moonlighted by narrating the official Tour de France race radio, providing live updates to teams from the car of race director Jean-Marie Leblanc. Once, as the two sat in the car before a stage, the journalist glanced out of the window to see a Colombian rider rummaging around for something in the back of his jersey. He watched as a syringe dropped out of one of his shirt pockets and rolled slowly across the tarmac before coming to a stop against the wheel of the race director's car. The young South American looked crestfallen. Several other people had spotted the syringe and were staring. He did not know what to do. Should he leave it lying on the road and pretend nothing had happened? The driver of the car opened the car door, and picked up the syringe. Handing it back, he said, 'Here take it, I was a rider, too.'[2] In the next day's paper, amidst the minutiae of the stage, there was no mention of the wayward syringe.

By the turn of the century, there was – at least in theory – a Chinese wall between the Tour de France and *L'Équipe*. Staff worked out of different buildings in Issy-Les-Moulineux, even if their offices were joined by a passageway. On the road, the newspaper's staff no longer stayed in the same hotels as the race employees, nor did they eat at the same dinner table any more. The socialising of the good old days only occasionally made a comeback when Leblanc – a man who had worked on both sides of the business – brought his jazz band to the office for an impromptu jam session.

Covering doping remained inherently difficult at *L'Équipe*. The first journalist to cover doping fell out with his colleagues after the Festina scandal. The clique of cycling correspondents spent half the year on the road with the riders they covered and were conscious they must tread carefully when going about their reporting; they could damage their working relationship with the athletes by repeatedly peppering them with questions

---

2 Philippe Bouvet, the journalist in the car, tells this story in the book *L'Equipe Raconte Le Tour de France,* 2015

about doping. Before long, after a few bust-ups in the newsroom, the doping reporter was shown the door. When the newspaper's editor asked for a volunteer to replace him, only one person put up his hand. His name was Damien Ressiot.

Ressiot had started out on *France Football* magazine, another Amaury publication, developing an interest for investigative journalism while working on a financial scandal at football club Olympique Marseille. Maybe he was a good fit for the doping story – he did not much like cycling. The paper sent him to Montpellier University to take a one-year diploma in performance-enhancing drugs in which he learnt about the science behind everything from blood doping to the effects of taking synthetic testosterone and cortisone. He was the only journalist on the course.

When he returned to the newsroom, bursting with knowledge about steroids and blood boosters, Ressiot took a desk in a corner under the strip lights of the white-walled office on a different floor from the cycling journalists. When he asked them for help in investigating Armstrong, they shrugged and turned the other way. Even with the backing of the editor, Ressiot was on his own and presented a sort of existential threat to the Amaury business. The bottom line was every time he dug up some dirt on cycling, it could undermine the sports side of the family firm.

In early 2004, a few weeks before the Paris–Roubaix race over stretches of cobblestones, Ressiot obtained a 3,000-page leaked police report based on interviews with the Cofidis team's riders and their wives that found evidence of widespread doping. It showed that the doping armistice after the Festina scandal six years earlier had not endured for all French cyclists. The temptation of taking performance boosters to keep up with the race leaders was too tempting.

L'Équipe decided to publish the story on its front page under the headline: 'DOPING: TERRIBLE CONFESSIONS'. Inside, on page 3: 'WITNESS STATEMENTS FROM HELL'. Over a whole broadsheet page, rider statements were laid out, with their denials or 'no comments' at the bottom. It marked a shift in the paper's usually 'see no evil, hear no evil' attitude to doping. For what was normally the sports paper of record, the story was sensational stuff and included the tale of a hotel chambermaid finding an unidentified rider in a coma after what appeared to be an accidental overdose.

The investigating magistrate was incensed by the police leak. He was still midway through the inquiry. He sent the Brigade Criminelle around to the *L'Équipe* office to try and identify the source. Known as *La Crim*, the police force was known for working on bombings, kidnappings and murders. Officers threaded a crime-screen tape around the newsroom's entrance and, slotting a memory stick into Ressiot's computer, sucked out reams of data.[3] Then they drove him in a squad car to his suburban home and carried out another search.

The story completely overshadowed Paris–Roubaix, forcing the withdrawal of the Cofidis team and casting a pall over one of the most important ASO events of the year. However, Amaury executives stood behind Ressiot. A company lawyer went to court to defend his right to publish.

While the Cofidis story was a tidy scoop, Ressiot had another target. Proving that Lance Armstrong was doping was like the

---

3 Author interview with Damien Ressiot

Holy Grail for investigative sports journalists. He had never met the brash American but when he said, 'Prove that I'm doping . . .' he felt like Armstrong was personally challenging him. 'It was like a game,' Ressiot said. 'I felt like I was playing a match against him.'

Over the past five years, Armstrong had been relentlessly efficient at the Tour de France. After a winter and spring of careful preparation, he put on his game face and with Oakley shades hiding his expression he got to work, grinding down the opposition with the help of his US Postal teammates. For journalists who were complimentary about him, he could be charming. For those who questioned whether he was riding clean, he was ferocious, staring them down and ordering them to come up with evidence. That was almost impossible, one said, unless you hid in his suitcase.

There must be a way, mused Ressiot. Through his contacts, he found out that scientists from the French anti-doping laboratory were working on a new test for EPO and were retesting dozens of frozen Tour de France samples from the two years before the first test for the wonder drug was introduced at the 2000 edition. These two years included the 1999 Tour de France, the year of Armstrong's first victory.

Of fifty-two samples still suitable for testing more than five years later, the scientists found twelve were positive for EPO. They had no idea to whom the positive urine samples belonged because, under anti-doping protocol, they were not identifiable by name, but by a six-digit code.

After each Tour de France stage, the race leader wearing the yellow jersey was pulled in to give a urine sample. That meant Armstrong would have been tested as many as fourteen times in 1999. If Ressiot could crack the codes, he would be able to find out if Armstrong was one of the dirty dozen who had used EPO. He managed to get to first base easily enough, obtaining the codes that had shown up as positive.

Next, he had to match the cyclists to the codes. There were a few sources who would have this on file: the Union Cycliste Internationale; the French Sports Ministry; and the French Cycling Federation. Ressiot knew there was only a slender chance they would break medical protocol to help him. So he went to the other possible source – Lance Armstrong.

As the 2005 Tour de France approached, Armstrong was planning to burnish his legacy before retiring from cycling at the age of thirty-three. He had become exceedingly rich – his base salary and bonus the previous year was $14.5 million.[4] On a sporting level, he had already passed the record mark of five wins held by the likes of Eddy Merckx and Bernard Hinault. He wanted one final victory to cement his place as the greatest Tour de France rider of all time.

For all his bluster about never failing a drugs test, conspiracy theories lingered about Armstrong. One of these was that, before the 1999 race, he was granted permission by the UCI to continue to use stimulants as part of his recovery from cancer. Some riders had a so-called Therapeutic Use Exemption (TUE) if they had a medical condition, such as asthma, and this information remained private. Ressiot contacted a lawyer who acted for Armstrong and worked out of an office in Monaco. He told him he wanted to write a story that proved that Armstrong did not have such an exemption and had competed on the same terms as everyone else.

---

4 Wheelmenthebook.com

The lawyer was initially receptive, but Armstrong's team manager was suspicious and shut down the idea. Trying a different tack, Ressiot phoned the Union Cycliste Internationale president, Hein Verbruggen. He was in China at the time, and was not able to talk for long, but agreed to hear him out. After some reflection, he said he had no problem sharing Armstrong's records – he knew that there was nothing to hide – but he could only authorise this with his permission. He would talk it over with his team manager, Johan Bruyneel.

Eventually, Verbruggen persuaded Bruyneel and Armstrong to let down their guard. Ressiot was on to second base. He travelled to the ruling body's headquarters nestled among the Swiss Alps to see the evidence that his sources thought would be a good-news story, but which he hoped would prove Armstrong was a cheat.

The offices adjoined an indoor velodrome in which cyclists zipped quietly around a pinewood track. Ressiot was shown to the office of the medical director, who laid out Armstrong's anti-doping forms. Ressiot carefully made copies. As he expected, the array of forms showed no evidence of drug exemptions, but that was not the point. Once he had left the offices, he matched Armstrong's code to six positive EPO tests at the 1999 Tour de France, including the opening-day time trial in which he had powered to victory. It was a home run for Ressiot . . . almost.

His story would unravel one of the greatest periods of dominance by an individual in any sport, and neither he nor *L'Équipe* could afford to get this wrong. If it was inaccurate, Armstrong could successfully sue for millions, maybe tens of millions, of euros and demolish the Amaury family finances.

Therefore, he needed a second source that confirmed this was indeed Armstrong's six-digit code in 1999. Easier said than done. Whatever he tried, he could not get his story over the line. Months passed without a breakthrough. He had begun to fear that all his painstaking work would be for nothing.

Meanwhile, business as usual, Armstrong won a record-extending seventh Tour de France. In a defiant victory speech on the podium, he railed against those who did not believe his story.

Among the sceptics was *L'Équipe*. The following day, its front-page headline '*IL RESTERA À PART*' ('HE'LL STAY OUT ON HIS OWN') provided faint praise by alluding to the lack of affection many felt for him in France. The subheading was also less than glowing: 'He leaves cycling with this unprecedented feat at the heart of the most troubled period of the sport.' In a front-page editorial, the newspaper went even further – it said that, after the Festina scandal, Armstrong did not represent renewal. The underlying message – we know your secrets.

During the Tour de France, Ressiot had stayed in Paris and stewed. His story was written but still on ice. He kept talking to his sources, seeking a way forward. Just as he was preparing to go on vacation on the coast of Brittany in the first week of August, he got what he needed. A second source confirmed Armstrong's code. Ressiot cancelled his vacation.

At 11.00 a.m. on a Monday morning in mid-August, the *L'Équipe* editor chaired the daily newsroom conference about what would go in the following day's newspaper. Senior staff discussed a story about tennis player Maria Sharapova and the daily staple of French football – PSG and Lyon were joint leaders as the season was getting under way. All pretty mundane stuff. As they were about to disperse, the editor said there was a chance something could change the news agenda.

'What's that?' one of the group said.

There was a big drug story about Armstrong, he said. Lawyers were going through the details. 'We're waiting for final confirmation,' he added.

Normally, the pages of the newspaper would be on view in the newsdesk secretary's office before being transmitted to the printing presses around France. But that day, the first four pages were blank in order to avoid leaks. As senior staff worked on the layout and headline with lawyers, Ressiot could relax a little. For the first time in months, he felt like the onus was no longer on him. His work was done.

'I'd done my job,' he said.[5] 'If there's a war tomorrow, then there's a war.'

The next morning, when Ressiot turned up to work there were dozens of television cameras and reporters in the car park outside clutching that day's newspaper. In live broadcasts, they showed viewers the front page with the headline: 'THE ARMSTRONG LIE'. Ressiot ducked into the building. At his desk, he was receiving calls every couple of minutes. He ignored call after call on his mobile phone but smiled at a one-word text from the editor who had hired him to cover doping. It said simply: 'Congratulations'.

Ressiot's evidence was laid out over the first four pages. An editorial read: 'For those who think that the Tour de France is more than a cycling race, for those who think the winner is

---

5 Author interview with Damien Ressiot

more than a champion, the revelations of *L'Équipe* are more terrible than the Festina and Cofidis scandals.'

Not far away, Leblanc, the Tour de France race director, was also being bombarded with calls. He was furious nobody had forewarned him about the story.

12

Heir

City of London

Growing up in Paris, Philippe Amaury's son, like many children of his age, was only vaguely aware of what his father did at work. As he and his school friends flicked through *Miroir du Ciclisme*, *Vélo* and *Sprint International* in the 1980s, they tried to outscore each other with their cycling knowledge and latest news about Bernard Hinault, and the new kids on the block: Greg LeMond and the Colombian climber Luis 'Lucho' Herrera. Little Jean-Étienne did not think to boast that his dad owned the Tour de France because, well, that was something difficult to get your head around for an eight-year-old boy. How can anyone own something that belongs to sixty million Frenchmen and women?

At the start of the summer holidays in 1985, his dad took him to the Tour de France for the first time.[1] Six million cars were expected on the roads, with most of the traffic heading south from Paris to the Côte d'Azur. In the family car, the Amaurys struck out west where there was congestion around the Breton village of Plumelec. The hamlet would host the opening-day

---

1 Author interview with Jean-Étienne Amaury

time trial. The Tour de France's travelling circus was based nearby at Morbihan. Parked in the streets were rows of television trucks with antennae, including a crew from CBS, there to analyse the progress of LeMond. As Jean-Étienne knew all too well from school playground chatter, LeMond had just signed what was billed as cycling's first $1 million contract to follow Hinault from Renault to La Vie Claire. The new team's riders sported aerodynamic gadgets like teardrop-shaped helmets, clip-in pedals and disc wheels – new tech to try and shave a few split seconds off their times.

On the four-mile course, the biggest crowds were massed on a wooded climb to the Côte de Cadoudal. For thousands of Bretons it was a family outing. Many of their parents, grandparents and even great-grandparents had done the same. Wearing giveaway sunhats from the Tour de France caravan, they feasted on picnics in the lush green fields, tucking into fresh baguettes, cheese and salami with red wine. Jean-Étienne drank in the atmosphere – the noise, the crowds and the adrenalin of a sports event. His father had given him a small green card which hung around his neck. On the bottom of the card were the logos of two newspapers – *Le Parisien* and *L'Équipe*. It gave him behind-the-scenes access – he might even receive a pat on the head from the Tour de France champion.

Starting out last as the previous year's winner, Hinault trailed the best time at the halfway stage but powered back. Spectators listened on transistor radios pressed to their ears to see how the local boy was doing, cheering as he tore past. When it emerged he had won by four seconds, the crowd roared. He pulled on the yellow jersey and received a hug from his parents, Joseph and Lucie, who had made the one-hour journey by car from the family farm.

Afterwards, the only way Hinault could get through the throng was with a car equipped with a police siren that parted the crowds. He smiled and waved as fans thumped the car roof in appreciation. Meanwhile, Jean-Étienne was mentally storing up the images of his first Tour de France to tell his friends when he got back to Paris. It never occurred to him that he was the heir to the race. Even today, he struggles to get his head around it.

When he grants an interview to the author in 2018, he is aged 41 and comes across as a quiet and thoughtful man with no arrogance or sense of entitlement. More like his father than his rumbustious grandfather. It is two weeks before Christmas. Outside it is chilly and the heating on the executive floor of the ASO office is turned up higher than perhaps necessary. He is polite and sweats slightly in a grey suit, small beads of perspiration on the dome of his balding head. When the discussion turns to the Tour de France, he describes his family as a guardian of the race.

'The Tour de France is the people by the roadside,' he says. 'It belongs first and foremost to the people.'[2]

At school, Jean-Étienne was good at mathematics and science and embarked on a computer engineering degree at one of the prestigious Écoles Central in Lille. The college prided itself on keeping pace with the development of science and society. He enjoyed problem solving and learning about a fast-developing new skill – website software. He thought perhaps that acquiring

2 Amaury interview, *ibid*

expertise in what in the late '90s was known as 'new media' might one day be useful for working in the family business.

L'Équipe and *Le Parisien* had set up their own websites by now but were struggling with the conundrum of how to have an online presence without eroding newspaper sales. 'I thought one day there could be some crossover between my career and the family business,' Jean-Étienne said. Perhaps in years to come he might become involved with digital newspapers or online streaming of the Tour de France, but it was only a vague notion. 'When and how I would work with the family business, there was never an exact idea.'

At age twenty-two, with a group of other fresh-faced graduates, he took a job as a computer engineer at Bloomberg in London. The financial news wire was earning billions of dollars from banks and finance professionals who paid $20,000 a year for its real-time data and analysis pumped out around the clock. This information helped banking titans keep track of their money, and spot ways to make more. Among them was Thomas Weisel, the Silicon Valley banker who financially underpinned the career of Lance Armstrong.

As Jean-Étienne flashed his new ID badge and walked into the office, he found a pantry stocked with juice and breakfast cereals to encourage staff to come to work before dawn. The company ethic was work hard, play hard. Some executives would mimic the bankers in the industry they covered by arriving for work at 6.00 a.m. in chauffeur-driven Mercedes limousines complete with slicked-back hair and red braces under their suit jackets. In the sales department, staff who connected bankers with this global financial ecosystem put little flags on their desk to show their nationality. The Italians stood up and gesticulated. The French and Spanish were more measured. Japanese staff worked stoically through the London night to service clients in Asia's financial markets. Little did the multinational staff know that Jean-Étienne was the heir to the Tour de France.

Bloomberg was developing financial news channels in Spanish, Italian, French, German and Japanese. It was an interesting time for the young French graduate whose boss was a New Yorker called Katherine Oliver. He helped to produce on-demand television through which Bloomberg clients could watch interviews and news conferences. It was a sort of Netflix for bankers. 'We were about twenty years ahead of our time,' he said. But instead of sexy blockbuster movies, the streamed interviews he helped produce were a little more dry – such as interviews with economists and bankers about 0.25 per cent interest-rate changes. 'We were focusing on the Internet, and the revolution that was going to happen.'

There was a lot of expensive trial and error. The multinational television stations which were burning through $20,000 for a two-minute live interview had little or no advertising income, so this became unsustainable, even for a financial giant. Eventually, all of them bar the English channel were shut down.

* * *

With blonde hair and blue eyes like her mother, Jean-Étienne's older sister Aurore was described by one colleague as smart and easy to get on with. At age twenty-four, she took a job in the Paris office of Mayer Brown, which specialised in corporate law litigation. For a couple of years, she worked out of the law firm's New

York office, developing an expertise in technology during the dot-com boom before returning home. Mayer Brown's posh Paris office was just off the Champs Élysées, a five-minute walk from where her grandfather had run his media empire at number 114.

Jean-Étienne and Aurore were pursuing their careers with some success when their father became gravely ill. Many years earlier, conscious of his inheritance battle in court with his sister in the 1970s, he and Marie-Odile created a *Société Civile* to control the family business. Under French company laws, the shares of this holding company called simply Amaury SC could not be sold. At a time when sheikhs and oligarchs were buying Premier League football clubs as trophy assets, the family was effectively putting up a barrier to a corporate raid. Even if a billionaire offered $1 billion for Jean-Étienne or Aurore's interest in the Tour de France, they would not be able to relinquish their stake.

In May 2006, Philippe Amaury died at the age of 66. The funeral was at 10.00 a.m. on the last Tuesday in May at Saint-Francois-Xavier church near the family home in the smart seventh *arrondisement* near parliament. Among the mourners was Bernard Hinault and Sports Minister Jean Francois Lamour. Jean-Étienne and Aurore read sections from the Bible. Marie-Odile, dressed in a black velvet tapered jacket, and carrying a grey shawl, followed the unadorned wooden coffin out of the church with her head held high.

A short note in *Le Parisien* that morning said the family would prefer not to receive flowers, requesting instead donations be made to Petites Soeurs des Pauvres, a Catholic charity run by nuns.

Before long, there were rumours swirling about a takeover of the family business, but Marie-Odile made her intentions clear. In a note to staff a week after her husband's death, she wrote: 'With the same determination as my husband, I will oversee the development of our business activities.'

She rehired two of her late husband's trusted lieutenants to run the sports and media assets respectively, and announced that Jean-Étienne would join Aurore on the board. Her son would oversee the sports assets, his sister the media portfolio. The business would remain proudly *en famille*.

Jean-Étienne was dispatched from his job with Bloomberg in London to take a Master's degree in business at Stanford in the Californian sunshine. He would have to learn about managing the family affairs fast. His departure left just Marie-Odile and Aurore in Paris. In the *Le Parisien* office, Marie-Odile could not always contain her grief as she got down to work again. There were no more rounds of golf with her husband, no more Sunday lunches with all the family. One day, while talking to a colleague, she let her iron façade slip as she broke down in tears.

'I feel so very alone since Philippe's death,' she said. 'It's hard to bear.'[3]

---

3 *Le Monde*: 1/10/2009

Part III

Chasing the Breakaways: the Tour de France in the Internet Era

13

Opportunity

Palo Alto & Vilvoorde, Flanders

The gentle climate, green hills and oak trees had once made this Californian valley attractive to Spanish settlers. They could fish in the rivers and streams, and catch deer and other game in the woodland. They camped around El Palo Alto, 'the tall stick', which was a landmark tree that soared into the sky. The more wealthy among them built ranches to live the good life. Entrepreneurs arrived from other parts of the US, establishing sawmills to exploit the trees on the hillsides. The upper classes from San Francisco also got wind of the inviting pastures and came by horse and cart to build country estates. At the end of the nineteenth century, they added vineyards to the rolling slopes.

The valley took on a new life when a man called Leland Stanford and his wife Jane opened a university with the family name in memory of their late son. As hundreds of students came to the university to benefit from the free tuition on offer, the city of Palo Alto was born. A comfortably well-off and educated middle-class community emerged in which the city leaders owned the supply of gas and electricity as well as water. In 1938, two men called William Hewlett and David Packard lived in the city. They began to make computer products and started the latest iteration of the land now known as Silicon Valley.

A few months after the death of his father in 2006, Jean-Étienne Amaury arrived here to start a Master's degree in business. Compared to the chill autumn of Paris, the weather was pleasantly warm. Everything seemed to be upbeat and go-ahead. In the Palo Alto suburb of Menlo Park, two Stanford PhD students had incorporated a company from inside a messy garage. Now, eight years later, Google was worth $600 billion and had just bought another start-up fifteen miles down the road called YouTube that was launched above a pizzeria. The young Frenchman, with a passion for high-tech, felt invigorated by a startup culture that made the business world back home in France seem prehistoric. 'There was so much going on around me,' Amaury recalled. 'It was super-exciting . . . everyone around me was willing to take risks.'

One day, walking down the street in Palo Alto he did a double-take as he saw Steve Jobs walking past. Financiers in the valley were willing to risk hard cash on ventures even if they knew there was a fair chance they would not succeed. Entrepreneurs behind the projects would just take the knowledge they had accumulated and move on to the next thing. This easy-going approach would become known as a 'test and learn' culture and it was an alien concept in France, where the fear of failure was much more intense. Even one flop was enough to stigmatise a young entrepreneur back home. French authorities maintained a 'blacklist' of managers at failed businesses that lenders could review when considering whether to advance them funds for another venture. Often, there was no second chance – at least until your name dropped off the list three years later.

As usual, Amaury did not announce himself as the heir to the Tour de France. He did not bring this up as he chatted with his fellow students as they walked from lectures, strolling through the sandstone arches of the university, and past the mosaic-fronted church built in memory of the founder. The modules Amaury covered included finance, accounting, operations, marketing and strategy, all of them areas that would be useful in running the cycling race. He was quietly spoken, polite and unassuming. As he was settling into student life, among the other visitors to Palo Alto was someone he was already familiar with – Lance Armstrong.

Here in the US, the waves from the *L'Équipe* scoop about Armstrong had not hit with any great intensity mainly because there was no official endorsement from cycling or anti-doping authorities that the report was accurate. For now, it was just a newspaper story in a foreign language. There was no conclusive evidence of wrongdoing. It was one person's word against another's. Besides, all the talk in the cycling world that autumn was of the just-finished race. Floyd Landis, Armstrong's former *domestique*, his support rider, had come out of the seven-time champion's shadow in spectacular fashion. Landis took the lead after eleven stages only to suffer a sudden collapse in the Alps. The next day, in an epic turnaround, he rode in a solo breakaway for 78 miles to the town of Morzine. That kind of 'Hail Mary' attack was almost unheard of in the modern era, in which the leaders did not mount their attacks until the final few kilometres of a stage. It was, according to the VeloNews website, 'one of the most audacious and bravest rides seen in the modern era of the Tour de France'. Just as fans reflected on an enjoyable race, it emerged Landis had tested positive for testosterone. Helping to take the heat off Armstrong, he was about to become the first winner to be stripped of the Tour de France.

Armstrong had got to know Palo Alto thanks to his friendship with the man who had financially underpinned his career. As a young man, Thomas Weisel had graduated from Stanford in 1963 when the relaxed vibe was not unlike that which Amaury was now experiencing for the first time. Suntanned male students wearing button-down shirts rode bicycles around to lectures. Female students from wealthy families in floral dresses drove open-top Oldsmobile cars. Many of them studied hard for their money – fees were around $1,600, a considerable sum. Computing studies was already part of the curriculum and the technicians who oversaw a sprawling IBM computer spoke in a code most people did not understand. After graduating, Weisel became an investment banker in San Francisco. His firm became one of a small group known as the 'Four Horsemen' who, in a city of few investment banks, between them underwrote dozens of initial public offerings of tech startups during the dot-com era.

Weisel was fanatical about sport; he had almost qualified for the Olympics as a speed skater. Still with a competitive instinct, he took up cycling in his forties, competing in veteran competitions. It was at this point that he began to become interested in professional cycling and his and Armstrong's lives would cross. He founded a company called Tailwind Sports which secured a sponsorship deal from the US Postal Service to bankroll an American Tour de France team around Armstrong.

In parts of the United States, Armstrong's success at the Tour de France had sparked a mini boom in cycling. For Trek, a bike maker that had started out in a barn in Wisconsin in the 1970s and made a range of bikes at different price points, sales of high-end bicycles rose as a portion of total sales to 28 per cent from 16 per cent. Every year, during America's hold on the world's most famous bike race, it sold thousands of $4,500 rides named after Madone, a climb outside Nice.

Weisel's other side project was bailing out the money-losing US Cycling, the national ruling body. As part of his rescue package, he set up a group called the Champions Club, which gave Silicon Valley hot-shots the chance to ride with Armstrong on the green hills around Palo Alto. A group of twenty-seven of these had agreed to sign up to this exclusive club, paying a $100,000 joining fee to ride wheel-to-wheel with the professionals. Together, they had a net worth of tens of billions of dollars. Five were among America's richest 400 people, including Wal-Mart heir Robson Walton and John Doerr, who had invested in Google after its birth as a Stanford University computer science project.[1]

As the sun went down below the Californian hills and wine glasses were refilled, Armstrong enjoyed chatting with these successful men, some of whom appeared slightly in awe of his star status. The Silicon Valley set gave him investment tips on how to spend his growing cycling fortune, and at one point he ventured $100,000 of his own money on a tech fund that went on to invest in the car-sharing app Uber.

---

1 Bill Gifford, *Outside* magazine: 'High Rollers', 1/6/2006

While a few of these billionaire bikers were super-competitive, most just rode to keep in shape. They were too old to be jocks. 'Cycling is good for middle-aged men,' one said. 'It's sociable and better on your joints than running.' Between them, they contributed $1 million a year to develop the next generation of American Tour de France prospects. The money covered the costs of sending young riders to learn their trade in the hard-as-nails cycling heartland of Belgium where, like students, the American rookies slept in bunk beds and shared a communal kitchen.

With his cycling fortune, Armstrong enjoyed the high life, travelling from coast to coast in a private jet. Raised by his mother in a 'soul-deadening' suburb of Dallas, he had not gone to university but, since signing his first million-dollar-a-year pay contract at age twenty-five, he had become familiar with the art of moneymaking. When he signed one of his first deals in the sport, worth a reported $2 million, he requested to receive part of his income as image rights through an offshore company in Luxembourg. Now, a decade later, with a fortune estimated at more than $100 million, Armstrong kicked about investment ideas as though he was a trainee venture capitalist. He read the *Wall Street Journal*. As they talked money, one Champions Club member, a hedge fund manager, complemented the Texan on his 'business mind'.[2]

Whenever talk of the *L'Équipe* story came up, Armstrong shot it down expertly. He and his inner circle had honed their defence skills over many years. Armstrong contended that because the story was from a French newspaper, it was not

---

2 Author interview with source

credible. He called the sixty-year-old Amaury family newspaper 'trashy'. His team of public relations advisers and lawyers muddied the waters as much as they could, saying the testing was unofficial and dubious. Generally, Americans believed and admired Armstrong, the dashing cancer survivor who hung out with George Bush and Bill Clinton, and commanded $250,000 for a speaking fee. Over the previous two years, Nike had sold more than 50 million yellow silicon bracelets at $1 apiece on behalf of his Livestrong cancer charity. Nike steadfastly stood by Armstrong, as did his other sponsors, from Trek bicycles to Oakley sunglasses, continuing to pay him millions of dollars in post-retirement endorsement deals.

More support came from a report commissioned by the Union Cycliste Internationale into whether to open disciplinary proceedings against Armstrong. It was a binary question and the answer was 'no'. The report found that the French anti-doping laboratory that uncovered the positive EPO tests had not followed the correct procedure. (They had not intended to, of course; it was always supposed to be a dry run.) There was no proof that the urine samples were not tampered with and therefore no action should be taken. As soon as the 130-page exposition was published, and even before reading it in full, Armstrong went on the offensive again, attacking *L'Équipe* and the Tour de France organisers who, he said, had failed to discredit him.

With the report helping to book-end his career in the way he wanted, Armstrong could kick back and relax wherever took his fancy. He was thirty-four, young, rich and single. He had recently divorced his wife and, after seven years following the monk-like existence of a professional cyclist (no alcohol, late nights or fatty foods), he could do all the things he had denied himself for so long. He dated pop star Sheryl Crow and fashion designer Tory Burch. He bought art for his homes in Texas and Colorado, and went on surfing vacations in Hawaii.

'He's a lot more fun and interesting off the bike, and lot cuter,' Sally Jenkins, the co-author of his memoir, told the *New York Times*.[3] 'The bike guy was this gaunt, driven fighter. Off the bike, he's this flip-flop-wearing, beer-drinking, serial-dating marquee idol.'

One evening, after a fundraising event for his cancer charity in New York, Armstrong was hanging out with Hollywood actor Jake Gyllenhaal at the bar of the Mondrian hotel on Park Avenue. The star of *Brokeback Mountain* was in talks to play Armstrong in a movie about his life, and was shadowing him for a few days to get a feel for what he was like. Over drinks, the pair got talking to one of the members of the Champions Club who had attended the auction, a hedge fund trader whose day job including investing on the stock market part of the Microsoft fortune of Bill Gates.

The conversation turned to cycling's business model and how, the trader suggested, it could benefit from a new ownership structure. This was a typical private equity move on Wall Street and in the City of London – find an undervalued asset, take it over, restructure it and take a share of the extra profits. In cycling, the biggest races were controlled by diverse owners, most of them like *L'Équipe* with links to sports newspapers such as *Gazzetta dello Sport* in Italy and in Belgium, *Het Nieuwsblad*. Their primary business was under attack in the age of online

---

3 Jenkins quoted in *New York Times* article by Allen Salkin: 'It's Not About the Bike', 22/6/2008

news and gossip. If investors bought them out, they could build a year-round cycling championship with a more compelling narrative which generated more revenue.

A deal with the Tour de France, perhaps even a takeover, would be the first part of any such strategy. Under the trader's proposal, teams would share some of the equity with Amaury Sport Organisation and reap the benefits from listing the championship on the stock market.[4] The trader was enthusiastic about the potential of the idea, but he did not have the time or money to bankroll the plan. He proposed that Armstrong set up a meeting with Tour de France executives to look into it and maybe interest some of his banker pals.

A few weeks later, Armstrong rounded up a few other members of the Champions Club to hear their views. In a private room at Spago, a fancy restaurant in Palo Alto, they discussed what it would take to launch a takeover of the Tour de France.

The group agreed there was an opportunity to transform professional cycling, even if in Armstrong's words it would require a 'big number' for the owners to sell an asset that had been in the family for more than half a century.[5] The sale price in 1956 – about $5 million in today's money – was before television had turned Le Tour from a national fête that sold newspapers to a sports property with global reach. It was now an asset not only for its status but its potential to make money. One Paris-based analyst who covered the leisure industry reckoned that the Tour de France could be worth as much as $1 billion.

The race's heritage put it on a par with other sporting

---

4 Author interview with source who attended the meeting
5 Author interview with Lance Armstrong published in *Breaking Away*, *Bloomberg Markets* magazine article, July 2012

assets like Ferrari's Formula One team, the heirloom owned by the Agnelli family since 1969. That might make it expensive but for the super-wealthy, a so-called 'big number' was all relative. A shortage of money was not a problem for the type of investors Armstrong hung out with. While learning to fly a state-of-the-art helicopter, one Silicon Valley magnate looked at buying – 'as a kind of hobby' – the aerospace company that made the machine and was worth billions of dollars. Another had commissioned a 126-metre yacht with a basketball court, helicopter pad and submarine. The cost – $200 million. When the author spoke to Armstrong about the talks in Spago, he was charming and expansive. He talked more like the bankers that he now mixed with than the cartoon-watching Texan kid who had arrived at the Tour at age 21. But he was also a little vague about the proposed Tour de France buyout. It sounded like it was a nice idea, but was unlikely to go any further.

Perhaps more important than the price of the Tour de France was another more incalculable barrier – would the French really let a bunch of American dudes buy a piece of their heritage?

Not far away from these high rollers, Jean-Étienne Amaury was buckling down to his studies in the winter months at Stanford, all the while staying in touch with his mother and sister back in Paris. The fees for a Master's degree now topped $30,000 and, like past generations before him, he did not want to waste such expensive tuition. For now, news was yet to reach him and his family about the American interest in buying the Tour de France.

★ ★ ★

Brussels Midi train station is a rail hub that links the Belgian capital with three of Europe's biggest cities: London, Paris and Amsterdam. The area around the station is down at heel, clogged with traffic, walls painted with graffiti. The feeble trees standing along the avenues here are fighting a losing battle against carbon emissions from exhaust fumes. There are multicultural shop-fronts – Spanish and Portuguese restaurants stand side by side with Turkish and Moroccan shops. It looks much more like a humdrum *arrondisement* of Paris than a district of London or Amsterdam.

A half-hour drive north and you pass the shabby-looking Brussels Royal Yacht Club, situated on the banks of a canal. Soon, you have left the urban sprawl behind and you come to a quieter area of red-brick terraced houses. Some of the buildings have a Dutch influence, with pitched roofs. The road sign that opens up to this part of the world says '*Vlaanderen*' (Flanders). From this point, the people are Flemish. This rainy and wind-swept land off the frigid North Sea breeds cycling nuts who speak a sing-song version of the more guttural Dutch.

Wouter Vandenhaute's television production office is based here in Vilvoorde in a whitewashed former factory which once manufactured machinery to make clothes. Opening the black iron gates, the stone courtyard is completely empty but, when you walk inside, there is a buzz of energy; trendy young staff chat in Flemish about last night's sushi meal. Multi-coloured cupcakes and flowers celebrate that today is Valentine's Day.

Walking up a back staircase, you come to Vandenhaute's top-floor office, which – as a joke – staff have nicknamed 'The Loft' after a Flemish language movie he co-produced in which five married men shared a penthouse to carry out extramarital affairs. The office is sparsely furnished with a modernist black table and bottle-green, straight-backed sofa. A few books are scattered about, one about Antwerp, another about Eddy Merckx. Vandenhaute is wearing flip-flops. This is where he comes up with his ideas. He calls himself a Futurist.

The six million inhabitants of Flanders are considered to be the most fanatical followers of professional cycling in no small part thanks to Merckx's long dominance of the sport. For the best part of a decade, he had elevated the sport above any other in this corner of the world. It was not just that the Flemish liked seeing their own win, they liked everything about cycling – the pain, the suffering and the glory. Greg LeMond found this out first hand. He made Flanders his temporary home at the height of his career, settling in a brick detached house in a suburb of Kortrijk. On the night of his first Tour de France win, waiting to welcome him home at 3.30 a.m. were 500 Flemish neighbours, and a twenty-one-piece band.[6]

On average, the Flemish state broadcaster Vlaamse Radio en TelevisieomroepOrganisatie (VRT) shows cycling on 119 days of the year. In 2005, a larger percentage of Flemish fans tuned in to the Tour de France than the French: each day's television coverage of the race on Flemish television often starts an hour before broadcasting begins in France. When the road cycling season shuts down at the end of the autumn, and the French forget about cycling for a few months, the Flemish flock to winter cyclo-cross events, drinking beer and eating chips slathered with mayonnaise as they brave the cold and rain to watch riders pedal through muddy fields. If cycling is a summer novella

6 De Visé, *ibid*

for the French, for the Flemish it is a year-round soap opera with dozens of storylines.

Nothing is too banal. When, over a buffet lunch at the 1976 Tour de France, the English writer Geoffrey Nicholson dropped into a conversation that he found Flemish rider Lucien van Impe a trifle dull, he received a death stare back across the table. A Flemish journalist corrected him. No rider, he said, is ever without interest if you have the patience to search for the facts. The interesting point about Van Impe was that one month before the Tour began he would put his watch one hour forward so he was not out of sync with French summertime when he crossed the border.[7] Thirty years later, the author found a reporter from *Sporza*, a Flemish sports channel, sitting alone in a television cabin on a rain-swept mountain several hours before anything exciting was likely to happen in that day's stage. Headphones on, he was crouched over a piece of paper trying to find meaning in the time intervals of some of the more obscure riders.

Flanders became the boot camp where talented young American riders would come for up to three months at a time, living like young soldiers – bunk beds, room inspections and daily four-hour training rides. On the weekends, they would test their race craft against their more experienced local peers in under-twenty-three category races. For the young men of Flanders, riding through wind and rain was second nature, just as it was in the neighbouring Netherlands. For generations, children had been sent on their bikes in pouring rain to primary

---

7 Geoffrey Nicholson: *The Great Bike Race,* 1977. Belgium and France had a different summer time zone until the early 1980s when the European Commission asked member states to harmonise their clocks.

school. Should they complain, their parents would come back with the refrain, 'You are not made of paper.'

Vandenhaute had started his career as a journalist on Flemish public television. He read the sports news. It was, of course, mainly about cycling. After growing a little weary of tracking the same races every year, he went on to set up his own production company that made quiz shows and reality television. The company, Woestijnvis, took its name from the Flemish word for Desert Fish. (It had once been the wrong answer in a quiz show – the right answer was Desert Fox.) It was successful. Several programme formats were sold abroad, making Vandenhaute rich.

Every July, in a break from work, he turned his attention back to cycling. He rode with a group of friends over the same Alpine climbs as the Tour de France riders, before taking in the afternoon's racing on television in mountain-top bars. Vandenhaute had just come back from his holiday – it was as enjoyable as any he could remember – and was back in his office leafing through *Vélo* magazine with a picture of Landis on the cover when he heard the bombshell news – the American had failed a drugs test. 'I was so disappointed,' Vandenhaute said. 'I was deeply convinced that cycling was run badly.'[8]

Landis denied any wrongdoing, stumbling through interviews trying to explain his failed test. At one point, he blamed a Jack Daniel's bourbon binge after his bad day in the Alps. Meanwhile, Vandenhaute threw himself into writing a new business plan for cycling, with CVC Capital Partners, a private equity firm. He was convinced that

---

8 Author interview with Vandenhaute

cycling needed a better year-round show. For years, most leading riders based their whole season around the all-or-nothing Tour de France, not bothering to show up to most other races that could not bring them the same kind of exposure or income. That was unheard of in other sports where the action lasted almost all year. Would American football be successful if the best athletes just participated in the Super Bowl? Could Formula One be a worldwide show if the most accomplished drivers just turned up for the Monaco Grand Prix?

Nominally, CVC was based in an office in tax-efficient Luxembourg but its network of bureaux was open for deals anywhere in the capitalist world, investing a trove of €31 billion on behalf of private investors who ranged from Saudi princes to state pension funds. A faceless organisation, with no logo or slogan, it was led by sharp financiers and accountants who preferred to go under the radar. The glass-fronted head office concealed staff from public view. Executives rarely gave interviews and the London public relations firm it retained almost always offered journalists the same response to questions about its inner workings: 'no comment'.

In essence, CVC took stakes in established companies and then helped them to make more money. Recently, it had taken control of Formula One, attracted by low overheads and healthy profit margins that it planned to make even more robust. To maximise returns from the series, it constructed a byzantine network of shell companies in tax shelters for the motor racing series that made it difficult for media to follow the money. Its profits were invariably impressive – it often made annual returns of 20 per cent for investors. (Over time, its earnings from Formula One would surpass $7 billion.) Depending on your view, CVC was either a slick operator, or a tax-avoiding capitalist monster.

Over the course of six months, Vandenhaute worked with two managing partners in the Brussels office of CVC on a business plan on their new project which they called Cycling 2020. They collected oodles of numbers – start-up costs, projected income, revenue distribution – and plugged them into an algorithm to gauge the chances of the plan making money. 'It was data, data, data,' Vandenhaute said. 'And then more data.' Satisfied with the numbers popping up on their computer screens, CVC decided it was willing to invest €100 million.[9]

Under the proposal cooked up by Vandenhaute for Cycling 2020, it would be compulsory for the world's leading riders to compete in the best races for ninety days of the year. While the Tour de France would remain untouched, the Giro d'Italia and Vuelta de España, the next biggest three-week stages races, would be cut in half to ten days to allow room on the calendar for sixteen one-day races.

As he worked through the plan, rumours reached Vandenhaute of the Silicon Valley talk to launch a takeover of professional cycling and he wanted to know if there was any synergy with what he was doing. On the last day of the 2007 Tour de France, he arranged a meeting with Armstrong in Paris to discuss ways of collaborating.

Alberto Contador was rolling into town in the yellow jersey after a feisty performance in which his persistent

9 Vandenhaute interview, *ibid*

attacks in the mountains were about to see him become the youngest Spanish winner of the race at age 24. He had only intended to aim for the white jersey, the category for younger riders but, a skinny livewire, his talent and ambition burned brightly. Time after time on the steepest mountains he would rise out of the saddle and, in the words of one commentator, start dancing on his pedals, as he kicked away. Sometimes, his surges gained him time on rivals, other times not, but after three weeks he had done enough to keep at bay second-placed Cadel Evans.

With the Tour de France in town, Armstrong and Vandenhaute met at the Hotel Crillon just around the corner from the finish line. The hotel was a luxury haven in central Paris with plush carpets, elaborate chandeliers, freshly cut flowers and gold-tapped bathrooms. The tinkle of piano music welcomed tourists laden down with designer bags. Further down the Champs Élysées, Contador kissed the winner's trophy, a dark-blue and gold porcelain bowl presented to him on behalf of President Nicolas Sarkozy.

There was a last-day-of-school buzz among the weary members of the Tour de France roadshow. The final day of the race was a time for partying and meeting old friends. Some of the riders ended up in Le Queen, a tacky nightclub just off the Champs Élysées once popular with drag queens. Exhausted riders would get drunk after a single beer, the alcohol going straight to their head. (The next day, those who had stayed up late would regret it, waking up in their hotel room with a pounding headache facing a long journey home.) Amid the convivial ambience, Vandenhaute and Armstrong bonded, exchanged contact details and agreed to stay in contact; perhaps some of his pals could become co-investors with CVC?

For Armstrong, the project seemed to be just another business proposition to chat about over a beer. For Vandenhaute it was something that kept him up at night. Turning the patchwork calendar into a seamless sporting and commercial operation would require not just money. Perhaps more important were the diplomatic skills to get the project off the ground. Without the support of other stakeholders, his Cycling 2020 plan was no more than paper – a thirty-five-page PowerPoint presentation marked 'Confidential'. In the corner of each page was a picture of his television company's logo – a flying pig. He made plans to visit cycling's stakeholders one by one to pitch his plan, and promised to keep Armstrong informed as to how he got on.

When Contador went back to Pinto, a suburb south of Madrid where he still lived with his parents, thousands of people crowded into the Plaza Mayor to hail his victory. He was suddenly coming to terms with almost everyone recognising him, wherever he went. His life had changed in the course of the last three weeks. 'I had a life before the Tour,' he told one interviewer. 'And another one afterwards.' As part of that package were persistent questions from journalists about doping – after Armstrong and Landis, some considered every Tour winner guilty until proven innocent. About one in every three questions he was asked by reporters about doping.

Meanwhile, Vandenhaute travelled regularly to Paris, a one-hour train ride from Brussels. In a series of meetings over the coming months, he spoke to no less than four of Marie-Odile Amaury's top executives. Under his plans, he

said, there was no need for the family to relinquish ownership of the Tour de France. The race would merely become
part of a newly packaged championship that generated more
income for everyone. The only material consequence for the
Amaury family, he explained, would be that one or two of
their smaller races could be relegated to a secondary championship for 'B' teams.

These races would include the Paris–Nice event that took
place in March at the start of the European season. Bridging the
winter and spring, the week-long jaunt was known as the 'Race
to the Sun'. Unlike the Tour de France, it made little money.
The family had acquired the race in 2002 after it had racked up
€500,000 of losses over the previous three years, but it had
begun turning an annual profit of about €90,000.[10] While it was
not a money-spinner, and did not seem a big deal to Vandenhaute,
the Belgian's proposal rang alarm bells in the tight-knit cycling
community. The Amaury executives were cautious, preferring
the current status quo to a step into the unknown outside their
control. They made non-committal responses to the man from
Flanders.

On a frigid January day in 2008, Vandenhaute took a plane to
Geneva and made his pitch to the teams in a hotel near the
airport before they travelled to the season-opening Tour Down
Under in Australia. He showed his PowerPoint presentation to
seventeen team managers, a polyglot lot who between them
spoke an array of languages besides English including Dutch,
Italian, German, Spanish, Basque and Danish. Usually, aligning
them on even minor rule changes was tricky. They had

---

10 ASO financial accounts

high-pressure jobs because of short-term sponsorship deals. They loved their work but they were constantly on the road, grinding out eighteen-hour days.

Fresh from a break over Christmas, almost all of them appeared to be at least interested in what Vandenhaute was trying to do. Some of them enjoyed the trappings of wealth: one owned a $2.5 million modernist mansion with a wine cellar overlooking a fjord in Denmark; another had a house on the outskirts of Madrid with an indoor gym and swimming pool. But they all wanted more stability. They were tired of the sport's precarious finances. They were fed up with living on the edge.

They wanted to make cycling a global spectacle that attracted the attention and money they thought it deserved. One or two were still around to tell the tale of how teams had made a short-lived attempt with an IMG executive to negotiate some of the Amaury family's television income in 1995. But that was before doping scandals had weakened their bargaining position. Over the intervening years, team managers came and left the sport without picking up the initiative again. Now this Flemish entrepreneur with a sing-song voice and flying-pig logo had arrived with a new business plan, and they were all ears.

14

Showdown

Paris, 2008

Cycling's ruling body was an organisation once so feeble its general secretary's salary had to be paid by *L'Équipe*.[1] There was no money in formulating the regulations and so, for most of the previous century, the Union Cycliste Internationale, founded in 1903, was run by a couple of national cycling administrators and the odd staff member. For most of its first sixty years it was presided over by French and Belgian officials. They convened the odd meeting with peers from around the cycling world to agree on rules and enjoy a slap-up annual dinner.

That jovial, amateurish way of operating was little different from football's FIFA, which started out nearby in rue Honoré, and motor racing governing body Fédération Internationale de l'Automobile, whose bureau still overlooks Place de la Concorde. It was only with the launch of the FIFA World Cup in 1930 that football's ruling body started to become a bigger fish. Meanwhile,

---

1 Jacques Marchand: *Quel Tour pour Demain?* (2013); René Chesal, general secretary of both the UCI and French cycling federation, received a 'complementary' salary from *L'Équipe* in the years after the Second World War, according to Marchand.

the cycling ruling body, without a major sports event to call its own, continued to live out an existence as a semi-volunteer organisation with hand-outs from *L'Équipe* editor Jacques Goddet, who recognised it could play a role in developing the sport globally.

By moving its headquarters to Geneva in 1969, the Union Cycliste Internationale sought to become more of an independent global organisation rather than a subsidiary of the newspaper that organised the Tour de France. But instead of consolidating its power, it diluted it by creating separate bodies – in Rome and Brussels – to oversee amateur and professional racing, respectively. At this point, cycling administration was becoming like boxing, with an array of sanctioning bodies jostling for space and influence. Even after more than one hundred years of history, cycling's ruling body was 'still running after the authority it never had', according to a French writer.[2]

In the 1980s, a Dutch president had given the UCI another makeover, merging the separate units in Italy and Belgium into one group. Hein Verbruggen, a former marketing executive for Mars, was excited by the globalisation of the sport. He began to market the world cycling championship, the biggest asset of the ruling body, and tinker with the season's format to increase the international audience. As he went about this exercise, he clashed with Tour de France executives who had pretty much done what they had liked until he arrived. Regulations he introduced in 1989 – the year of LeMond's second victory – meant the

---

2 Marchand, *ibid*

Amaury family was no longer in charge of handing out all the invitations to its own race. From that point, UCI rankings determined the first eighteen entries; the Tour picked four wildcard teams.

In an effort to get Verbruggen on their side, the Amaury family twice offered him the job of Tour de France director. However, he turned down the approaches, saying it was a job more suited to a Frenchman. Instead, he built up the governing body from a staff of four to a team of a hundred with lawyers, administrators and marketing staff. In 2002, these staff moved into a new $18 million headquarters in Aigle, Switzerland, with its own velodrome. The Dutchman said he had turned the ruling body from a 'chip shop into a restaurant'.[3] By 2008, at the age of seventy, he had stepped down from his presidential role, even if he was still busily advising Pat McQuaid, the Irishman who moved into his office overlooking the Alps.

As an ex-pat in Switzerland, McQuaid was still finding his way as the ruling body's president, and getting to know the local customs. A cheerful Irishman in his late fifties, he found the Swiss perfectly pleasant but a little quiet. He was the eldest son of ten children – his Catholic father and Protestant mother left Northern Ireland for Dublin because of the difficulties of what was considered a mixed marriage. He became an amateur rider, like his father, and then explored the racing scene as a manager and then as an administrator. He missed the camaraderie of the pubs back home, and appreciated it when, one day, he received an invitation for lunch from Wouter Vandenhaute to discuss his project, Cycling 2020. Over a couple of bottles of wine in a

---

3 Hein Verbruggen: *De Waarheid van Hein Verbruggen* (2018)

high-end restaurant in Annecy, the two men got on well, sharing anecdotes.

The Irishman did not have the business-school poise of the slickest sports executives and some journalists lampooned him for his lack of style but, he explained, he was trying to find a middle way between preserving cycling's heritage and taking it to new territories. And amid the scenery, fine food and bonhomie with the Belgian, McQuaid made one thing clear – it was his mandate to organise the professional cycling calendar and, as the leader of a not-for-profit organisation, plough any profit back into the sport.

In fact, McQuaid was already in discussions about just that. He had met the top Amaury Sports Organisation executive recently to discuss bundling races together into a championship. That meeting at a restaurant in Lyon also involved good food and wine but his dinner guest was not quite as amiable as Vandenhaute. Patrice Clerc, a Frenchman with sandy hair and blue eyes, had remained sternly impassive as the chatty Irishman outlined his plan. When McQuaid had finished, Clerc turned his nose up as though there was a foul smell in the air. 'He was not interested in anything outside France,' McQuaid said.[4]

The more Clerc heard of the various plans to create a season-long cycling championship, the more he became paranoid. Having replaced Jean Claude Killy as president of ASO, his job was to protect the interests of the Amaury family. Wherever he looked, he saw threats.

At stake was the right to set the dates of ASO races, including not only the Tour de France but also a dozen smaller races

---

4 Author interview with Pat McQuaid

including Paris–Nice and the Tour de l'Avenir that others wanted to push around to fit their own purposes. This was a financial threat to the Amaury sports events, the most profitable part of the family empire, and fear was setting in. 'They were afraid,' one insider in the talks said. 'They were afraid that cycling's model would change, and they would lose everything.'

French teams and sponsors were also fearful. These smaller ASO races helped offer year-round exposure for them. The events built a domestic framework for professional cycling from March to October. They were important to team sponsors like insurer AG2R, lender Cofidis and lottery company Française des Jeux. For these mid–size companies most, if not all, of their business was in France and they were not interested in a shift towards a global show with races dotted around the world. They did not sell insurance, credit or lottery tickets in New York, London or Tokyo.

When French teams competed in provincial France, the regional branch managers of Française des Jeux came to back-slap and chat with Marc Madiot and his riders. It was a nice little treat to boost staff morale. During the lean years since the last French victory in the 1980s, Française des Jeux's sponsorship had won plenty of goodwill among the French public. 'If you fight honestly and lose,' a team insider said, 'it's more attractive than winning ugly.' At one point, amid the foreign takeover talk, the chief executive of Française des Jeux became worried that the Tour de France could fall into foreign hands. Christophe Blanchard-Dignac sent a message to the Amaurys to tell them his company was interested in buying the race if they wanted to sell. It would keep the race 100 per cent French. The Government was also sounded out about the proposal, according to one company insider, and 'considered it to be a good fallback option'.

That was not necessary, at least for now. At the bank, the Amaury family remained strong. Its finances were more robust than those of the sport's ruling body. The Union Cycliste Internationale had reserves of €12 million, less than the family picked up each year in ASO dividends. Nevertheless, the UCI had some muscle: it was the sport's leader, at least on paper. Part of the Olympic movement, it was recognised by governments around the world. McQuaid was negotiating with China about adding a race in Beijing. And, in parallel, he was quietly working on a new commercial unit, Global Cycling Promotions SA, which would go into competition with ASO.

By the start of the 2008 season, Clerc had heard enough of all the machinations going on around him. In a fit of pique, he took all of the family's races out of the ruling body's jurisdiction, and then – raising the stakes further – he banned the new champion Alberto Contador from defending the Tour de France. It was not a personal slight, it was just the Spaniard's new team – Astana – had been at the centre of a series of doping controversies in recent years that had consistently undermined the race. In the score-settling, Contador and the new team boss Johan Bruyneel were collateral damage.

Reporting on the news, a television crew followed Contador as he raced in a tune-up event in Majorca – preparing for a season now shorn of the biggest race. In a fit of anger, he raced away from the rest of the field, drew up alongside the camera and yelled into the lens: "Astana. At. The. Tour . . ." The year ahead for the newly crowned Tour de France champion was now half-empty. McQuaid was also furious. He fired back, writing to teams to inform them that they would be punished if they competed at Amaury events. Clerc's decision to go rogue, he said, was 'unacceptable insubordination'.

With the 9 March start of ASO's Paris–Nice looming, the battle lines were drawn. The teams had long ago booked their airline tickets to Paris, brought over team cars and prepped their race plans. A day before the eight-day race was scheduled to begin, team managers arrived at the Millennium Hotel, a bland facility with 1970s décor near Charles de Gaulle Airport. They were going to meet to decide whose side they were on. Already pacing up and down the hotel's carpeted corridor was Clerc's junior envoy, Christian Prudhomme, the Tour de France race director. On the Tour, he conducted proceedings from the back seat of the race director's car, a red Skoda Octavia with a radio link to each team. On the seat next to him was his trusty, battered brown leather briefcase and a mobile phone containing the phone numbers of dozens of government officials and mayors from around France. Expert at fighting fires, he was good at smooth-talking nosy journalists, panicky officials and angry farmers.

But, on this day, there was more at stake than a minor *contretemps* that could be skilfully worked out. It was potentially one of the biggest moments in the history of cycling politics. The teams had to make a binary choice – did they support the governing body or the Tour de France organiser?

Over the phone, Prudhomme spoke to six French team managers and what he heard back from them was encouraging. Even if they did not always agree with him, they retained a certain loyalty to the Amaury organisation. They were united by language, culture and a certain bonhomie. 'It's a "*franco-français*" thing,' one of them said. 'We're bound together.' The French teams had too much to lose from a falling-out. Come July, they might find themselves barred from the biggest race of them all. The Tour de France gave teams almost all their exposure and ensured the sponsorship money that paid their salaries. None of them could afford to miss those three weeks in July.

While the French teams were committed to starting Paris–Nice, the intentions of the fourteen foreign teams were less clear. They did not have the same affinity with Prudhomme as with his freewheeling predecessor, Jean-Marie Leblanc, who liked a drink and a chat, and played clarinet in a jazz band. In contrast, Prudhomme was a former television sports presenter who was friendly but a bit dry, taking care never to put a foot wrong. 'Prudhomme,' sniffed one team manager, 'is a politician.' There was, observers said, a golden opportunity for the foreign teams could use the stand-off as a negotiating tactic to wrest some long-lost authority and financial strength from the Amaury family.

The team manager with the biggest grudge at this point was Bruyneel, whose new team was excluded from a dozen races without any due process, and no right of appeal. With a dimple in his chin that gave him a vague resemblance to John Travolta, he was raised in Flanders but, after racing for Spanish team ONCE, married a woman from Valencia and settled in Spain. His greatest moment during an unremarkable career as a cyclist was when he took the yellow jersey for one day in 1995. Bruyneel saw much more of the yellow jersey as manager of Lance Armstrong's team, overseeing each of his seven wins.

Following a longstanding tradition, a family in Brittany shares a picnic and watches Tour de France riders go by. *(Vincent Amalvy/Getty Images)*

Jean-François Naquet-Radiguet, with a master's degree from Harvard, modernised the Tour de France too quickly for many of cycling's old guard and was soon ousted. *(Patrice Halley/Presse Sports)*

Marc Madiot (left) sports the European flag on his maillot at a minor race – at the Tour, he cut the emblem from his race number in solidarity with his father and other French farmers struggling with Brussels red tape. *(Landrain/Presse Sports)*

Coca-Cola pom-pom girls with Greg LeMond. Coke replaced Perrier as the drink sponsor when the Tour de France became more international in the late 80s. *(Presse Sports)*

In a rare public appearances, Philippe Amaury hands a memento to Miguel Indurain to mark the Spaniard's record-equalling fifth Tour de France victory in 1995. *(Fablet/Presse Sports)*

Jean-Claude Killy, the ASO President, confers with Richard Virenque at the start of the 1998 Tour de France in Dublin after police found a stash of doping products in the car of his Festina team. *(Fablet/Presse Sports)*

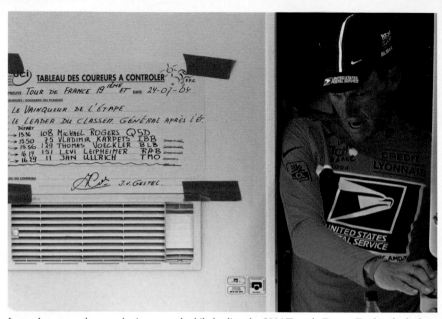

Lance Armstrong leaves a doping control while leading the 2004 Tour de France. By then he had switched from using EPO to blood doping, which was not clearly detectable in sample analyses. *(Martin Bureau/Getty Images)*

Lance Armstrong and team manager Johan Bruyneel celebrate a seventh straight Tour victory in 2005, shortly before *L'Équipe* published evidence that he had doped. *(Tim de Waele/Getty Images)*

Flemish entrepreneur Wouter Vandenhaute is among foreigners who have tried to persuade the Amaury family to change the business model of the Tour de France. *(Tim de Waele/Getty Images)*

After ending a power struggle between their organisations, Marie-Odile Amaury (ASO chairwoman) and Pat McQuaid (UCI President) made an effort to remain on friendly terms. *(Rapon/Getty Images)*

Française des Jeux team manager Marc Madiot chats to the lottery company's CEO Christophe Blanchard-Dignac, who looked into buying the Tour de France to keep it out of foreign hands. *(Martin/Presse Sports)*

On his comeback, the 37-year-old Lance Armstrong strains to keep up with teammate Alberto Contador, 26, on an Alpine climb. *(MONS/Presse Sports)*

As doping allegations continued to weigh on the credibility of the Tour de France, Marie-Odile Amaury attends the unveiling of the 2011 race route. *(Rapon/Presse Sports)*

Bradley Wiggins celebrates becoming the first British winner of the Tour de France with his Team Sky teammates. *(Bryn Lennon/Getty Images)*

A house in Yorkshire painted in the red polka dots of the 'King of the Mountains' jersey to mark the passing of the 2014 Tour de France through the north of England. *(Doug Pensinger/Getty Images)*

Marie-Odile Amaury with children Aurore and Jean-Etienne in 2019. The only shareholders of the Tour de France's parent company, they are thought to be unable to sell their stakes without each other's consent. *(Seguin Franck/Presse Sports)*

This gave the journeyman pro, already sure of himself, a swagger like Travolta in *Grease*. None of his peers could match that record. Bruyneel could be a little arrogant, but whether they got on with him or not, most of the team managers felt a certain solidarity with him over the unilateral punishment he had just received.

In the corridor outside the meeting room at the Millennium Hotel on the eve of Paris–Nice, Prudhomme huddled with team managers, beseeching them to be at the start line. The show must go on, irrespective of political differences. The team managers said they would talk it over, before shutting the door, leaving him to wait outside.

Inside, any fighting talk soon fizzled. One by one the French team managers turned on their microphones to speak, and confirmed they would be at the start line. So did a few of the foreign squads. Even the most rebellious among them did not see much point in going home. Seven of the fourteen foreign teams voted to race under the jurisdiction of the French Cycling Federation. The other seven abstained from voting, displaying only a minor show of defiance. As the team mangers filed out of the conference room, Prudhomme called his boss to relay the good news.

Clerc had no intention of easing the pressure on the Union Cycliste Internationale. Both sides were by now only communicating by legal letters and sniping at each other in the media. Every week, it seemed, a new 'cease and desist' email would arrive in the Irish president's inbox from the ASO lawyer as he continued with his plans for a new global championship.

In an extraordinary snub, McQuaid would not receive an

official invitation to that year's Tour de France. (He turned up anyway.)

When the Tour de France came around, all the cycling politics was forgotten and all the attention turned to the race. It began in Brest on July 5, without Contador and no clear favourite. With the chop-chop of helicopters, the tooting of car klaxons, and the buzz of swarming crowds, the atmosphere was noisy and stressful for cyclists. There were more journalists than in other races and extra pressure to perform. Riders handled the extra burden in different ways. Carlos Sastre, an introvert from a village in the Spanish hinterland, went further into himself. He barely spoke to his teammates, many of whom spoke languages – Danish, French and German – he did not understand. He spoke only faltering English. But he did not need many friends. He was happy on his own, a mountain man who liked to block out the world and climb.

During most of the year, Sastre trained in the mountains around his village El Barraco (population: 2,165) in the Alberche valley. It was a typical Castilian outpost: a few stone houses around a small town hall flying the Spanish flag. As far as the eye could see there were mountains, part of the Sierra de Gredos range stretching west towards Portugal. There were eight peaks of 2,000 metres. There were no helicopters, barely any traffic and only the odd hiker. He did not like the strict training regime imposed by his team. Instead, he preferred to train alone in what he called this 'natural paradise'.

During the 2008 season, there was some tension within the CSC team over who they would support when the season climaxed with the Tour de France: would it be Sastre, described as a 'lonely swallow' by one teammate, or would it be the popular and chatty Schleck brothers, Andy and Frank, from Luxembourg. All three probably had the potential to win, but there was no clear decision made public. They would work it out, it seemed, as they went along. With five stages left, Frank wore the yellow jersey. Sastre was fourth, 49 seconds further back. Andy wore the white jersey as best young rider.

The trio rode in a group of five CSC riders towards the Alpe d'Huez and what would be the moment of reckoning. The eight-mile climb would be one of the last shakeouts of that year's race — a brutal ascent determining who had the most energy and determination left after 18 days in the saddle. Sometimes, the race, a whole career even, could come down to less than an hour on the bike. At the base of the climb, Sastre glanced over to Frank and began to kick steadily away. Only one other cyclist followed. There was some way to go, 45 minutes of climbing up a gradient of as much as 10 percent. After opening up a gap of 100 metres, the Castilian drifted back towards the other leaders. Then, he kicked again and pulled away and began steadily opening up a gap.

Now it was Carlos Sastre against everyone.

There was the din of the crowd, and the heat. People leant in to scream encouragement in his ear, others ran alongside him for as long as they could keep up. A couple of near-naked Danes sprinted next to him wearing just red underpants and bucket hats, trying to grab a few seconds in the spotlight. Orange-clad Dutch, who had painted names on the tarmac with white paint, clapped and cheered exuberantly. A third group was dressed as wizards: pointy hats, white beards and capes.

Sastre blocked out the waves of noise and paced himself as he did on his training rides near El Barraco when there was nobody in sight, perhaps just the odd eagle silently gliding above or a few goats grazing by the side of the road. It was a hot day, like the dry summer days in Castile. He unzipped his maillot and squirted water from a bottle on the back of his neck and kept churning the pedals. The lead was getting bigger, increasing to more than two minutes. The Schlecks could not muster the energy or resolve to launch their own breakaway to try and catch him.

Sastre kept his rhythm and crossed the finishing line, raising his arm for no more than a second or two to celebrate. That solo ride was enough for him to win the Tour de France that year, and define his career. A couple of years later he retreated to his small town, and set up a bike shop a few miles away in a warehouse on an industrial estate, forever proud of becoming one of the French race's winners.

While the Tour de France was the pinnacle of the sport, there were two other three-week stages races that were also pillars of the cycling season.

The Giro d'Italia was owned by RCS, a Milan-based publisher. Its salmon-coloured sports newspaper *Gazzetta dello Sport* that founded the event was as much an institution in Italy as *L'Équipe* was in France. The Giro race leader had worn since 1931 the same pink on the leader's jersey as the colour of the newspaper. The country's greatest riders, such as Fausto Coppi and Gino Bartali, were ingrained in folklore as much as the Giro. Even today, arguments regularly break out in cafés across Italy about who was the greatest Italian cyclist of all time. For some Italian riders their home race was as important as the Tour de France, perhaps more so.

La Vuelta a España, the other major stage race, had more of a patchwork past. Five different organisations had owned the Spanish race since 1935, including a now defunct newspaper called *Ya*. Meanwhile, the colour of the race leader's jersey had changed eight times since, from orange, yellow, white and red to gold. Television station Antena 3 had inherited the Vuelta almost by accident in 2005. While the race posted a small annual profit of €5 million, its owner was not committed to developing the race, preferring to invest in the more profitable production of soap operas and quiz shows. The Vuelta offices in a Madrid suburb reflected its status; they were situated by the tradesmen's entrance at the back of Antena 3's sprawling television studios. The race director's cramped room looked like that of a school teacher – an old wooden desk, books piled high and a cheap plastic sunblind to keep out the blazing summer sun.

The greatest of all Spanish cyclists was Miguel Indurain, who had a resting heart rate of 28 beats per minute and the pedal-stroke consistency of a metronome. Indurain won the Tour de France from 1991 to 1995 and picked up two victories at the Giro d'Italia. His career achievements clearly showed the pecking order of the three Grand Tours. Even in his prime, winning all three in a single year was next to impossible. If there was one to sit out, he had decided it would be the least prestigious – his home race. He never won La Vuelta a España.

Under the plans of Cycling 2020 – the flying-pig prospectus – the Vuelta would shrink to just ten days from twenty-one, rendering it even less important on the calendar and perhaps threatening its future. Clerc, the ASO chief executive, talked to his peers at both the Giro and Vuelta as he sought alliances against the UCI. While he was told that buying a stake in the Giro was not possible, Antena 3 was willing to sell part of La Vuelta. The Amaury family agreed to acquire a 49 per cent stake to further buttress themselves against whatever business risks were around the corner.

The widening rift within professional cycling had become an affair of state, an international diplomatic incident.

In the summer of 2008, French president Nicolas Sarkozy intervened personally to call a truce, asking Marie-Odile Amaury to iron out their differences.[5] Sarkozy's request would certainly have worried Madame Amaury. She and her executives worked hard to nurture a good relationship with the Government. If they should ever lose access to public roads to put on their races, well, there would be no Tour de France. Perhaps the only person she took orders from was the President of France.

In the middle of the holiday period, she took charge of managing the dispute. For the matriarch to step in was highly unusual and showed her concern for the way the conflict was escalating. She agreed to meet McQuaid at a neutral venue in Switzerland.

One day in August, Madame Amaury and McQuaid were welcomed by Jacques Rogge, President of the International Olympic Committee in Lausanne. In his office, the Belgian told of his concern about the infighting in cycling. He then gathered some papers, got up and prepared to walk out. 'I would love to think that, at the end of the day, you might

---

5 McQuaid interview, *ibid*

come to the basis of a solution,' he said quietly, before closing the door behind him.

Madame Amaury and McQuaid and their entourages quickly found common ground. After a second day of discussions a few weeks later, they sealed a truce. The matriarch agreed that her races would come back under the UCI's jurisdiction. In return, the Irishman agreed not to undercut the autonomy of her races.

In an effort to end the bad blood, Madame Amaury fired Clerc, replacing him with her son Jean-Étienne. She then made another business trip, this time to Madrid.

The Vuelta, the family's newest business interest, was building to a climax with a penultimate day time trial in the mountains outside the capital. Contador, barred from the Tour de France but able to race the Vuelta a España, was leading the 11-mile time trial by more than a minute as he wound through the pine forest to the Alto de Navacerrada. For the *madrileño*, this mountain was his backyard, where he trained throughout the year with a motorbike pacer. His team were confident of victory and gaining a measure of revenge for missing the Tour de France. They had a cushion; the second-placed rider Levi Leipheimer also rode for Astana. So, with the race result more or less settled, team manager Bruyneel left his sports director in charge and drove to a hotel at Madrid airport fifty miles away to meet Madame Amaury.

She was introduced to Bruyneel and the other managers by Prudhomme, shaking hands with each of them. Then, speaking in French, slowly but deliberately she began to discuss the troubles of recent months and how she wanted them to put their differences in the past. Bruyneel was impressed by her poise, and relieved to hear that his team would have a way back to the next Tour de France. 'She was very firm and clear,' Bruyneel said.[6] 'It was a clear-the-air meeting.'

Continuing her quiet diplomacy, she maintained cordial relations with McQuaid, setting a follow-up meeting over lunch at a modest Paris brasserie.

★ ★ ★

Barely had she returned from Madrid in the autumn of 2008 than Marie-Odile Amaury was pulled into another crisis meeting, this time about a threat to another column of the family business – *L'Équipe*.

The broadsheet newspaper had enjoyed a quasi-monopoly in France for most of its sixty-two years. Its few post-war rivals soon folded, leaving a single daily covering sport in the Hexagon. The red masthead at the top of page 1 had not changed since its foundation, and it remained one of the best sellers on newsstands. However, average daily sales had slumped by almost 8 per cent the year before to 323,000 amid competition from online media. More bad news was to come. A group of investors announced the launch of *10 Sport*, a sports tabloid costing 50 cents – 35 cents cheaper than *L'Équipe* – that looked destined to erode the broadsheet's already-thin profit margin.

Madame Amaury's executives called a crisis meeting. They had already accumulated some relevant experience. Eighteen months earlier, *Le Parisien* heard of plans by Berlin-based publisher Axel Springer to launch a 50-cent French version of its tabloid *Bild*. Borrowing a Quentin Tarantino movie title, they

---

6 Author interview with Johan Bruyneel

drew up an internal plan called 'Kill Bild', in which *Le Parisien* would launch a cheap version to handicap the French *Bild*. In the end, it was not necessary. Blaming prohibitive production and distribution costs, Axel Springer dropped the project.

With the arrival of *10 Sport* weeks away, in his notebook, one of Amaury's news executives jotted down three words: 'Kill *10 Sport*'.[7] Marie-Odile Amaury's daughter Aurore was called on to the action team. After winding down her short career as a corporate lawyer, she had joined her brother in the cut and thrust of the family business. It was the first time most of the newspaper staff had worked closely with the thirty-three-year-old heiress and they were impressed by how personable and intelligent she was.

At meetings with senior managers, they considered making *L'Équipe* a tabloid, cutting its cover price and adding a football pull-out. In the end, they decided to maintain the newspaper untouched, and launch their own 50-cent tabloid. It was like building a lightweight destroyer to protect a historic ship. *Aujourd'hui Sport* would be produced by fifty editorial staff out of the *Le Parisien* office. A blitz of ads on the radio and at newspaper kiosks to promote their title would seek to smother the exposure of *10 Sport*. And cheaper advertising – nicknamed '*neuf et demi*' rates internally – would put yet more pressure on the start-up. On the first Monday in November, the rival tabloids launched, both displaying front-page pictures of football stars Karim Benzema (*10 Sport*) and Nicolas Anelka (*Aujourd'hui Sport*). Neither title did particularly well. By the end of the

---

7 French competition regulator: written decision following a complaint by the owners of *10 Sport*; ruling published 20/2/2014

month, *10 Sport* was averaging 48,000 daily sales, to 38,000 by the Amaury title.

For someone investing €7 million of her family's wealth in the project, Marie-Odile Amaury was not very enthusiastic. She sniffed at the shift downmarket from the more respectable *L'Équipe*. 'I am not in favour of low-cost newspapers,' she said. 'Serious news is enlightening, original and comes at a price.' Her daughter was more combative, saying the family would 'explore this market until the end'. By April, the average daily sales of *10 Sport* had tumbled to 21,500 and, by the summer, it had given up the fight and become a weekly. The executive who had jotted down 'Kill *10 Sport*' in his notebook, added another note: 'mission accomplished'.

The exercise showed how aggressive the latest generation of the family could become when defending its business interests, but it would land the Amaury family a €3.5 million fine for anti-competitive practices.[8]

★ ★ ★

The steady drumbeat of doping scandals continued in cycling, giving Marie-Odile Amaury a lingering headache about the damage it was causing her business. It seemed like almost every time she opened *L'Équipe* she read news of another controversy, under the by-line of Damien Ressiot, the man who had nearly brought down Lance Armstrong.

In May 2008, Spanish police were eyeing an apartment block in a tree-lined street in Madrid where five-bedroom homes went for €1 million. In one of them lived a

---

8 Written ruling, *ibid*

haematologist. Undercover officers had staked out the apartment block at 92 Calle de Zurbano for weeks, watching well-heeled residents and housekeepers come and go during the day. Posing as workmen, they fixed a video camera to the front of the building to gather evidence about who was visiting the haematologist.

Since the introduction of a test for EPO six years earlier, many of those who doped had switched to having blood transfusions to boost their count of oxygen-carrying red blood cells. They had their blood taken and stored during the off-season, and then reinfused before big races to boost stamina. Although this was officially cheating under anti-doping rules, there was no way of identifying the infraction with a urine or blood sample, unless you reinfused somebody else's blood by mistake. Seeking a boost, riders had come from across Europe to Madrid to use the services of this doping clinic.

Acting on a tip-off from a whistleblower in cycling, the police had seized more than a hundred one-pint bags of blood stored in a freezer. The blood bags were marked with code names, but it was abundantly clear from the police investigation that many of them belonged to professional cyclists. Internally, the police's Operación Puerto – 'Operation Mountain Pass' – drew up a list of fifty-eight riders suspected of involvement. Doping was not a crime in Spain, like in France, but there was no way prosecutors could ignore something of this magnitude. They decided to draw up a case against the ringleaders, accusing them of a crime against public health. It was legislation dating back to 1978 that was more frequently used in the prosecution of traffickers from Galicia who used the rugged north-west coast to import boatloads of cocaine into Europe.

After the haematologist and a sports doctor were arrested, there were no plans to charge the cyclists, who in the eyes of the law had not committed a crime.[9] If there were to be any proceedings against them, it would come through sporting sanctions. Over the coming months, the spectre of doping weighed on the sport as the investigation into the blood doping ring continued on different fronts. And at the next year's race in 2009, there was no let-up in cheating. Five cyclists failed drug tests and, again, Astana was at the centre of the storm. In an anti-doping test, its star rider Alexandre Vinokourov from Kazakhstan was found to have someone else's blood in his body.[10] Meanwhile, an Italian rider on French team Cofidis, Cristian Moreni, was arrested on the Col d'Aubisque mountain pass after he tested positive for testosterone. After an initial denial, Moreni acknowledged wrongdoing, agreed to pay a fine of one year's salary and said he wanted to return to cycling 'on a more honourable note'. Amid the maelstrom, German public broadcasters ARD and ZDF pulled live coverage midway through the race. 'We are meant to be broadcasting a clean race,' one executive said. 'Not a race of people using doping products.'

---

9 The haematologist had the charges against him archived on the grounds that he had early-stage Alzheimer's disease. The sports doctor was convicted in 2013 but cleared on appeal in 2016, when a judge ruled that the reinfusing of blood was not a serious medical risk.

10 *Le Monde,* 28/7/2007. Vinokourov was fired by his team and suspended by his national cycling federation in Kazakhstan after the failed doping test. He denied wrongdoing, saying, 'You would have to be mad to do what I am being accused of.'

In one corner of the *L'Équipe* office, Damien Ressiot continued his detective work, trying to piece together exactly who was cheating. It was serious, well-researched journalism but doping stories put off newspaper advertisers, and did nothing for the image of the Tour de France that, not for the first time, was facing a widening credibility deficit.

One morning in March 2008, Marie-Odile Amaury invited five members of the *L'Équipe* newsroom to her office at *Le Parisien*. The Société des Journalistes was a legacy dating back to her father-in-law's ownership of the newspaper. Most French newspapers had something similar, a way for employees to let off steam. At these meetings, they discussed staff issues like working hours, salaries and editorial independence.

Sitting at an oval table in the large office, Ressiot was among the journalists who had travelled across town for the meeting. He had kept a low profile since his Armstrong scoop three years earlier, rejecting offers to appear on television. He preferred to work in the shadows. This was his first face-to-face encounter with the Tour de France's matriarch.

In the few meetings she had had with staff she did not know well, Madame Amaury tended to have a no-nonsense, business-like approach that hid her natural shyness. After welcoming the group of employees into her office, she spent no time on pleasantries and small talk. They got straight down to business, going through the agenda point by point. Halfway through, she raised an issue that was bothering her.

'I wish that that Ressiot would shut up,' she exclaimed. 'I am fed up of doping stories in the paper.'[11]

---

11 Author interview with Ressiot

Ressiot shifted uneasily in his seat. A colleague cleared his throat and interrupted her. 'Madame Amaury, let me introduce you to Damien Ressiot.'

She looked up from under her blonde fringe for a moment, nodded to acknowledge him, and continued talking as if nothing had happened.

Subsequently, according to Ressiot's version of events, *L'Équipe* decided to give less prominence to doping stories, relegating them to back pages – where advertising rates were cheaper – alongside niche stories about sports politics and business that often did not have accompanying pictures because their subjects were men in suits. Ressiot was a little put out. It looked to have killed his chances of appearing on the front page – as he had with 'THE ARMSTRONG LIE' – but at least he would not be silenced. He could carry on with his investigative work. Madame Amaury has always maintained the journalists she employs have complete editorial independence, but claims of a less confrontational approach to doping by *L'Équipe* reached Armstrong's entourage, who liked the idea.

Armstrong was planning his return to the Tour de France after a four-year absence – with the Astana team, no less – and was keen to avoid talk about doping. As part of a carefully orchestrated public relations campaign, Armstrong intended to focus on promoting his Livestrong cancer charity and his age-defying challenge. If he won the Tour de France at age thirty-seven, he would become the oldest winner in its history.

The PR campaign swung into action in New York. At a black-tie charity event at the Waldorf-Astoria to promote world peace and tolerance, he sidled up to Nicolas Sarkozy. The French President was in town to receive a Statesman of the Year award after helping to heal a US rift with France over its refusal to endorse the Iraq War, a decision that led to the revival of the 'cheese-eating surrender monkeys' insult coined in *The Simpsons*. In a bridge-building speech in Washington a year earlier, Sarkozy had extolled his admiration for American icons from Elvis Presley to Ernest Hemingway, and Marilyn Monroe to Neil Armstrong.

As a sports fan, Sarkozy was delighted to meet with the other Armstrong and chat about his comeback. It was the start of a charm offensive in which Lance – whose return was initially greeted with scepticism by Amaury Sport Organisation – sweet-talked ASO chief executive Yann Le Moenner, a keen amateur triathlete. Together, the pair went for a ride to chat. Armstrong made it clear that the Astana team 2.0 would be clean and his return would be fantastic publicity for Le Tour. Armstrong invited a photographer from Amaury-owned *Vélo* magazine to his home for a soft feature that included him doing the school run. Amid this new *fraternité*, any talk of Armstrong and his Champions Club buddies buying the Tour de France was, of course, off the table.

Armstrong kept in contact with Sarkozy. On another occasion, a week before ASO picked the wildcard entries for the 2010 race, he was invited to the Elysée Palace for lunch. He came bearing a gift – a Trek Madone racing bike. The machine featured red, white and blue details on the stem and wheels to represent the French Tricolore. On the top tube was the logo of Armstrong's Livestrong charity.

This soft power play, as it had done before in the US with

Presidents Bush and Clinton, helped to eclipse the whispers about Armstrong's dark past. All the talk now was how the world's most prominent anti-cancer campaigner was back for an against-the-odds challenge. It was a great water-cooler story – could grizzly old Lance beat the younger generation?

15

Protectionism

Paris, 2010

As a chauffeur-driven saloon car glides into Monaco, Lance Armstrong is sitting in the back seat, which is upholstered in white leather. As he looks down from the road above the principality, he peers into the amphitheatre of Port Hercule, where yachts bob in the Mediterranean. Today, in the usually tranquil streets, cycling fans in t-shirts and shorts dance to elec-tropop coming from the advertising caravan. The start of the 2009 Tour de France is a couple of hours away. 'Welcome to the party,' Armstrong says to filmmaker Alex Gibney, who is making a movie about his comeback.

As he readies for the nine-mile opening time trial, he looks fit but also much older than everyone else, a man approach-ing his 40s. He is 16 years older than when he first partici-pated in the Tour de France. He plunges off the ramp, sweeps past the Monte Carlo Casino and climbs up to the Moyenne Corniche road before descending back into town. He is fast but not that fast. He finishes tenth out of one hundred and eight riders, respectable but not outstanding. Over the coming days, it is clear that he is just off the pace. As he flops onto the fresh linen of a hotel bed after one week he tells

Gibney: 'This is going to be a lot harder than I thought it would be.'

Wherever Armstrong goes, a pack of journalists follows. As he weaves through the crowds on his bike after each stage, the pack sprints after him. In the team bus he shovels down rice with chicken to replace burnt calories, gets a massage for his tired limbs, rolls up compression socks to his knees to improve blood circulation, and comes out to speak to reporters. He is more relaxed than in his prime and brings a bit of a rockstar vibe to the race. It is as though Mick Jagger has come out of retirement for a farewell tour; Armstrong is *the* story of the Tour de France.

Despite his star status, it turns out he is not even the top rider on the Astana team. Alberto Contador is quicker, both in the opening time trial and when the race reaches the Pyrenees. Johan Bruyneel has the complicated job of managing the ambitions of both men. One night at the start of the second week, he informs the riders that the plan for the next day was to maintain the status quo. In other words, no attacking. Even so, Contador sprints away from the older man – eleven years his senior – and gains 22 seconds. In front of television cameras, Armstrong appears graceful in losing time. When they were alone on the team bus, it was another story, according to Contador. He says Armstrong stared at him and growled: 'Don't fuck with me.'

By the penultimate day, which was to end with a 15-mile climb to the top of Mount Ventoux, Contador was in the yellow jersey with a comfortable lead of four minutes over second-placed Andy Schleck and, barring a disaster, had all but wrapped up his second victory in three years. Armstrong, meanwhile, was clinging onto third place, with Bradley Wiggins and Frank Schleck within 40 seconds.

The mountain road in Provence to the summit of Ventoux starts in the shade of pine trees. It is here that Frank first tries to make a break to snatch a podium place. Armstrong follows right behind him, eyes fixed on his back wheel. He then hauls himself up into his sightline as if to say: you're not going to beat me. Eventually, the trees make way for an empty lunar-like landscape where there is no shade from the summer heat, and by now every rider is suffering. They swig from water bottles. Wiggins is unable to keep up, dropping off the pace despite a desperate effort to fight back. Armstrong hangs on, crossing the finishing line just ahead of Frank, to guarantee third place. Not winning has made him more popular than during all those years when, under a cloud of suspicion, he hammered the French and everyone else. Four years after uncovering him as a cheat, *L'Équipe* makes an about-turn. On its front page the next day, it says 'CHAPEAU, LE TEXAN'.

It turned out that just like the Festina scandal in 1998, the Armstrong comeback of 2009 did not make a significant impact on ASO's revenue for that year. The family income from the Tour was boringly but reassuringly steady. This was because it was based on long-term deals with sponsors like Nestlé's Vittel and Crédit Lyonnais, as well as the France Télévisions contract that paid out the same amount every year. With most revenue fixed, the main variable was merchandising – branded shirts, caps and other trinkets – and that made up only a small fraction of total earnings.

With little potential for big jumps in revenue, the most important thing for the Amaurys was to keep these deals ticking over year after year and protect the Tour against the existential threat of mass doping that had led German television to suspend coverage. For now, the drugs scandals of the recent past seemed to have subsided and, by one non-scientific benchmark, the peloton was cleaner; two Frenchmen finished among the top ten in the general classification for the first time in years. A few riders may still have been doping but, according to several anti-doping experts, this was now through micro-dosing, a de-escalation of the pharmaceutical arms race.

Armstrong decided to have one final season in the saddle. Gibney, the film director, kept shooting the images of him to make his movie, travelling with him on a private jet. While his strict training routine meant he was not able to hang with the Champions Club in Silicon Valley anymore, Armstrong managed to fit in some time with business high-rollers if they could fall in step with his schedule.

Every now and again the conversation turned to the business of professional cycling, the conservative nature of the Amaury family and how CVC was backing a plan to form a new championship that would squeeze much more cash out of the sport for everyone.

That kind of distraction was strictly off limits for Armstrong as he followed the monk-like existence of a professional rider but the chatter kept humming in the background, irritating some in the French establishment.

For decades, the government had fretted about the effects globalisation was having on France, and a succession of presidents had led a counter-attack against foreign influence. Jacques Chirac had cited a threat to competition in blocking Coca-Cola's attempted takeover of Orangina, the French soft drink launched in the 1930s that was still decanted at bars and cafés across the country from the same orange-shaped glass bottles. The humble French yoghurt pot had also become part of another Franco-American corporate tussle. French politicians had also mounted an offensive to protect Danone from a hostile takeover by PepsiCo as a former Danone chief executive said, 'Danone is like Chartres cathedral and you can't buy Chartres cathedral.'

This protectionism occasionally spilled over into the Tour de France. When it emerged that ASO had agreed that a wine maker from Chile had become the Tour de France's official drinks partner, vintners from the Languedoc-Roussillon region wanted to know what the hell was going on.

Languedoc-Roussillon, near the Spanish border, is a peaceful part of France that produces some delicious fruity wines, and the most militant winemakers in the world. In Sète, a quiet port town with some pretty canals running through its streets, local *vignerons* – members of the Regional Committee of Viticultural Action – arrived one August night wearing balaclavas and armed with crowbars. They smashed their way into two warehouses and emptied gallons of mass-produced foreign wine from giant vats.

The Languedoc wine men were as hostile to the Spanish stuff down the road as to the plonk from the New World. 'Each bottle of American and Australian wine that lands in Europe is a bomb targeted at the heart of our rich European culture,' one veteran said. Amid this tense climate, they had no plans to give the Tour de France an easy passage; they threatened to block the race route. It would need all of race director Christian Prudhomme's diplomatic skills to dial down their angry rhetoric. At an agricultural show, he pacified the vexed wine-makers by offering them a deal under which they could, free of charge, show off their products at the start and end of each day's stage.

Aside from supporting local food and wine, the Government was working on a list of objects of historic value that must be protected at all costs. They included hundreds of traditions ranging from the building of traditional wooden-beamed homes in Normandy to the sport of *pelota* played in the Basque region in the south-west of France. The Tour de France itself was not officially on the list as *patrimoine national*, but to many lawmakers it was as good as. There was a group of politicians in the upper house of the French parliament who had formed a group called *Les Amis du Tour de France* and they were on standby, whenever needed, to rush to the aid of the race.

Madame Amaury and her family business nurtured the relationship with the Government as carefully as her father-in-law had done when he handed Charles de Gaulle a scrapbook of cuttings of his wartime speeches that he had published clandestinely during the Nazi occupation.

On some mornings during the Tour de France, a small group of Government ministers and the odd mayor eased back into the leather seats in a Falcon 7X business jet at Paris-Le Bourget airport for a day out at the race. In the twenty-seat jet, they settled back and chatted to the other guests, executives of ASO's major partners. On arrival at their destination, they were divided into even smaller groups and ferried by five helicopters to different points along the route of that day's stage. The Amaurys spent an estimated €250,000 each year on these de luxe day trips for politicians in Paris who – apart from a pleasant excursion – used their appearance at the race as a way to polish their patriotic credentials with voters.[1]

Over the years, one or two left-wing politicians had sniped at how the Tour de France was a burden on public coffers, draining funds from police and local authorities to serve what was a private business owned by the Amaurys. In 1977, the mayor of Rennes complained about the cost of hosting a stage of the race, calling it a 'commercial enterprise, which over-shadows a sporting contest'. In 1981, the sports minister objected to the blizzard of ads on the jerseys of riders. The playing of 'La Marseillaise' at the yellow-jersey podium cere-mony, the minister noted, was sponsored by a real-estate company. But such sniping was isolated, and barely resonated with the general public, especially in rural parts where the Tour de France was tied up with millions of happy memories. The race's importance was elevated to celestial levels by *Les Amis du Tour de France* in the senate. The race 'is a sacred history', said the group's founder, a senator from a Pyrenean hamlet of 106 residents. 'Those sleepy villages are suddenly revived and thrust into the spotlight.'

A combination of this misty-eyed traditionalism and the Amaury family's hard-nosed executives had thwarted the project of Wouter Vandenhaute. While foreign team managers had listened with interest – and dollar signs in their eyes – to his Cycling 2020 plans, however much he spoke to the ASO managers he could not seem to make any headway. 'It was not specifically one person who was against the idea,' Vandenhaute

---

1 Author's estimate based on advertised rental costs of Falcon 7X; 12 round trips to and from Paris at a cost of €10,000 per hour, not including helicopter trips.

said. 'It was the French culture of conservatism that stopped any progress.'[2]

Frustrated by not getting anywhere, he suspended his partnership with CVC and lowered his target; he would try to consolidate cycling in his own corner of the world. In a joint venture with the newspaper publisher which owned *Het Nieuwsblad*, he focused on bundling the rights to six one-day races in his homeland, including the Tour of Flanders. The race, which fell around the same time as Easter, he considered 'a holy day' for the Flemish people. Some 600,000 people came out to watch – 10 per cent of the region's population. The century-old race even had its own museum, which ran a video loop of riders struggling up the cobblestone Koppenberg climb.

As he sat in his office in a former factory in Flanders a few years later, Vandenhaute continued to muse about taking his plan global. The success of his repackaged Flemish races – revenue now having increased five-fold to €5 million – made him more sure than ever that the premise of his Cycling 2020 business plan was sound. He was adamant that if it worked in his homeland, it could work on a global scale. After a three-hour discussion fuelled by three espressos and as many croissants, he said he would continue working on the plan despite the cultural challenges in France. 'I can't control the stars,' he said. 'But I like dreams.'

★ ★ ★

Without a business plan of their own, cycling teams were all over the place in terms of strategy. One Dutch team manager

---

2 Vandenhaute, interview

was amazed to turn up to his first meeting with his peers to find there was no chairman and no agenda. This was quite unlike the polished corporate meetings he was used to attending in his previous job at a bicycle manufacturer. The flurry of topics under debate swung wildly, without any structure or predetermined objective as tempers frayed among the biggest egos in the room. The bad vibes were never more intense than when Johan Bruyneel and Marc Madiot traded insults.

More often than not, arguments would revolve around which teams were bending the rules – drafting behind cars, possibly using motors to power their bikes, or resorting to the oldest method of cheating – doping. Leaving the room after one of these meetings, the exhausted Dutch manager felt he had just wasted an hour and a half. 'The only thing that was well organised was the dinner afterwards,' he said. Two days later, in another demonstration of the sport's persistent infighting, he witnessed half the team managers walk out of a meeting to protest a regulation change, leaving the president of the ruling body staring into space in a nearly empty conference room at the Brussels Sheraton.

Another of the more cerebral managers frustrated by this lack of progress was Jonathan Vaughters. The son of an attorney from Denver, he was the antithesis of an American sports jock. A socially awkward kid with Aspergers who had been bullied at school, he did not have the natural confidence of some of his peers who, like a schoolkid, aimed jibes at him and tore into his holier-than-thou attitude about doping. Vaughters read *New Yorker* magazine and was a wine connoisseur.

As a homesick young pro in Spain, when he grew tired of

training on his bike for six hours a day, week after week, month after month, he would shut himself in his apartment for three days to work on oil paintings. But the bullying continued on the road; when his eye swelled up because of a wasp sting to the size of a tennis ball, he was ribbed for not taking an anti-inflammatory drug in case it broke doping rules.

Growing up in the land of the NFL, he knew as well as anyone how the collective bargaining model in US sports allowed athletes and teams to have a real say in the direction of their sport. In cycling, however, it seemed like race organisers held all the cards and the teams and riders just had to do as they were told. All he had on the balance sheet to show for all his hard work was the money from short-term sponsorship contracts that underpinned the payroll of twenty-nine riders and paid their food and travel costs, as well as about $1.5 million-worth of fancy bikes. If the sponsors ever decided that they had had enough, Vaughters would be left with nothing but some second-hand equipment.

Vaughters and his staff sent out forty pitches a year to potential sponsors hoping they would keep the team in business. Meanwhile, he sat at the wheel of the Garmin-Cervelo team car and coaxed riders to bring home the results to satisfy the tech and bike company sponsors paying their wages. It was, he said, 'a tightrope act with no net'.

His working life was similar to Bruyneel's. Vaughters toiled over a laptop and BlackBerry in hotel rooms and on the team bus. With the twenty-nine cyclists competing at as many as three different races at any one time, logistics were worked out on a colour-coded Google Docs spreadsheet. However, there was one major difference between his approach and that of

Bruyneel – Vaughters marketed his team as doping-free. His mantra was more akin to Madiot's – better to lose cleanly than win by cheating.

Vaughters himself had dabbled in doping as a cyclist but he was repentant and had gone halfway to confessing his sins as a rider on the US Postal team when he gave an off-the-record interview to the *New York Times* saying he was one of two of Armstrong's teammates who had doped – on the condition the newspaper did not identify him. Now, he said, he wanted to play his part in reforming the sport.

Over the years, Vaughters had developed a thicker skin against the bullies and had learnt to revel in being a geek. He wore purple New Balance sneakers and sported sideburns. He liked to bring outsiders on to his team and dressed them in a kit with an argyle design popular with middle-aged golfers. He also liked to use his brain to outwit the more backward teams with their dead-wood thinking. Riding for a French team, Credit Agricole, a decade earlier, he found the team manager did not seem to have developed any type of strategy. 'He would say, "Hurry up and do well,"' he said. 'It was a stagnant environment.'[3]

As he sought to follow a smarter approach, he took particular pride in hiring a twenty-two-year-old Lithuanian rider who, he said, French teams assumed was doping because of his standout results in junior races. The morning after his latest win, Vaughters put the young man on a plane, ran a private battery of doping tests on him, and measured his watts-per-kilo power data. When the results came back, they found he was clean, and stronger

---

3 Vaughters interview with *Cycling News* website, 29/11/2010

than his best climbers. 'I went with that,' Vaughters said, 'as opposed to the rumour and bullshit.'[4]

On a rest day of the Tour de France, Vaughters welcomed a gaggle of journalists to the wine mecca of Châteauneuf-du-Pape. It was where John XXII – a Pope in the fourteenth century – had built a castle near the seat of the Catholic Church in Avignon. It was a sort of holiday refuge for the Popes and a pretty garden and vineyards were built around the castle. After the Holy See moved to Rome, the château fell into disrepair but was revived as a historic monument at the end of the nineteenth century. Occupied during the Second World War, the Nazis blew it up with dynamite as they fled.

The small town that had grown up around the castle still boasted a lot of history, including a church, a chapel and the vineyards that produced the local wine which had earned a reputation of enduring quality. Some said the secret was the pudding stones covering the land that absorbed the Provençal sun by day and released its warmth overnight, helping to ripen the grapes. Today, this small winemaking area of 8 miles by 5 miles has become one of the protected historic assets of France, guarded down to the last centimetre. At one point, a public inquiry was opened about a patch of unused land smaller than a basketball court. After the plot's owner had died, the town hall agreed that the state should buy back this tiny bit of almost sacred territory.

Under an azure sky, Vaughters held a press briefing within this celebrated *domaine*. The press had been asked to convene at a yellow mansion at the end of a dusty track cutting through a

4 Mark Johnson: *Argyle Armada, Behind the Scenes of the Pro Cycling Life*, 2012

vineyard. With the sound of crickets chirping, the group sat under the shade of conifer trees. Over a Franco-Mexican lunch of burritos paired with the local red, Vaughters expounded on the cultural clash between foreign teams and the French cycling establishment. Perhaps because of the fine wine coursing through his veins, he was more revealing than he might normally be. He explained how he had tried unsuccessfully to engage Marie-Odile Amaury in talks about revenue-sharing over *canapés*.

Over the last few months, Vaughters had mulled over the conundrum of the teams' tightrope business model and figured that, for now, the Amaury family still held the upper hand.

There was still some light at the end of the tunnel, however. Even as Vandenhaute suspended his collaboration with CVC, taking up to €100 million off the table, there was another plot in the works. This one was being prepared not in Flanders, but in England.

★ ★ ★

The Rothschild banking dynasty was founded in 1838, making the Amaury family almost nouveau riche in comparison. Still swinging in the breeze outside its ultra-modern office today in the City of London is an iron badge of five intertwined arrows, representing the five brothers of a German family who went their separate ways to seek their fortune. They ended up in Paris, Frankfurt, Vienna, Naples and London.

This pan-European network allowed them to set up an unrivalled network of money, information and contacts. When the Rothschilds bankrolled the Duke of Wellington's defeat of Napoleon, it helped establish them as a powerbroker in international finance. Nowhere more so more than in London, where the office was around the corner from the Bank of England, which, when cash-strapped in 1826, was bailed out by the Rothschilds.

Over the last 150 years or so, the family's assets were broken up and the once-great dynasty was overtaken by Wall Street giants like JP Morgan and Goldman Sachs, which had decamped their staff from the City to bigger offices in Canary Wharf. As the dynasty splintered over time, Rothschild in London became a sort of boutique finance firm. It was still a player but a smaller one; staff brokered billion-dollar mergers and acquisitions, taking a cut of the deals. The executive chairman was Alexandre de Rothschild, the sixth generation of the founder.

To get to the gleaming glass and steel building housing the Rothschild office in the heart of London each morning, Majid Ishaq would walk down St Swithin's Lane, a narrow passageway which was still owned by the Rothschild family. A tall man with a noble air and well-kept beard, he was the son of a science teacher who came to Bradford from Pakistan. He and his brother played rugby league, a tough sport played most passionately in northern England. He captained the school team. Later, the family moved to Cardiff and finally settled in east London. Along the way, his sporting talent – he became an accomplished goalkeeper – helped him to integrate with each relocation. In the capital, he worked in a greengrocer's as a teenager but now, approaching middle age, any trace of a working-class accent had long gone; he sounded much more like the privately educated colleagues alongside whom he now worked.

Driven and intelligent, he was working himself up through the ranks at Rothschild and had become the head of the Consumer, Leisure and Retail department. His work involved brokering takeovers of restaurant chains, hotels and breweries, along with the occasional sports industry deal.

A few years earlier, he had helped to get the Glazer family's pursuit of Manchester United over the line. The buyout was deeply unpopular and, as the broker, Rothschild became a target for vitriol. Activist fans shut down the bank's computer network for a few hours and broke into its Manchester office. Ishaq and his colleagues working on the deal took to using assumed names to protect themselves. When, on the scheduled day of the acquisition, financing from three New York hedge funds did not come through because of a clerical error, Ishaq sent Rothschild's funds to underwrite the deal for 45 minutes to ensure the £790 million pound agreement did not collapse.[5] It earned Rothschild a generous brokerage fee and an invitation to Ishaq – a United season-ticket holder – to become the Premier League club's chief executive. He politely turned down the offer.

With his small team of university graduates, Ishaq had run a mass of financial data into a computer program and turned it into a business proposal for the century-old sport of cycling that had most of its history on the other side of the English Channel. The plan for World Series Cycling was now in the hands of another Englishman called Jonathan Price, who had first brought the idea to Rothschild.

A decade or so earlier, Price had helped turn Manchester United into a commercial superpower by replacing regional advertisers at Old Trafford stadium with global brands following

---

5 Mihir Bose: *Manchester Disunited, Trouble and Takeover at the World's Richest Football Club*, 2007

its listing on the London stock exchange. Boosted by the dawn of the Premier League, United's revenue quadrupled within a decade. Clubs across Europe looked on enviously. After Price left United, a Spanish businessman called Florentino Perez hired him as a consultant in his successful bid to become Real Madrid president. Now in middle-age, Price was seeking to turn cycling into a global business. Price noted that, as football was embracing globalisation, about half of the Tour de France's sponsors remained mostly domestic French brands like supermarket chain Carrefour and mineral water Vittel.

Before the start of the 2011 season, Price had invited eight team managers to Rothschild's headquarters for a meeting to explain how World Series Cycling would help their sport to become a truly global championship. The managers felt a bit out of their comfort zone in the heart of London's financial district. They wondered what to make of these two Englishmen standing before them in a wood-panelled meeting room.

Price explained the concept; he was the project leader and so he opened the meeting. He planned, he said, to have a global circuit of races, with new events on the east and west coast of America, as well as in Asia. The Tour de France would still be the pinnacle of the season but, under his plan, the bottom line was that teams would share in 64 per cent of cycling's equity. Their current return? Zero.

By the fifth year, it was projected that World Series Cycling would be generating €85 million in net income, giving each of the participating teams just shy of €4 million.[6] That was three times more than the forecast for Cycling 2020. One of the team

---

6 Copy of Rothschild pitch seen by author

managers liked Price's idea, but couldn't help feeling he was selling them air. 'He wasn't the guy with the money,' one of them said. 'He seemed like all he had was an idea.'

In fact, according to another version, it wasn't even his brainwave. 'He just stole my idea,' Vandenhaute claimed.[7]

For his own groundwork in getting World Series Cycling off the ground, Price wanted a 10 per cent cut. Price had done well for himself; a recent project to start a youth-team tournament for Europe's top football clubs in Malaysia had earned him £2 million. He lived in a top-floor apartment called The Penthouse in London's South Kensington, near Harrods.[8] But he did not have enough financial firepower on his own to launch the championship and he was looking for an investor to take care of the startup costs in return for the remaining 26 per cent stake.

Many of the cycling managers desperately wanted a new business model and with all this rebellious talk in London they felt emboldened. They were fed up with flirting with bankruptcy. In each of the last three years, at least one of their peers had failed, disappearing into the graveyard of defunct team names when their mid-size company sponsors pulled the plug: Gerolsteiner (2008); Barloworld (2009); and Milram (2010).

Like his peers, Vaughters feared his team might be the next to vanish. The previous winter, a lack of resources had led him to merge with another team. At the 2011 Tour de France, the new Garmin-Cervélo team arrived with a bunch of talented misfits that included David Millar, a reformed doper from the UK with

---

7 Vandenhaute, interview
8 Companies House, UK corporate registry

a troubled past, and Thor Hushovd, a giant Norwegian who wore the rainbow jersey as road-race world champion.

The day before the start, Vaughters was told by ASO officials that for some stages over the next three weeks he would need to put a dashboard camera in his car to improve the television coverage. The opening stage would cross the Passage du Gois, a two-and-a-half-mile pathway from the island of Noirmoutier to the west coast of France. The tarmac road was covered by the sea most of the day, with the Atlantic waves only subsiding for a few hours to allow traffic to pass.

Twelve years earlier, Vaughters had crashed on this same slippery, seaweed-covered road, fracturing his chin. The idea of the dashboard camera was to capture dramatic moments like these, giving an extra dimension to the global broadcast feed of France Télévisions. It would show horrified reactions from staff in the team car when a rider fell or their whooping when he surged to a stage win.

Vaughters was tired of being told what to do by the all-powerful Amaury family executives as his team danced with death at the end of each sponsorship deal. And he was determined not to give away those in-car television rights for nothing.[9] For once, he was in control. His response to the ASO officials was succinct – '*Non*'.

---

9 Author interview with Vaughters

16

Uprising

City of London, 2012

Before long, the World Series Cycling plans had leaked out and were being chewed over in the media. 'THE GREAT CYCLING POWER GRAB,' a UK magazine yelled in a headline. In the US, website VeloNews flagged the breaking news as important: 'Must Read: Breakaway Cycling League Forming'.

In Paris, Jean-Étienne Amaury was by now familiar with the gripes of team managers. While his mother stonewalled them, he humoured them by listening to their grievances. He assured them he would take their views on board. But, they found out, their conversations with him did not get them anywhere. Amaury, a gentle soul, seemed to be more of a thinker than a doer to the team managers. 'He has his head in the clouds,' one said. But when he heard about World Series Cycling, the Tour de France heir was unusually firm. Some of the eight team managers involved had raced or managed teams during cycling's darkest doping years. How could they be in charge of the future of the sport?

One of the eight plotters, Bjarne Riis, had recently become the first Tour de France winner to admit doping during his career. Riis, from Denmark, had won the race in 1996, at a time when he was nicknamed by some as 'Mr 60 Per Cent' for his hematocrit level which suggested artificial boosting of his red blood cell count. (The average is closer to 40 per cent.) Two of the other managers, Bruyneel and Vaughters, were also having their cycling records picked over as by prosecutors and special agents with the FBI and the US Food and Drug Administration investigating Armstrong's seven-year winning streak in France that was partly funded with public money.

One by one, former American riders on the US Postal team including Vaughters, Landis and Armstrong's close friend George Hincapie were subpoenaed to give evidence to the federal investigators under oath. Over the course of the coming months they would confess to doping, and implicate Armstrong and Bruyneel as central to the deceit in cycling's most prestigious race between 1999 and 2005. The witness statements helped investigators to assemble a picture of years of systematic doping on the team: EPO, testosterone, cortisone, human growth hormone, blood doping. Usually, the witnesses said, Armstrong and the others lay down on their hotel-room beds while, behind locked doors, the team doctor reinfused their blood. Once, when running late during the 2004 race, the driver of the team bus faked engine trouble on a remote mountain pass and parked on the side of the road so that the 'entire team' could have a transfusion.[1]

---

1 Floyd Landis affidavit published on US Anti-Doping Agency website. In his affidavit, Hincapie said 'most of the riders' on the team had blood transfusions administered on the bus at that year's Tour de France. José Azevedo, another cyclist on the team, told the *Correio de Manhã* newspaper in 2012 he never saw any of his teammates dope.

The revelations smashed through Armstrong's façade of credibility that he had defended so aggressively. While the federal government decided not to prosecute, largely because the US Postal Service had not suffered material damages, the US Anti-Doping Agency used the momentum to call in the riders for questioning, eventually producing a damning report that it made public in 2012.

The mounting evidence about to bring down the House of Armstrong did not change anything, as far as Jonathan Price was concerned. The way he saw it much of the scandal dated back a decade. It was history. He continued working hard to get the other twelve teams on board with his future project. When he had an objective in sight, Price was, in the words of one of his business partners, extremely tenacious – 'a bit of a rottweiler'. Price was trying to court one cycling squad in particular – Team Sky.

Sky was owned by BSkyB, a broadcaster that, from the site of a former biscuit factory near London's Heathrow airport, pumped out news, sport and entertainment programmes from a cluster of hangar-like studios.

BSkyB's sports output was as British as roast beef and Yorkshire pudding, focusing on cricket, golf and, above all, football. For most of the last twenty years, its Sky Sports channels were overseen by a former tabloid newspaper reporter from County Durham who ventured abroad for just two weeks a year, to a holiday home in the former British colony of Cyprus. As a young man, Vic Wakeling had edited the Saturday sports supplement of the *Evening Mail* that hit the streets in Birmingham packed with match reports, statistics and league tables a couple of hours after the final whistle of Saturday afternoon football matches. In the 1980s, he went on to work in London for the *Sun* at a time when the paper was at its most jingoistic.

After moving into television, Wakeling was able to use his football contacts to help BSkyB snag the first broadcast rights to the Premier League in 1992. Over the next few years, he helped to shape the league's schedule to suit his employer's commercial interests, staggering weekend games over Saturday, Sunday and Monday to maximise viewership. Thanks to the success of the Premier League, the broadcaster now brought in an annual revenue approaching £7 billion and employed 23,000 staff.

Cycling was hardly a draw for most Britons, compared to cricket, golf and football. The Tour de France did not even appear on British television in highlight form for most of the twentieth century. In 1974, the French race made its first visit to England for a solitary and unspectacular stage near Plymouth to promote a new ferry service from Brittany. The *Daily Mirror* was distinctly unimpressed by the sight of a procession of riders pedalling along the A38 road, asking the next day, 'The Tour de France: can 40 million Frenchmen be wrong?'

The serendipitous route to BSkyB owning a Tour de France team had started in Manchester, known for its buzzy music scene, including hipster bands the Happy Mondays and Oasis. In this rainswept corner of north-west England, football was as deeply embedded as its industrial past. This heritage was epitomised by L. S. Lowry's iconic paintings of matchstick men converging on a stadium against a backdrop of chimneys pitching out black smoke. In 1993, city authorities found themselves putting together a bid to host the Olympics and, to bolster its chances, they felt the city needed to add something more to their pitch than two big football stadiums and the Hacienda nightclub.

Instead of building a brand-new swimming pool or athletics stadium, the city council opted for a cheaper alternative – a velodrome. At the time, the UK did not have a single indoor cycling track, although cycling as a sport was not completely unknown. There was the Manchester Wheelers Club, an amateur group with whom Chris Boardman, an unemployed carpenter, had honed his time-trial skills on countryside roads. A year earlier, at the Barcelona Olympics, Boardman had won a gold medal in the individual pursuit.

The £10 million velodrome was to be built on derelict land once used by a coal-fired power station. On a summer's day, the top Olympic official left his hotel suite overlooking Lake Geneva to inspect the venue. The seventy-two-year-old Spaniard, Juan Antonio Samaranch, arrived in a private jet and was whisked by car to a muddy building site. Even though it was a summer's day, it was overcast and drizzling and work had barely started. As a British Olympic official shielded his immaculate white hair and charcoal suit from the rain with an umbrella, only the odd crane showed any sign of building work. Ever the diplomat, he said Manchester had a 'very, very high' chance of hosting the 2000 Olympics. A few weeks later, Sydney was chosen as the host city.

Work on the velodrome went ahead anyway. When it was ready, locals who lived in redbrick terraced houses across the road were bemused. From the outside, it looked like a white spaceship; inside, there was a 250-metre oval with a giddying gradient of 42 per cent at the highest point. Still, may as well make the best of it. The British Cycling Federation moved its six full-time staff from an office above a kitchen showroom in Kettering, a provincial Midland town, into the space-age venue, but they soon found they could not afford to pay annual gas and electricity bills. With few cycling races to host, they rented it out for a car launch, a Conservative party rally and a cat show.[2]

After two years, the Federation's board grimly discussed shutting the velodrome. Despite their best efforts, they were going to have to concede defeat; Manchester was not destined to be a mecca for cyclists in skintight Lycra suits and aerodynamic helmets. The UK could sustain ninety-two professional football clubs, but it was unable to manage the upkeep of a single velodrome.

Two weeks before the planned shutdown, a lifeline arrived from the Government. It came thanks to a new National Lottery game. Just as the velodrome opened its doors for the first time, the lottery launched with a Saturday evening draw on television. It was wildly popular. Half of the enormous ticket sales went back into a prize fund, and about 25 per cent was shared with selected charities and not-for-profit organisations from the arts and sport. Within eighteen months, £2 billion had reached these so-called good causes – track cycling was seen as one of the many worth recipients, a way both to encourage the British public to do more exercise and boost the nation's count of Olympic medals.

If the first lottery grant kept the lone UK indoor velodrome's lights on, the second and third handouts developed a pattern. In the four-year cycle before each summer Olympics, a generous

---

2 Author interview with Brian Cookson, then a board member and later the Federation's president

grant from the lottery flowed into the British Cycling Federation's bank account to help get British track cyclists ready for the world stage: Sydney in 2000; Athens in 2004; Beijing in 2008. Within a decade, the Federation received an eye-popping £34 million in funding. There were no more cat shows at the velodrome.

To benefit from all this lottery money, a group of talented riders from around the British Isles moved to Manchester, among them a nineteen-year-old raised on a council estate in London's Kilburn neighbourhood called Bradley Wiggins.

In the offices adjoining the velodrome, performance director David Brailsford and his team worked on everything from helmet design to posture to cut the track times of his young, talented cohort of riders by as many milliseconds as possible. Thanks to the appliance of a scientific approach, Britain became the world leader on the track and its only indoor cycling venue was transformed into what the *Manchester Evening News* called 'an Olympic medal factory'. Wiggins went on to win five medals at the Athens and Beijing Olympics, more than most countries managed with their entire team. In the small world of two wheels, Britain was a modern-day titan.

After a decade of solid success, the Olympic ideals – *citius, altius, fortius* (faster, higher, stronger) – gradually lost some of their appeal for Brailsford. The Welshman had for some time wanted to channel his energy into having a go at starting a British road-racing team and, more specifically, trying to win the Tour de France.

By now, cycling was fashionable in Britain. BSkyB chairman James Murdoch, Rupert's youngest son, was among the men in their thirties who had taken to cycling. He was a globetrotter and environmentalist who was born in London, went to school in New York and liked to spend time in Italy. In tune with an offbeat side to his sober nature, he had installed a life-size model of Darth Vader in one corner of his BSkyB office. For Murdoch Junior's generation, cycling was just as much about riding the mountain passes themselves as reading about the adventures of the Tour de France riders in newspapers or magazines, or watching them suffer on television in their living rooms. As with amateur golfers who hit the fairways in the morning and watched the pros on television battle it out in the afternoon, cycling enthusiasts wheeled their own carbon-fibre bikes out of the garage at dawn and were back in time to watch racing on their iPads.

This upwardly mobile crowd helped lure tech companies like Belkin and Garmin to sponsor professional cycling teams. A familiar refrain was becoming more widely heard – cycling is the new golf. For the growing middle-class audience, there were books published in English about famous climbs in France, Italy and Spain, as well as websites dedicated to bike kit and the gradients of mountain passes. Tomes were released in English about storied riders of the past: Coppi, Merckx and Hinault. And when London was chosen to host the Olympics, BSkyB joined the party; it agreed to sponsor the British Cycling Federation, adding yet more financial firepower to its medal quest.

To leverage its investment, BSkyB encouraged the public to take up cycling by arranging rides around the country. It set up a bike shop at its London headquarters, encouraged staff to ride to work and built showers for them to wash off the urban grime after their commute. BSkyB was all in, and it was easy enough for Brailsford to persuade its executives to support his quest to win Le Tour.

Team Sky was born – BSkyB would later change its brand name to Sky – and one of the first things Brailsford did as manager was go about signing Wiggins, his velodrome protégé. Sky paid compensation to the middle-ranking American Garmin team to release him from his contract. It was a financial transaction more common in football. Wiggins had already spent a few years riding for modestly funded French teams and the off-season transfer to Sky was, in his words, the cycling equivalent of moving to Manchester United. For one of Team Sky's first races, Murdoch Junior flew in to watch Paris–Roubaix, taking a helicopter charter for the last part of his journey to the muddy fields of northern France.

Murdoch said Team Sky intended to 'push the envelope' in road cycling,[3] while Brailsford began to apply the same attention to detail on the open roads. That meant addressing everything from designing the most aerodynamic skin-suits to adding mood lighting in the team bus and lugging a dozen mattresses around Europe to help each rider get a good's night sleep. Brailsford initially set a five-year target to win the Tour de France and, thanks to a budget of some €25 million per year and advanced analytics and training methods, it was soon clear that they were a force to be reckoned with.

As cycling finally took off in the UK, it was already decades into a slow decline in France. Dozens of velodromes had shut down since the 1950s, including the famous pair once owned by the Goddet family. The Velodrome d'Hiver closed its doors

---

3 *Cycling News* website, 11/4/2010

in 1959 after a fire; the outdoor Parc des Princes was rebuilt in 1972 without a velodrome around the football pitch. France still held the all-time record for the most Olympic track cycling medals, but it was only a matter of time before it was overtaken. For some time, the French had generally viewed chic sports like skiing and tennis as more aspirational than cycling. Doping had eroded the appeal of the sport even further, as had a persistent failure of French riders to win the summer race that was embedded in the national psyche. Not since 1985 had a Frenchman won the Tour de France.

Of course, no one was more invested than Marc Madiot in trying to end this barren run. All the talk of Sky's scientific approach rankled him because it made the French teams like his seem old-fashioned and, well, stupid. To visitors of his Française des Jeux team bus, with leather upholstery in the colours of the Tricolore, he gestured to a stack of power meters piled in a corner which his riders used for training. 'We use them just like Sky,' he said. 'But we don't shout about it all the time.'[4] Even without the hype, the facts remained – the host nation's last Tour de France win was a quarter of a century ago, and much of the dry spell in between was on his watch as manager of the *de facto* French team. Now, horror of horrors, it looked like the English were closing in on winning the Tour. Dressed in black, Team Sky riders rolled relentlessly through the countryside of France.

★ ★ ★

In his old job, David Brailsford had time and space to work on performance in his minimalist office next to the Manchester

---

4 Madiot, interview

velodrome. A few metres away, cyclists whirred quietly around the Siberian pinewood track. His new job as Team Sky manager was on public roads, sometimes against a backdrop of noise – car horns, chatter and arguing. He chose to avoid the exhausting back and forth of cycling politics, bypassing the team managers' meetings whenever possible. Although he was fluent in French, he would usually limit his interaction with his peers to a brief '*bonjour*' or '*bonsoir*', infuriating Madiot, who complained that the British team 'lived on its own island'. Even worse, as part of their non-conformist approach, the Brits declined to use difficult-to-pronounce French words long embedded in cycling's lexicon; for example, '*soigneurs*', the backroom staff who massaged the limbs of riders became known, in Team Sky parlance, as 'carers'.

On a spring day in 2012, Brailsford could not swerve politics any longer. He was summoned to the BSkyB boardroom for a meeting with a cluster of senior executives. This room was where all the big corporate decisions were made. It was where the board decided how many hundreds of millions of pounds to bid for football rights. Outside in the hall, along with pictures from Premier League matches, TV series and movies, a black Pinarello bike hung on the wall. Brailsford was the only one not wearing a suit. The Welshman's go-to clothing was perhaps to show others he was just a sports guy. He was dressed in his loose-fitting Team Sky-branded casual wear which the American manager Vaughters dismissively suggested was 'Tony Soprano chic'.

Waiters served lunch to the dozen people around the table and, on a large screen, Jonathan Price began his PowerPoint presentation about World Series Cycling.[5] He was addressing a

---

5 This segment in based on an interview with a BSkyB source

sharp crowd; for example, Robert Tansey, the marketing director, had a Master's degree from Oxford University. Most of the executives barely spoke; it was Brailsford who asked the most questions. When Price began to expound on the possibility of organising World Series Cycling outside the remit of the sport's governing body, one man cleared his throat. Brian Cookson, the most senior administrator in British cycling, told the group he had a conflict of interest. He was also vice-president of the Union Cycliste Internationale, which had come out against Price's project. Cookson left the room and waited in the corridor.

The international ruling body had already aggressively shot down Price's plans, labelling World Series Cycling a rebel breakaway league. This kind of tension was a concern for BSkyB. It did not want Team Sky involved in a power struggle that deflected attention from that summer's Tour de France.

Over the previous couple of years, Brailsford's staff had gathered a reliable set of data from the Tour de France and could now gauge how Wiggins stacked up against his rivals. On training rides in Tenerife that spring he was in superb form. They estimated that his power output made him a contender to win the French race, if only he could keep going under extreme fatigue in the final week. That was a tantalising prospect and the BSkyB marketing director did not want politics to get in the way of sport. He advised his colleagues not to join the project straight away, but revisit it at the end of the summer.

★ ★ ★

The lush green landscape of the Pyrenees was cloaked in mist, and the temperature was a cool 15 degrees. Overnight, truck drivers had dragged all the paraphernalia of a Tour de France mountain stage up the winding road to 1,600 metres above sea level; advertising hoardings, broadcast vans, and small portable rooms for the doping control and press conference.

Everything was in place around the only tarmac road of a small ski resort that was hidden in a dip in the mountains. Following the travelling convoy over three weeks were 45 trucks and 11,000 smaller vehicles carrying everyone from team managers to TV commentators and undercover police. Then there were the fleet of five helicopters carrying VIP guests, and planes hired by France Télévisions circling over the 180 cyclists to transmit live satellite signals for television.

On the mountain passes, traffic was restricted and so it was quiet up here among the clouds, the snowless ski runs and stationary lifts. The most fanatical cycling fans were massed further down the mountain road on the Col de Peyresourde. Caravans had taken up position along the edge of a narrow grassy precipice, near the top of the 10-mile ascent. Here there were no metal crash barriers and they would be within touching distance of the riders. Flags representing France, the Netherlands, Denmark, Belgium's Flanders region and Spain's Basque country fluttered in the wind. Basque names were daubed in white paint on the tarmac. There was also a flag that was less familiar on this well-known climb – the Union Jack of Great Britain.

It was the final mountain stage of the race. By the end of the afternoon, the winner who would wear the yellow jersey on the Champs Élysées in four days would be all but confirmed. Some 50 miles away, Wiggins, wearing the yellow jersey, had just scaled the day's first mountain surrounded by his Sky teammates. Along the route, fans yelled, 'Allez, Wiggo!' as the

Londoner, clenching his teeth, methodically pedalled towards his destiny.

If Wiggins could defend his race lead over 25 miles of climbing today, he would in all likelihood become his country's first Tour de France winner. In fact, such was Team Sky's dominance that they were on course not only to take first but also second place. Chris Froome was second overall, comfortably ahead of Italy's Vincenzo Nibali.

Striding across the narrow strip of tarmac among the clouds was Jean-Étienne Amaury. He could be proud of all the *savoir-faire* that went into the event management that was needed each day at the Tour de France. It was a daily logistical triumph.

Up here in the Pyrenees, Amaury had a bird's eye view of the race without being part of the cut and thrust of daily decisions around the peloton down below. His five-minute speech every autumn in a convention centre in Paris was the only fleeting reminder that the race was controlled by his family. The first time he got up in front of the dais to address the audience he had looked like a choirboy reading from a church lectern, far younger than his thirty-one years, as he told the audience of riders and dignitaries that 'ethics remains an absolute priority', a reference to cleaning up doping scandals.

Aside from Amaury's annual speech, race director Christian Prudhomme was the public face of the Tour de France. He was a more gifted public speaker than the Tour de France heir. Amaury was, after all, a computer engineering graduate from an École Centrale. He was a logical thinker, a left-side-of-the-brain guy – his favourite subject at school was maths. His speeches didn't have the same creative sparkle as the urbane former television journalist. Sometimes, Amaury resorted to borrowing his employee's turns of phrase. When asked his favourite rider, he named Bernard Hinault. 'As Christian Prudhomme says,' Amaury said, 'the champions of your youth are the champions of your life.'[6]

This year, as Wiggins closed in on the race victory, Amaury could reflect on what was turning out to be a successful race; for a start, there had been no drugs busts or failed doping tests. Of course, the patriot in him would like a French winner of the race as had happened during his childhood, but the arrival of Team Sky was at least good for the race's business outlook. The arrival of more spectators from across the English Channel was proof the race was unlocking a new audience. It had taken more than 100 years of the Tour de France to generate this kind of interest in the UK.

In the thin air of the Pyrenees, a mile or so from where Amaury was watching the action on a small television screen, Team Sky's relentless pursuit of victory encountered an internal disfunction. Froome's job was to shepherd Wiggins to the finishing line. However, flouting team orders, he began pulling away from him, impatiently looking back over his shoulder at his teammate in the yellow jersey. He easily opened up a gap of 10 metres.

This insubordination threatened to upend months, if not years, of planning. BskyB was much more closely aligned with Wiggins, having backed him as an Olympian and road racer. They had built their team around him. In contrast, twelve months earlier Froome had been a disposable Team Sky *domestique* on an annual salary of £100,000. Brought up 6,000 miles

---

6 Amaury, interview

from London on the dusty, dirt-red roads of Kenya, he was little known by the British public. But here he was showing that he had the ability to take the yellow jersey.

This was not the first time that he had struggled to keep his ferocious ambition in check during the race. The previous week, he had launched another sudden burst of speed on another steep climb to leave Wiggins flailing. It had left the team managers horrified. In the Team Sky car, the sports director held the team radio to his mouth and spoke first with incredulity and then anger to Froome: 'I'm hoping you got the OK from Bradley for that . . . Froomey, Bradley is hurting . . . What the fuck is going on?'[7]

Even before the race began, there had been rumours of tension in the team. According to the gossip, Froome believed his power output numbers to be better than those of Wiggins, and yet his teammate was receiving special treatment. After his first rebellion at the Tour, he backed down. He was summoned to the back of the team bus to explain himself. Now, the same scene was playing out, again.

Froome, wearing black, paused and turned to look back over his right shoulder at the yellow jersey. What would happen if he ate into his teammate's two-minute advantage? It was not only personal glory that was at stake, there was also a lot of money on the line. The financial chasm between winning the Tour de France and finishing second or third equated to several million pounds. And even if he did not win this year, if he could show his potential as a prospective winner, his next contract could be worth at least another million pounds.

---

7 Sean Yates, filmed in the documentary *Bradley Wiggins: A Year in Yellow*, 2012

No wonder, halfway up the incline, he was in two minds about what to do.

Television commentators watched with amazement. 'I don't understand,' one said, 'how in a team as organised as Sky there could be such chaos.'[8]

After barely a minute, Froome called off his attack. For the last 400 metres, he allowed Wiggins to ride in his slipstream. As the Londoner crossed the finishing line, he let out a sigh of relief. He was in touching distance of an objective he had had for most of his life. Four days later, Wiggins did what no other Briton had achieved in 109 years – he won the Tour de France. No compatriot had finished in the top three before. Many of the fifty or so British entrants over the years had failed to even finish the race. Tom Simpson, one of only a couple to earn a top-ten finish, tragically died in an attempt for glory under a scorching sun in 1967, amphetamines found in the maillot pocket on his prone body after his collapse on Mount Ventoux.

Wiggins played down the magnitude of his achievement with some classic English deadpan humour during a victory speech on the Champs Élysées. He picked up the microphone and, addressing the cheering crowds around him, he said, 'We're just going to draw the raffle numbers now . . .' In terms of advertising value to BskyB, one estimate put the value of the break-through British win at $100 million.

Wiggins followed up by winning the time trial at the London Olympics eighteen days later. The back-to-back successes were a marketing bullseye for Sky. While its name was not on his red, white and blue skinsuit, it had spent four years carefully aligning

8 Carlos de Andrés, Television Española

its brand with the British cycling team. For perhaps the first time, everyone in Britain seemed to be talking about cycling, with some of the glory reflecting on Sky. On the day of his time-trial victory, even the *Daily Mirror* was getting excited. On its front page, it printed a picture of the sideburns of Wiggins, inviting readers to cut them out and show their support. Forget the new golf; for a moment, cycling was the new football.

After the warm glow of such a successful summer, BSkyB executives began to explore the World Series Cycling plans in more depth. In the winter, two representatives of the broadcaster were sent from London to the latest team meeting at a hotel in Geneva.

★ ★ ★

During the secret talks about World Series Cycling in Rothschild's office in the City of London, the possibility of a Tour de France boycott was occasionally floated. There were knowing nods about the Wimbledon industrial action when eighty-one of the best players of the era stood up to the tennis establishment, wresting power from the blazers that ran the sport. Some of the cycling team managers – and even one or two riders – had quietly talked amongst themselves about taking the nuclear option.

In 1973, the tennis revolution had started when a Yugoslav player called Nikola Pilic was told he was not welcome at Wimbledon because, according to a typed telegram from the All-England Lawn Tennis & Croquet Club, he was not on 'good standing' with his national tennis federation. Pilic had shirked a poorly remunerated Davis Cup match for his country to play for a bigger pay cheque in a Montréal tournament that was part of a new circuit – World Championship Tennis – organised by a Texas oilman called Lamar Hunt.

Hunt's offer of bigger pay cheques, therefore, was very attractive to players. Tennis had only turned professional five years earlier and there were still thin financial pickings. If you got through qualifying into the main draw of the French Open, you received 'six shirts, a vest sweater, a regular sweater, socks and that's about it,' one player said. Even the Wimbledon winner took home only £5,000.[9]

Hunt had gone to the tennis ruling body in London to explain that he was trying to modernise tennis with players in more colourful kit and female stewards dressed as cowgirls. British tennis officials were horrified and wanted to teach Pilic and his peers that such poor taste would not be tolerated. The plan backfired spectacularly. When Pilic showed the telegram to the American leaders of a new player union – the Association of Tennis Professionals – they declared war, enlisting more player support and encouraging them to boycott Wimbledon.

Among the eighty-one rebels was Stan Smith, a blonde, moustached Californian who had already travelled to London when the boycott was announced. As a hastily rearranged draw was plugged with amateurs and journeymen, Smith did a spot of shopping in the West End of London, looking as though he did not have a care in the world. Within weeks, the increasingly flustered tennis suits backed down and granted players the right to play where they wanted; they even cleared space on the

9 Official Wimbledon website: https://www.wimbledon.com/en_GB/about_wimbledon/prize_money_and_finance.html

calendar for Hunt's made-for-television tournaments. It was the birth of the modern tennis circuit.[10]

A Tour de France boycott was not an easy option. The cycling teams and riders had more at stake than the tennis players of the 1970s. Team bosses risked losing millions of dollars in sponsorship that they used to pay salaries and underpin their operations. A boycott of a race that generated some 80 per cent of the exposure could easily mean sponsors refused to pay up, starving teams and riders of income.

A second problem was that the riders were poorly organised when it came to negotiation. The riders' union was led part-time by a former cyclist from Milan called Gianni Bugno, who wore expensive shades and could fly a helicopter but spoke broken English and was not a natural leader. (His other job was flying crews of technicians to fix power lines.) Being a union leader in cycling was made more difficult because most riders did not think much beyond 'Where am I going now?' . . . 'I have to get on a plane' . . . 'How am I going to make a splash this season?' . . . 'I need to be razor sharp in July'. Because a whole season could be defined by one climb over 25 miles on a summer afternoon, they devoted their energy to preparing for that moment.

Typically, fewer than a dozen riders bothered to turn up to listen to the union's annual meeting. Instead of complaining about their share of the sport's revenue, most riders had become hard-wired to negotiate pay with their team managers and not the Amaury family. Over the years at the Tour de France, there had been strikes over lack of rest time, and because of police

---

10 Stan Smith is today much better known for a line of Adidas sneakers

searches of their rooms for doping products, but industrial action over pay was extremely rare.

In 1971, there was a stand-off with race organisers over prize money when riders had to cover a three-leg stage with finishes in Basel (Switzerland), Freiburg (Germany) and Mulhouse (France). The gruelling stage raised revenue from each of the cities for organisers but, while there was a short gap in between each leg for a massage and shower, the riders felt that they were being exploited. After an impromptu negotiation, Félix Lévitan agreed to increase the prize money for each leg.[11] A second short protest followed a few days later based on claims that that year's 470,000-franc prize money equated to only 15 per cent of Émilien Amaury's race profits. (This may have been little more than a rumour; the Tour was not profitable until 1974, according to Lévitan.)

For the past forty years, there had been hardly a whisper about a strike over money. When it came to the merits of such a course of action, American team manager Vaughters identified another flaw. He suspected that if there was a boycott, it could turn out to be a costly waste of time. The Amaury family, he reckoned, would invite French amateur teams instead and, just like they had done every summer for the last century, the public would bring their baguettes, brie and red wine and flock to the roadside to watch the peloton fly by. At home, millions more would still tune in to watch the action on television, whoever was competing.

While the teams considered their options, Jonathan Price had

11 Félix Lowe, Eurosport Re-Cycle podcast, June 2021: 'When Rini Wagtmans denied teammate Eddy Merckx to become the accidental yellow jersey'

gone one by one to cycling stakeholders to sell the idea of the series – just like Wouter Vandenhaute before him. In Paris, Amaury Sport Organisation executives waved him away, telling him to talk to the ruling body. In Switzerland, the ruling body's leader told him to move along please, we are not interested. Despite hundreds of calls, emails and meetings across the rest of Europe, Price found he was making little headway with half of the teams. They refused to come on board even provisionally, fearing they would burn their bridges with the Tour de France. Price was frustrated but people close to him still believed in the strength of the joker that could still be played by the teams. A boycott could rip out half of the field from the race, removing much of the world's best talent and making the Tour little more than a parochial event with a field of weekend warriors.

All of a sudden, there appeared to be a breakthrough. On a winter's day in Geneva, two BSkyB executives walked into the meeting room of a hotel where the rebel team managers had gathered. Vaughters felt something was afoot. Until now, Team Sky had studiously avoided the World Series Cycling project. The appearance of two corporate hot-shots produced a frisson. 'They looked,' Vaughters said, 'like people to be taken seriously.'[12]

The two men were Richard Verow, head of legal for BSkyB's sports unit, and Graham Bartlett, a business consultant who had recently left his role as chief commercial officer of Liverpool Football Club. As the team managers listened to the corporate men, they were impressed by what they heard. Rather than spinning rumours, gossip and chatter that were the staple of team meetings, the executives showed PowerPoint presentations based

---

12 Interview, Vaughters

on research incorporating, for example, the potential value of cycling's television rights. This data was based on desk work by staff back at the broadcaster's headquarters in London.

BSkyB's lawyers were also mobilised to discuss the legal implications of World Series Cycling for teams, and whether they could be disciplined for staging a new championship that was not officially sanctioned. Over the course of the coming weeks, the owner of Team Sky let it be known to other teams it was interested in becoming an investor in the project, taking on a say in the management of the series, and sucking up a bigger cut of the profits. This made some sense – BSkyB had the know-how to run a made-for-television championship. It had, after all, helped craft the success of Premier League football.

BSkyB was keen to keep its interest in World Series Cycling under wraps; there was no competitive advantage to go public with the plans. When a reporter found out about the attendance of the two English executives at the Geneva meeting, Sky's public relations team swung into action to try and downplay its significance.

17

Surrender

Avignon, 2013

From a red-brick detached house in Tring, a pleasant town 40 miles north-west of London, a brand consultant had an idea for a start-up company. Simon Mottram had grown up watching the Tour de France on television, buying the rather ugly maillots of teams more out of devotion to his sport than for their aesthetic appeal. On work trips, he visited cycling shops across the world, and became convinced there was a gap in the market for stylish apparel. A Yorkshireman in his thirties, he had attended dozens of marketing meetings as a brand expert – he advised Burberry and Chanel, among others – and spoke eloquently in pitching his idea to launch a new cycling business. Not many people shared his vision; it took 200 meetings to round up £140,000 of investment.[1]

In the UK, a chain specialising in auto and cycling equipment called Halfords had been the biggest retailer in cycling for decades. It was a budget brand that fitted with the archetypal English cyclist of the 1980s, a bearded school teacher who rode to work with the *Guardian* newspaper, a thermos of tea and a

---

1 *The Guardian*, interview with Mottram, 25/1/18

Tupperware box of sandwiches. The cycling clothes Halfords sold were practical but hardly chic. Cycling was, according to Mottram, seen as 'something weirdos did'.

When he saw photographs of post-war Tour de France riders, he was intrigued by how stylish they looked. In the evenings, he sat at the kitchen table making sketches of cycling clothes. Eventually, he had enough money to begin producing high-end gear, making it at a factory in Hungary and selling £150 gloves and £250 jackets via a website. With a nod to the sport's French heritage, he named the company 'Rapha' after a French team of the 1950s that had been sponsored by St Raphael, an apéritif maker for whom Émilien Amaury had once placed ads in Paris newspapers.

Mottram was in the right place at the right time. It was the start of the British cycling boom. In 2010, a market researcher had coined the term 'Mamil' ('middle-aged man in Lycra'), to identify a new consumer trend that was under way. The typical Mamil enjoyed fine living, took his $10,000 Italian-designed Campagnolo bike on holiday to France and wanted the right gear to go with his lifestyle. To help connect with him, Mottram started a magazine called *Rouleur*. The arty coffee-table publication gloried in the freedom of the open road, the beauty of the mountains and the rich history of cycling.

Mottram opened a store in Soho, London and in San Francisco's Marina district to cater to bike fashionistas. With a minimalist design and exposed brick walls, the stores were a place where urban Mamils could browse clothes, flick through the arty in-house magazine, sip a cappuccino and dream of mountain passes. To critics, Rapha was a victory of branding over tradition that grated with the sport's more humble origins.

They ridiculed Rapha customers, many of whom worked in finance and enjoyed a little conspicuous consumption like the much-derided yuppies of the 1980s.

The Mamil was an alien concept across the English Channel. French cyclists had tended to come from the working classes. Some of the first professional riders were miners or farm labourers, used to enduring hard work and suffering. Riding for hours over potholed roads was not a pastime for the urban bourgeoisie. Cycling had largely remained a sport steeped in the simple country life in France. Perhaps, as a result, there was no such thing as a hipster bike shop in Paris. Mottram tested the waters for $180 Lycra shorts in the birthplace of bike racing by opening a pop-up store, but it did not lead to a permanent shop.

Across France, cycling clothing was often bland and inexpensive. Who would spend £250 on a cycling jacket when Decathlon sold the same kind of gear at a fraction of the price? Despite this, Rapha stores followed in Amsterdam, Berlin, Copenhagen, Hong Kong and Melbourne and, in 2013, Mottram agreed a deal to sponsor Team Sky. The Rapha logo was positioned in small letters on the team's kit.

After the first mountain stage of that year's race, the Rapha logo was on the yellow jersey. Wiggins could not defend his title because of a chest infection and knee injury, leaving Froome as the undisputed team leader. Froome dominated the race from the moment it entered the mountains. Head down, gently rocking from side to side, he barely showed any emotion, even when he powered away from his rivals on the steepest slopes. With one remaining stage that finished atop the majestic Alpe d'Huez, he led by more than four minutes.

The mountain is set among jagged, snow-capped peaks over-shadowing Le Bourg-D'Oisans, a small town at the heart of a lush valley, brimming with fauna and wild flowers. The region's once bountiful mines are reputed to have produced crystal used to make the chandeliers at the royal palace of Versailles. The smooth, well-preserved tarmac road heading north-west turns into a series of sharp bends. On a map, the squiggles charting the twenty-one switchback turns of the road look like the spikes of a heart-rate monitor.

Froome was guided up the zig-zag ascent by a teammate whose job was to ensure that his rivals did not erode his lead. One of the longest straight stretches of the road, two-thirds of the way up, has become a party destination for orange-clad young men and women from the Netherlands after its riders won year after year there in the 1970s and '80s. For cyclists, riding through thousands of beery Dutch crowds is like cutting through the middle of an out-of-control stag party.

The Team Sky pair parted a narrow gap between the crowds in single file, cutting through the barrage of noise and outstretched arms, any one of which could have brought them crashing to the tarmac. It was after navigating the orange-clad masses that, with three miles left of the climb, something unex-pected happened. Froome ran out of energy.

As he suddenly lost power in his legs, Froome lifted his hand in the air anxiously appealing for help. Thankfully for him, it was soon forthcoming. His teammate drew up alongside the team car to collect a sachet of energy gel that he delivered to the team leader. It was all he needed. He refuelled his empty tank sufficiently to allow him to cross the line safely. He even extended his lead by an extra minute because his closest rival also struggled on the mountain. The dip in performance turned out to be just a scare, an anecdote on the road to Paris.

Now, as he arrived at the team hotel, Froome was confident of victory. The next day, Friday, was a rest day and on Sunday afternoon he would become the race's second British winner in 110 years. To capitalise on the UK cycling boom, the Amaury family business had already decided to start the following year's race in Yorkshire, in return for fees totalling £4.5 million from local authorities.[2] More than one million people would line the route in England, more than matching the enthusiasm in France: one Yorkshireman festooned the white façade of his roadside cottage in red polka dots, another painted the five-bar gate to his country pile in the colours of the Tricolore.

But for now it was time for Froome to start thinking about how to leverage his position as the next Tour de France champion. As for much of the last century, the Tour de France was not a means in itself to get rich. In 1972, Eddy Merckx, considered by many to be the greatest cyclist of all time, received only the equivalent of about a third of Stan Smith's £5,000 for winning Wimbledon that year. Prize money for both summer events continued to grow at a steady pace but, in 1990, the Tour's growth suddenly stopped. According to research by Jean-François Mignot, the winner's purse declined over the next two decades when benchmarked against the average salary in France.[3] In other words, the television money earned by the Amaury family's business during the modern-day sports rights boom did not translate into direct financial benefits for cyclists.

---

2 *Cycling News* website, citing *Yorkshire Evening Post,* 1/2/13
3 Jean-François Mignot: *Histoire du Tour de France,* 2014

The prize money of €450,000 waiting for Froome was a quarter of the cash reward that Andy Murray had just secured for winning Wimbledon. After French income-tax deductions and splitting the prize money with eight Sky teammates, as was customary, there wasn't much left. When asked why the Amaury family was not more generous with prize money, its executives trotted out the same argument on several occasions over the years – why reward riders after so many of them since the 1990s had sullied the race's image with doping scandals?

Like their predecessors, Froome and his peers believed that their only negotiating tactic when it came to pay was their performance on the bike. They had leverage if they performed well, and they could climb the team pay scale by increasing the amount of media exposure they were able to secure for team sponsors. Merckx's team sponsor when he won the Tour in 1972 was Molteni, an Italian salami maker that would have been delighted to see its name displayed across newspapers and television.

Froome's breakthrough second place at the Vuelta a España in 2011 had already made him a millionaire. On the back of that performance, he bartered a twelve-fold salary increase with Sky, lifting his pay to €1.2 million.[4] In terms of a pay rise, it was like being promoted from middle manager to chief executive. The same year, he moved to Monaco with his girlfriend Michelle.

Now as Tour de France champion-in-waiting, there was plenty more money on the table for him; the man in the yellow jersey could command a salary of $5 million. But, after negotiating his wage, he was on his own when it came to how he made some extra cash on the side. So Michelle, who doubled

---

4 Richard Moore, *Sky's the Limit*, 2012

up as his business manager, arranged a meeting for him with a Dutchman called John van den Akker in the lounge of the hotel where the team was staying atop the Alpe d'Huez.[5]

Froome was still finding his way around the strange ways of European cycling. He had heard about criteriums, of course, but did not know much. They were cycling's version of World Wrestling Entertainment (WWE), contests that were stage-managed so that fans could see their heroes in the flesh but with little or no sporting merit. The idea was that riders did not have to push their already exhausted bodies any more than was necessary.

In the weeks after the Tour de France there were as many as 120 criteriums in the 1960s as fans clamoured to see stars like Merckx. But the exhibition races on street circuits were becoming obsolete because enthusiasts today could see riders in high definition on television and, with foreign travel more accessible than ever, real fanatics could join French locals lining the route. There were still a smattering of criteriums in Belgium and the Netherlands and Van den Akker, a former rider, was the go-to man who hooked up cyclists with criterium organisers.

As the man in the yellow jersey, Froome could command a premium fee, Van den Akker told him. With little time to spare, they quickly worked out an outline plan for the two weeks after the Tour.

On the day he sealed victory in Paris, Froome went out on the town until 5.30 a.m. to celebrate. Barely had he rested his head on the pillow in his hotel when an alarm woke him at 8.00 a.m. He was, of course, feeling more than a bit groggy. 'The first thing I noticed was that I didn't have to think about which

---

5 Author interview with John van den Akker

mountains we would do or what that day's stage looked like,' he said to journalists at a news conference the day after his win. 'The stress was completely gone.' It was time to cash in. He had signed up to eight criteriums, guaranteeing him about €250,000 in appearance fees. He got up, drank a coffee and took a private jet to collect his first pay cheque as Tour de France champion in the provincial Belgian town of Aalst.

★ ★ ★

For every Tour de France winner there are 150 or so cyclists jostling for lesser levels of recognition. A *domestique* could be on as little as €60,000 a year. Just like the *crème de la crème* of the peloton, their only negotiating tactic was how they performed on two wheels. In cycling, your value to the team rose and fell throughout the year like the stock market, but July was when you had to try and hit form; many contracts were negotiated in the weeks after the Tour de France.

The best way for the average French rider to boost his modest salary was by providing solid support to the team's leading rider. His place in the general classification was practically irrelevant. Instead, his remit was to help in the mountains, even sacrificing his own bike, if necessary. Besides this selfless toil, the only other way to stand out from the crowd was to snatch a stage win and secure maximum exposure for the team's sponsor.

Brice Feillu was one such rider. As a twenty-three-year-old rookie, the young man from the Côte d'Azur had announced himself in the sport by winning a stage in the Pyrenees at the Tour de France with the Agritubel team, bringing valuable publicity to the backer, a supplier of feed racks and fencing for cattle farms in rural France.

There was only one problem – he forgot to zip up his shirt before he crossed the finishing line to show the sponsor's name on the front. As photographers snapped him raising his arms to celebrate, you could only see his bare chest and maillot flapping in the breeze. Agritubel probably missed out on hundreds of thousands of euros in media coverage.

However, the win confirmed he had potential and earned him a more lucrative deal the following year with Vacansoleil, a Dutch package holiday company. Over the previous three years, Feillu had lived off one-year contracts and was still searching for a second Tour de France stage win. For the 2012 season, Feillu rode for the Saur-Sojasun team sponsored by two mid-sized French companies, one specialising in water treatment and the other in soya food production.

At that year's Tour de France, he would plumb the depths of despair in his new job. A few hours after he navigated the opening-day prologue of that year's Tour de France, he fell violently ill with gastroenteritis. He had a 40-degree Celsius temperature, accompanied by vomiting and diarrhoea. After a sleepless night, he found he could not hold down any breakfast. He called his girlfriend Maud on the south coast to say he would probably have to head home.

Just before the team bus left for the start line, the team asked him to try and tackle the stage on an empty stomach. Feillu agreed and grimly rode near the back of the field for five hours, dousing his head in water from his bidon to try and keep his fever at bay; he took vitamin drinks to avoid dehydration. 'I felt terrible, very low,' he said.[6] He crawled across the finish line on

6 Author interview with Brice Feillu

his own, ten minutes off the pace. By the time he arrived, the other riders were already on the way to their hotel.

The next day, he decided to tough it out again on a diet of only potatoes. Riders usually consume several plates of eggs, rice and cereal at a pre-stage breakfast and refuel with cereal and glucose bars while riding. The humble potato only has about 150 calories of the 4,000–9,000 calories that cyclists burn off in a stage, so he was effectively running on petrol fumes.

On the hilly course, still suffering enormously, in a group of five stragglers, he finished 16 minutes, 29 seconds behind Peter Sagan, the sport's biggest showman. Sagan was feeling so comfortable that, before he crossed the finishing line in first place, he took his hands off the handlebars and, imitating Forest Gump, pumped his arms like pistons as though he was running at full speed.

It was only on the seventh stage that culminated with the climb to La Planche des Belles Filles that Feillu felt well enough to do what he was paid for – pace his team leader up the ascent. Finally, he was starting to feel a bit stronger. In the final week, he decided to go for a stage win, reckoning that it could double his salary the next season to €120,000. Over the last week he had regained a kilo of weight, his illness was behind him and he was feeling fresher. He had added chicken to his potato diet.

The stage he targeted traversed the storied Pyrenean climbs of Aubisque, Tourmalet, Aspin and Peyresourde. Four miles from the top of the second climb he made a solo attack and was joined by Thomas Voeckler. The two Frenchmen rode together, cresting two mountain passes at the front. For more than half an hour, *France Télévisions* cameras tracked the pair as their pursuers whittled away the gap.

On the final Peyresourde climb, Voeckler attacked, striking out on his own. As he pulled away, Feillu could not follow him. He negotiated the final descent alone, was caught by a couple of other chasing riders and finished that day's stage in fifth place. After a two-week struggle skirting the depths of despair, he had come close to perhaps doubling his pay, only to fall short.

After giving an interview to a couple of journalists, he was overcome with emotion and broke down in the arms of his team's *soigneuse*. One thing was forever true at the Tour – there were many more losers than winners.

★ ★ ★

Froome's dominance of the Tour de France was great publicity for Rapha, but not so much for Jonathan Price, the World Series Cycling entrepreneur.

With Team Sky beginning what appeared to be a period of sustained domination, many cycling insiders were exasperated by its financial might and how the sport was no longer a level playing field. Some did not like how the British did things differently. One journalist of Agence France-Presse, the state-owned news agency, was riled by how Team Sky threw an iron ring around its staff to protect them against nosy reporters sniffing around for gossip. This was quite unlike the homely teams from France and Belgium who invited the media into their hotels for drinks and treated them like part of the family.

Who wanted the Brits to tell them how to run the sport?

As it turned out, not even the Brits themselves. Cycling fans on the north side of the English Channel who had grown up watching the Tour in the 1980s on Channel 4 tended to be traditionalists who had fallen in love with the gentle rhythms of the season and did not like the idea that World Series Cycling would give the sport a corporate makeover. They felt Price's concept of a new championship risked undermining historic races in Europe with soulless, commercially driven new events in the New World. 'The main problem is,' the UK magazine *Cycling Weekly* said, 'the organisers don't understand cycling.'

In an effort to alter this damaging narrative, Price hired public relations firm Burson-Marsteller and delivered a round of friendly media interviews, but his charm offensive had little effect.

Jonathan Price was also facing other obstacles in his bid to get a new championship off the ground. ASO's chief executive Yann Le Moenner refused to sit down with the Englishman and negotiate, referring him in the first instance to the sport's ruling body, a route which they both knew was a dead end.

Le Moenner sported a military-style buzz cut to complement his no-nonsense attitude, and a lean physique thanks to regularly competing in triathlons. His job, like that of his predecessors, was assertively to protect the family's income and to enforce the citadel-like prevention of disclosure. ASO accounts tucked away behind a paywall on a corporate registry showed that, since 1999, almost without exception, the family had paid itself dividends: these averaged out at around €20 million per year. The financial data did not separate the Tour de France's income from other sports events like the Paris marathon and Dakar rally, but there was little doubt the cycling race was the most lucrative of all the family's sporting revenue streams. Much of the race income still came from French companies – state television, a bank and a supermarket, for example – but a sizeable amount of the estimated €100 million in annual revenue was derived from abroad, from sponsors such as Czech carmaker Skoda and television networks like Eurosport.

Just off the Rothschild-owned, cobbled St Swithin's Lane in London's financial district, retail and leisure executive Majid Ishaq was losing interest in Price's plans even as Britain was in the middle of its biggest cycling boom. By now, the project was two years old and progress had been slow. Amid talk of a Tour de France boycott, managers had filed into the wood-panelled offices for Price's presentation and marvelled at the history around them. It was true, BSkyB had now shown an interest in helping to get the project off the ground, but Ishaq could not wait for ever.

At any given time, he and his team were typically juggling four projects. These were mostly run-of-the-mill corporate moves such as mergers and acquisitions of beer makers and hotel chains. Typically, only one in four of these would succeed and earn Rothschild a brokerage fee. Cycling may have been fashionable – some of Ishaq's colleagues had taken to cycling to work on the same carbon-fibre racing bikes used at the Tour de France – but Rothschild was in the business of making money. Part of his job was to know when to pull out when one of the projects was floundering. He stopped taking Price's calls, having a junior member of staff field them instead.

BSkyB had gone over the plans for World Series Cycling for months since Wiggins had won the Tour de France, weighing up the pros and cons for their business. Back at headquarters in London, the army of Sky planners had done their due diligence on the risk-benefit analysis of World Series Cycling, and decided that, at that point in time, there was more risk than benefit. Just before Froome embarked on what would be another successful

Tour for Team Sky, BSkyB consultant Graham Bartlett sat down to dinner with Vaughters to discuss how to proceed.

Since Bartlett had walked into the team meeting in a hotel in Geneva, the two men had got to know each other quite well. As they dined before the opening of that year's race in Corsica, they agreed to start looking at a different approach. Instead of trying to blow cycling's television-and-sponsorship business model out of the water, they figured that they should focus on the Internet.

The Amaury family had built its empire on the back of newspapers and guided it through the television era. Now, in the age of disruptive innovation, there was an opportunity for the teams to wrest back some control and money without having to be confrontational. Apps created in Silicon Valley were changing the world around them – Uber had begun to erode the hegemony of London's black cabs, and Airbnb had started to alter the commercial landscape of Paris by forcing small hoteliers to sell up. A few weeks later, on a rest day in Avignon, Tansey, the BSkyB marketing director, briefed other teams about the company's new vision.

On the outskirts of the ancient walled town, the eight team managers listening to him figured that BSkyB's decision made sense. Hardly any of them felt comfortable with the idea of a Tour de France strike; few of them had the same appetite for risk as Stan Smith and his easy-going tennis pals. They agreed to join Sky in pulling the plug on the project. Instead, they would become less confrontational. It was a relief. 'We felt like we were turning a corner,' one of them said. 'It was no longer necessary to fight fire with fire.'[7] With this decision, the foreign

---

7 Author interview with team manager

team managers were retreating from their Waterloo, effectively giving up on the bid for a share of the sport's television income. After two years, the threat of a Tour de France boycott was over.

The only manager who seemed really disappointed by the volte-face was Oleg Tinkov, who had acquired the team of Bjarne Riis just as the boycott was being taken off the table. For the next two years, the entrepreneur railed against the business model he had bought into, making threats about a boycott in the media, even though the other teams had already moved on. Tinkov said he felt like Don Quixote tilting at windmills. He was on his own, shouting into a void. After growing increasingly frustrated, he hurled a few jibes at ASO executives before also giving up.

As most of the team managers saw it, pulling the plug on World Series Cycling was not a major U-turn. The battle had not yet turned ugly and they could always regroup and attack at another point in time. It was, however, a blow for Jonathan Price who had spent much of the last two years running around Europe trying to align the teams and now would have nothing to show for his efforts. To help finance his travel and expenses, he had a credit line from a private investor, one of the owners of Ronnie Scott's jazz club in London.[8]

Without the support of the teams, Price was just another entrepreneur with an idea. And the idea was now worth nothing. During the meeting on a hot summer's day in Avignon, his World Series Cycling plans had evaporated.

---

8 Interview with Michael Watt, Ronnie Scott's co-owner, who said he gave an interest-bearing credit line to Price

Epilogue

The grand corner building at 114 Champs Élysées where Émilien Amaury ran his empire for thirty-three years is today one of the most expensive pieces of real estate in Paris. Long ago sold by the family, it is owned by a German private equity company and leased to Apple for €14 million per year to house a flagship store and offices. On a typical day, the ground floor is teeming with tourists eyeing up iPhones. The marble staircase with its timber balustrade, which Jacques Goddet climbed up in 1944 to strike a deal with Amaury, has been restored. You can still walk in and admire the hallway with its *beaux-arts* features. On the top floor where Amaury oversaw his publishing empire, Apple staff work quietly away on its French business. In a modern twist, the interior atrium is topped with shimmering solar panels.

The former *L'Équipe* office in Montmartre with its creaking wooden staircases where the Tour de France was run for forty years by Goddet and Félix Lévitan has been razed to the ground. In its place is a minimalist, sandblasted office block whose tenants include the management of an Australian bar chain. This part of rue du Faubourg-Montmartre is a hotchpotch of old-school classic Parisian architecture and modernist design, still not quite sure of its place in the world. There is no plaque to mark what was once the most influential sports newspaper in the world.

The ugly white office block with harsh strip lights and partitioned floors by the Paris ring road where reporter Damien Ressiot worked on his scoop that proved, for the first time, that Lance Armstrong had used stamina-building drug EPO has been demolished to make way for a sleek new tower housing a tech services company. Ressiot left *L'Équipe* in 2014 and took a salary cut to become head of testing at the French anti-doping agency. By then, Armstrong had got his comeuppance. After he was stripped of his seven titles because of evidence provided by former teammates, and lost nearly all his sponsors, he confessed all in an interview with Oprah Winfrey. Over the next few years, he downsized his lifestyle, settled lawsuits and put multiple homes up for sale.

To find the heart of the Amaury business empire today, you must take the C-Line train. From central Paris, the route skirts along the Seine for three miles past grand Hausmann buildings to 40 Quai Point du Jour in Boulogne-Billancourt. Today, *L'Équipe* and Amaury Sport Organisation staff work here in a glass-fronted, eight-storey office overlooking the dirty brown river.

In the subsidised ground-floor café, a dozen staff in trendy casual clothes gather in small groups to knock back cheap espresso shots and chat quietly. A screen shows the *L'Équipe* television channel that, on a typical morning, repeats niche sports like handball. On the top floor is Le Club, an executive suite with a terrace overlooking the city's grey slate rooftops.

Here, there is a bar and kitchen and waiters dressed in starched white uniforms attend to Marie-Odile, Aurore and Jean-Étienne Amaury.

Today, their media business is more beleaguered than ever. In 2015, the family sold the *Le Parisien* newspaper, once the cornerstone of the family empire, to the fashion brand LVMH for a modest €50 million.[1]

The Amaury family continues jealously to guard what is now by far its biggest asset. Having bought back the 25 per cent of the family business owned by Lagardère for €91 million, the family took back control of all the equity in the Tour de France for the first time in thirty years. And it continued to receive unsolicited bids. In 2016, billionaire Wang Jianlin – then China's richest man – became the latest person to make an overture about buying the race. He was in the midst of a $15 billion buying spree that included Sunseeker, the luxury yacht maker featured in James Bond movies, and a Claude Monet oil painting. A man of 'Napoleonic ambition' according to *The Economist*, 5ft 5in Wang let it be known he also wanted to buy the family's heirloom.

The story goes that Wang asked for a one-on-one meeting with Marie-Odile Amaury, without any of their entourage present. Point blank, he is said to have asked to buy the Tour de France. She told him the race was not for sale and, after an uncomfortable silence, he left. It's not clear whether the fabled meeting actually took place but, either way, Wang got short shrift.

---

1 The family's media troubles extended to *L'Équipe*. In 2021, the newspaper announced 47 job cuts, having posted a financial loss in nine of the twelve previous years. *France Football* was scaled back from a weekly magazine to a monthly one.

In a speech at Oxford University at around the same time, he said he was having difficulty making any acquisitions in the European sports industry, which had all 'basically been carved up'.[2]

In 2020, Marie-Odile Amaury promoted her children Jean-Étienne and Aurore to become general directors of the family business, ceding her executive power to them. The eighty-year-old widow took a step back, becoming president of the holding company. The generational handover had been fifteen years in the making since the death of her husband.

As he surveys the rooftops of Paris from his top-floor office on a winter's day, Jean-Étienne says the family's strategy for the Tour de France remains the same as it has been for decades. They are guardians of the race on behalf of the French people, and the state. When asked about the fleeting interest in the race by a group of Silicon Valley high rollers all those years ago, he shrugs and then reflects for a moment. 'The Americans,' he says, 'think everything is for sale.'[3]

★ ★ ★

And what became of the team plans to exploit the Internet era? Well, they started off by setting up a company called Velon Teamco Ltd. The Anglo–French – combining *'vélo'* and 'on' – was a nod to a more collaborative attitude between the British and French cycling fraternities. Graham Bartlett, the Sky consultant, was appointed chief executive of the organisation and moved into a two-desk serviced office in London's Kensington High Street. To make himself feel at home, he hung

2 Speech to students at Oxford University's Saïd Business School, 23/2/16
3 Amaury, interview

up a black Team Sky jersey on one wall, and began searching for new sources of income in the digital age. One of his objectives was to make money for the teams from data. As the British mathematician Clive Humby said in 2006, 'Data is the new oil,' if you knew how to refine it.

Data collection in cycling had evolved rapidly since the 1980s, when a German engineering student made the first power meter, a brick-like object he taped to a ledge under his handlebars, earning him the nickname of 'Game Boy' when he used it in amateur races because of its similarity to the Nintendo console.[4] His first clients included Greg LeMond and the Soviet Union's $23 billion space programme which planned to use the device to track the fitness of astronauts.

Each time LeMond pressed down on his pedal, a piece of metal on his crankshaft would transmit a charge through a wire taped on to his bike frame to the brick that converted it into watts, via a mathematical formula. The brick had a couple of buttons and was too unwieldy to use in races because it would sometimes become dislodged and crash to the tarmac. Instead, cyclists used it when they trained. Even then, many insiders did not know what on earth to do with the mass of information. One rider emailed an Excel sheet of his power data to a coach in the late 1990s, but said, 'To this day, I don't know if he looked at it.'[5]

Now, with cloud storage and high-speed Internet, data can be gathered and processed from riders – power, heart rate, cadence and acceleration – in real time within seconds, wherever you are in the world.

---

4 Slowtwitch.com interview with Ulrich 'Game Boy' Schoberer, the student engineer who founded Schoberer Rad Messtechnik (SRM), 1/5/2012
5 Bobby Julich, interview

Cycling teams began to collect this data from their riders, running it through specially designed computer algorithms to fine-tune race preparation. Not long after Wiggins won the Tour de France, Team Sky hired the sport's first data scientist to sort through millions of data points. His analysis was so detailed it factored in the sugar intake of the little bag of Haribo sweets that Froome liked to suck on after each Tour de France stage.

But this data, or some of it, might also one day be sold to the cycling fans to make money. Selling it would allow, for example, amateur enthusiasts to track their form against professional riders. Bartlett asked the Velon teams to get their riders to put an addendum on their contracts, waiving the rights to exploit their personal data. Then he arranged for them to fix a black box the size of an iPhone under their saddles and began mining for the new oil, sucking up huge volumes of information about their bodies and performance.

The Velon teams were not sure about what to do when Bartlett asked them to hand over all this private data; some were happy to release this kind of information, others were not so sure. Team Sky felt that rivals might gain an edge by plotting a graph of Froome's physiology to identify the moment of extreme fatigue when he was at his weakest on the bike. A compromise was reached and readings on heart rate and watts were shown only for 15 seconds every 15 minutes in order to limit the amount of information entering the public domain. Eventually, this information began to appear on a new Velon app. (The age and location of the cycling fans that logged into the app was duly collected.)

In his office, Bartlett was not just focused on the new oil. He had three goals; he stuck a piece of A4 paper on the wall of his tiny office bearing the words 'Excite-Inspire-Explain'. In another initiative, he arranged to fit GoPro camera footage to the bikes of teams during races, giving fans a new perspective of the action that showed riders sharing jokes in quiet moments, shouting encouragement at their teammates, and descending mountain passes at 60 miles per hour on 1 inch-wide tyres. The images were collected by Velon, edited into short segments and posted on YouTube. Like the data, this content was given away for free, with a view to making money at some undefined point in the future.

In a third enterprise, Velon launched its own racing series. Instead of buying up struggling races across continental Europe, it decided it would tailor its own mini championship to suit fans in the Internet age. The Hammer Series was a bit like a relay race – in cycling parlance, 'dropping the hammer' was when a cyclist sprinted. For a sport with an ageing demographic that was experiencing a gradual decline in much of continental Europe, it was the first major new race in ages. Because it was over a short circuit, filming the action was relatively cheap compared to a typical one-day race over 200 miles. The championship opened with an event in the Dutch province of Limburg and was streamed on Facebook Live.

All these new ideas were greeted with some enthusiasm by the new generation of the sport's aficionados but the problem for Bartlett remained as old as some of the vines at Châteauneuf-du-Pape. However many new ideas he and the teams came up with, he would find himself facing the same gnarly problem. The Amaury family business was as defensive as ever. Every time the teams brought in a new concept, ASO seemed to come up with something similar of their own. It signed its own deal with GoPro to film inside the peloton and made an agreement with another company to track the data of riders. For Bartlett, making progress on behalf of the teams was like trying to ride a bike around the living room of a tiny Parisian apartment.

For all the talk of a new start, the tension between teams and organisers continued to pervade the sport. Increasingly frustrated by a lack of progress, Bartlett found himself in a shouting match with the unyielding ASO chief executive Yann Le Moenner. By 2021, after seven years of endeavour, one of Velon's founding directors conceded that the venture had 'lost its bite' and was not making headway as planned.[6] With marginal revenue, it was still listed as a small business on the UK company register.

In Paris, Marie-Odile Amaury was still going to work after turning eighty years old, and continuing to advocate for the family business to minimise risk. Among the items on the bookshelf of her office one summer day in 2021 was a paperback copy of her father-in-law Émilien's biography, and what looked like, alongside a bottle of water, to be lunch: a couple of bread rolls wrapped in tin foil. A few weeks earlier, ASO increased its financial reserves to €142 million to guard against unexpected adversity. The Tour de France's mother hen was still watching over the coop for her children and, maybe one day, her grandchildren.

---

6 Jonathan Vaughters quoted by *Cycling Tips* website, 22/4/21

Bibliography

Abt, Samuel: *In High Gear – World of Professional Bicycle Racing*, 1989

Beevor, Anthony: *D-Day, the Battle for Normandy*, 2010

Beevor, Anthony & Artemis Cooper: *Paris After the Liberation: 1944-1949*, 1994

Bose, Mihir: *Manchester Disunited – Trouble and Takeover at the World's Richest Football Club*, 2007

Breakaway – On the Road with the Tour de France, 1985

Dupuy, Micheline: *Le Petit Parisien, Le Plus Fort Tirage des Journaux du Monde Entier*, 1989

Endeweld, Marc: *France Télévisions, Off the Record – Histoires Secrètes d'Une Télé Publique Sous Influences*, 2010

Books by *L'Équipe*

L'Équipe Raconte L'Équipe, 70 Ans de Passion, 2015

L'Équipe Raconte Le Tour de France, 2018

50 Ans de Coupes d'Europe, 2005

Fotheringham, Alasdair: *The End of the Road – The Festina Affair and the Tour that Almost Wrecked Cycling*, 2016

Fotheringham, William: *Fallen Angel – The Passion of Fausto Coppi*, 2009

Roule Britannia: Great Britain and the Tour de France, 2005

Futterman, Matthew: *Players – The Story of Sports and Money, and the Visionaries Who Fought to Create a Revolution*, 2016

Garcia, David: *La Face Cachée de L'Équipe*, 2008

Goddet, Jacques: *L'Équipée Belle*, 1991

Greilsamer, Laurent: *L'homme du Monde – La Vie d'Hubert Beuve-Méry*, 2010

Johnson, Mark: *Argyle Armada – Behind the Scenes of the Pro Cycling Life*, 2012

Jones, Colin: *Paris, Biography of a City*, 2004

Laborde, Christian: *Robic 47*, 2017

Lacroix-Riz, Annie: *La Non-Epuration en France, de 1943 aux Années 1950*, 2019

Lancry, Roger: *La Saga de la Presse – D'Émilien Amaury à Robert Hersant*, 1993

Lecasble, Valérie & Airy Routier: *Le Flambeur – La Vraie Vie de Bernard Tapie*, 1994

Leonard, Max: *Lanterne Rouge – The Last Man in the Tour de France*, 2013

Louy, Xavier: *Sauvons Le Tour!*, 2007

Un Nouveau Cyclisme, Avec Greg, Lucho et Wang, 1986

Madiot, Marc: *Parlons Vélo*, 2015

Manso, Benjo: *The Sweat of the Gods – Myths and Legends of Bicycle Racing*, 2005

Marchand, Jacques: *Quel Tour pour Demain?* 2013

Les Patrons du Tour, 2003

Jacques Goddet, 2002

Mignot, Jean-François: *Histoire du Tour de France*, 2014

De Mondenard, Jean-Pierre: *La Grande Imposture*, 2009

Moore, Richard: *Slaying the Badger – Greg LeMond, Bernard Hinault and the Greatest Tour de France*, 2012

Sky's the Limit: Cavendish and Wiggins, the Quest to Conquer the Tour de France, 2011

Mosley, Max: *Formula One and Beyond*, 2015

Nicholson, Geoffrey, *The Great Bike Race*, 1997

Nouzille, Vincent & Alexandra Schwartzbrod: *L'acrobate, Jean-Luc Lagardère ou les armes du pouvoir*, 1998

Penot, Christophe: *Ces Messieurs du Tour de France*, 2003

Perier, Denis: *Le Dossier Noir du Minitel Rose*, 1988

Petrov, Vladimir: *Money and Conquest, Allied Occupation Currencies in World War II*, 1967

Reed, Eric: *Selling the Yellow Jersey – the Tour de France in the Global Era*, 2015

Remy, Jaqueline: *Arnaud Lagardère, L'Heritier qui Voulait Vivre Sa Vie*, 2013

Rendell, Matt: *King of the Mountains – How Colombia's Cycling Heroes Changed Their Nation's History*, 2003

Roussel, Bruno: *Tour des Vices*, 2001

Schwartzenberg, Emmanuel: *Spéciale Dernière, Qui Veut La Mort de la Presse Quotidienne Française?*, 2007

Seidler, Edouard: *Sport à La Une*, 1986

Singer, Daniel: *Prelude to Revolution – France in May, 1968*

Thogmartin, Clyde: *The National Daily Press of France*, 1998

Thompson, Christopher S: *The Tour de France – A Cultural History*, 2006

Vadepied, Guy: *Émilien Amaury – La Véritable Histoire d'un Patron de Presse du 20ᵉ siècle*, 2009

Vaughters, Jonathan: *One Way Ticket – Nine Lives on Two Wheels*, 2019

Verbruggen, Hein: *De Waarheid van Hein Verbruggen*, 2018

De Visé, Daniel: *The Comeback – Greg LeMond, the True King of American Cycling, and a Legendary Tour de France*, 2018

Wilson, Elizabeth: *Love Game – A History of Tennis, from Victorian Pastime to Global Phenomenon*, 2015

Acknowledgements

I would like to thank all those who were generous with their time including Jean-Jacques Bertrand, Johan Bruyneel, Brian Cookson, Xavier Louy, Marc Madiot, Pat McQuaid, Daam van Reeth, Damien Ressiot, James Startt and Wouter Vandenhaute. The Amaury family prefers not to be in the public eye but Jean-Etienne Amaury was polite and helpful, and so was the family's public-relations advisor Lara Maitre.

Some of the information comes from when I worked at Bloomberg News, which let me cover the Tour de France – surely one of the most enjoyable gigs in sports journalism. During those years, Jonathan Vaughters was always a pleasure to talk to about the financial mechanics of the race.

I sourced information from many books but Guy Vadepied's biography of Émilien Amaury was particularly helpful in assembling an outline of his life. The histories of *L'Équipe* and the Tour de France by the newspaper's own staff were reliable pathfinders.

Margherita Orlando at the Bank of England's archive went out of her way to send me once-classified documents dating back to the Second World War when I was unable to visit during lockdown. Staff at the Bibliothèque Nationale in Paris were unfailingly efficient. My father Peter Duff and brother-in-law David Walker read early drafts of the book and provided valuable tips. Andreas Campomar was a charming and very able torchbearer at Constable.

Finally, there were several well-placed sources who preferred to talk to me off the record. You know who you are. Thank you.

Index

305